ANOTHER DARKNESS,
ANOTHER DAWN

Another Darkness, Another Dawn:
A History of Gypsies, Roma and Travellers

Becky Taylor

REAKTION BOOKS

To my parents, for their love, so freely given

Published by Reaktion Books Ltd
33 Great Sutton Street
London EC1V 0DX, UK
www.reaktionbooks.co.uk

First published 2014

Printed and bound in Great Britain
by TJ International, Padstow, Cornwall

A catalogue record for this book is available from the British Library

ISBN 978 1 78023 257 7

Contents

PREFACE

DESPITE THEIR PRESENCE across the world Gypsies, Roma and Travellers are some of the most marginalized and vilified people in society. They are rarely seen as having a place in a country, either geographically or socially, no matter where they live or what they do. Part of their marginalization stems from the fact that they are excluded from mainstream histories. At the same time, they are rarely granted a separate history, but rather seen to exist in a time-less bubble, unchanged and untouched by modern life. It remains that, despite a growing amount of research and writing, overall they are 'part of the historically inarticulate'.[1]

This book aims to serve not only as an introduction to the history of Romani peoples but crucially to show how their history is as intimately tied to the broader sweep of history as the rest of society's. Understanding their history is to take in the founding and contraction of empires, Reformation and Counter-Reformation, wars, the expansion of law and order and of states, the Enlightenment and the increasing regulation of the world: it is as much a history of 'ourselves' as it is of 'others'. In such a short volume it is not possible to cover all times and all places in the depth demanded by the subject. Instead, what I offer here is a way into under-standing both the experiences of Romani peoples, and how settled societies have dealt with their presence. Inevitably this has meant focusing on some areas to the exclusion of others, but always with the aim of revealing the most significant trends and events affecting Gypsy history. The period to the end of the sixteenth century tracks movement across both place and time, taking in possible departures from north-west India, gradual migration to the Balkans and their reception across Europe in the early modern

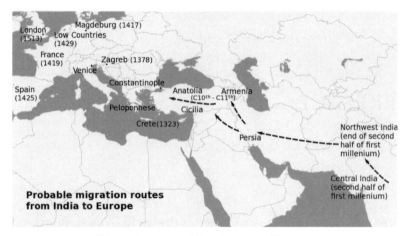

The main routes of Gypsies across Europe.

period. From this point onwards the amount of available evidence to historians increases significantly, allowing us to consider how they established themselves in Europe despite banishment and execution, as well as their arrival in the New World.

For the modern period, I have largely focused on the developments in four particular countries – Britain, Germany, France and Bulgaria – as a way of providing some focus and consistency to their history. These countries have been chosen as a way into exploring how different kinds of societies and states may have affected the reception, treatment and experiences of Romani peoples in modern times. Germany's experience of nationalism has had very different meanings and outcomes to that of the multi-ethnic Ottoman Empire from which Bulgaria sprang; while emerging ideas of citizenship and welfare played out differently in republican France, communist Bulgaria or in Britain's relatively stable liberal democracy. In this way we can see how near universal stereotypes of Gypsies as marginal, criminal, deviant or romantic had diverse outcomes in different national contexts. Consequently this book acts as a springboard into thinking about the history of Gypsies while also opening up the question of how different societies saw themselves and the minorities in their midst. So, rather than implying that the experiences of Spanish, Polish, Scandinavian, American or indeed Argentinian Gypsies are any less worthy of study, I aim to provide a map that might be used by others to explore the countries beyond the scope of this volume.

Writing this book was a salutatory lesson in the dangers of believing in a progressive view of history: things don't always get better, especially if you belong to a marginalized ethnic group. But neither were they always necessarily as bad as they first appear. We will see how the institution of slavery for Gypsies coexisted under the Ottomans alongside remarkable cultural diversity and autonomy; how branding, mutilations and 'Gypsy hunts' occurred at the same time that Gypsies established themselves across Europe; and how despite developments in education and attitudes towards minorities the modern world has failed to engender anything like acceptance of the place of Romani peoples within its societies. The lack of any simple, linear story of progress is illustrated in an examination of seventeenth-century executions of German Gypsies written in 1932. The writer's outraged account was prefaced with the following observation:

> It is, perhaps, a difficult matter for the modern mind, moulded by generations of increasing humanistic toleration, to imagine with sufficient realism some of the processes instrumental in the forming of our present European civilization. But here and there glimpses of the past are preserved, presenting vivid evidence of the manner in which Authority enforced Law and Order.[2]

The irony of this observation, written at a time when the German National Socialists were poised to tighten anti-Roma and Sinti[3] legislation to fatal effect across the Third Reich need not be laboured. More recently, attacks on Roma across the former Soviet bloc since 1989, the expulsion of Roma from Italy and France, as well as high-profile evictions of Irish Travellers from Dale Farm in the UK all serve to demonstrate how, centuries after their first arrival in Europe, Roma, Gypsies and Travellers remain unwelcome, with the legitimacy of their presence highly contested. This is no simple story of progression from brutal repression and marginalization in the early modern period, through attempts at assimilation and settlement in the nineteenth century to an inclusive and open world of early 21st-century multiculturalism.

Europe in the sixteenth century.

INTRODUCTION

In Search of the 'True Gypsy'?

BEFORE I GO ANY FURTHER it is worth making plain that there is no one word that can cover the multitude of peoples who have been called, or might call themselves Roma, Gypsy or Traveller, or any of the national variations of these words over time and place. Recent work has confirmed exactly how problematic it is to label 'people known as Gypsies', with meanings often heavily contested and certainly not 'politically neutral'.[1] This is not simply a matter of semantics, since individuals and whole communities are still routinely deported, moved on or discriminated against on the grounds that they are, or are not, Gypsies/Roma/Travellers.

When Gypsies first arrived in Europe they were known fairly consistently throughout the Continent as 'Egyptians', having been believed to originate in 'Little Egypt' in Greece, hence the consequent term 'Gypsy'. Over time variations on the Greek appellation 'Astigani', such as 'Tsigane' and 'Gitano' also became current. However, as Gypsies established themselves in different national contexts and became entwined in these societies, new names emerged reflecting this. So, in France, they also became known as 'Bohemians' owing to their supposed origins in Bohemia in the Czech Republic, with particular groups such as the Manouches arising, who had ties in Belgium and Germany. Similarly in Germany and northern Italy the Sinti and Jenische emerged as separate groups from the sixteenth century, with their Romani dialects containing many loan words from German. In contrast, the Irish and Scots Travellers do not claim Romani heritage, but rather an indigenous nomadic tradition, but nevertheless have often maintained close family ties with English and Welsh Romanies who do. In addition, as we shall see time and time again, governments and legislators often lumped them together with other social groups seen as undesirable – 'counterfeit Egyptians', vagabonds, vagrants, errants, nomads, those of no fixed abode, travelling people – in order to control, assimilate or remove them from society.

Broadly, although national variations of the word 'Gypsy' have been traditionally used to describe these communities, because of the strongly pejorative overtones – most often tied to associations of dirt, thieving and antisocial activities – recent waves of Roma activists have challenged the use of this term, proffering the alternative Rom/Rrom ('man' or 'person' in Romani) for an individual, and Roma for the collective identity. However, this term remains most closely associated with the communities of southeastern and eastern Europe, so in Britain, for example, the rather clunky term Roma/Gypsy/Traveller (or Romani when referring specifically to English and Welsh Gypsies) is often used in preference, and as a way of making explicit the heritages of the different communities.

While these developments are helpful in raising the profile of different communities with linked but dispersed heritages, they create a number of difficulties for historians. As we shall see, much of the evidence of the very early years is either genetic or linguistic, which presents us with a problem: while we may be able to chart the development of language across time and place, what we cannot know is how those who used the different variations of these languages thought of themselves. Indeed, this extends beyond the use of linguistic evidence to take in the written accounts we have of Gypsies' interactions with others. Essentially, whenever we look at a source, whether an account from the Byzantine Empire of 'Astigani' acrobats, seventeenth-century descriptions of 'Gypsy hunts' or twentieth-century police reports of 'Gypsy' evictions, we are usually dealing with outsiders' definitions and impressions rather than those of the people being written about. While sometimes we are told that the people concerned 'called themselves "Egyptians"', mostly we are left with the fact that it is the outside observer who was describing the subjects in a particular way and using a particular label. The people in question may well have thought of themselves as 'Gypsies', but we also need to be aware that they might have thought of themselves in a range of different ways – by their occupation (as travelling horse traders or knife grinders, for example), or in relation to their extended family group –

while at the same time possibly accepting, or rejecting the fact that others saw them as 'Gypsies'. Added to this is the fact that there were clearly times across history when hiding Gypsy identity was a matter of life or death, as well as times – for example when presenting oneself as a fortune teller – when emphasizing 'Gypsyness' was a distinct advantage.

Overlaid onto the puzzle of outsider definition versus self-ascription is a further difficulty, that of the 'impure' or 'half-bred' Gypsy. Already by the sixteenth century, legislators were grappling with the idea of 'counterfeit Egyptians', suspect both for living as Gypsies and for not actually being Gypsies: vagrants and others from settled society who 'became' Gypsies were seen as presenting a profound threat to social hierarchy, as they opened up the possibility of another way of being. In order to understand the genesis and significance of this we need to look at the history of writing on Gypsies itself. While Gypsies attracted attention from commentators and legislators from the outset, evidence about them tends to be patchy until the late eighteenth century, when Enlightenment scholars such as Hermann Grellmann started exploring both their origins and their place in European society. From this point there is a veritable flood of writing, much of it stimulated by members of the Gypsy Lore Society and made accessible through the *Journal of the Gypsy Lore Society*.

This society was established in 1888 and had its home at the University of Liverpool. It published and supported the work of an international body of amateur and academic scholars who styled themselves 'gypsiologists' and who carried out field research and archival study across Europe and North America. Central to the identity of many of these scholars was their acceptance as individuals within Gypsy circles as a 'Romani Rai' (Gypsy gentleman). An article of 1892 defined a 'Romany Rai' as 'acting as private secretary, legal, medical and spiritual adviser, general arbiter and tobacco jar to his Romany friends', with one writer comparing 'a Romany Rye surrounded by a group of eagerly enquiring Gypsies . . . [to] Christ sitting in the midst of his disciples'.[2] While it is easy now to wince at the patronizing tone with which Gypsy 'disciples' were positioned in relation to the god-like scholars, it is the undoubted case that much of what we know about Gypsies stems from their work. This is, however, a double-edged sword: while gypsiologists have bequeathed us a body of evidence and detail, we need to understand that their scholarship was often conducted through the heaviest of rose-tinted spectacles.

Along with artistic attempts to capture a lifestyle centring around picturesque caravans, interest in Gypsies focused largely on recording their origins, language and customs. Gypsiologists were largely preoccupied with the ancestry of Gypsies and with developing theories about their 'pure bred' nature that often tied pure blood lines to Romani language use and 'proper' nomadic living, certain marriage customs and cleanliness taboos. Confinement between four walls was thought to be unendurable to the Gypsy tribe, while wanderlust was transmitted by birth, and death was marked by the superstitious burning of possessions.[3] All this was entwined with a quest for understanding their relationship with, or rather separateness from, modern society.

Gypsiologists were intent on discovering and recording the language and culture of Gypsies before they disappeared. In this they were part of the wider Victorian phenomenon of classifying and understanding the physical and social worlds, but they were equally inspired by a nostalgic desire to capture ways of life apparently threatened by urbanization and industrialization. It was often from a medley of 'back to the land', early caravanning and arts and crafts movements, and preservation and conservation societies that many of the supporters of Gypsies and their romantic lifestyle were drawn. A main preoccupation of these groups was the benefits gained from escaping from civilization and its cares, and conversely the joys of becoming at one with nature. Resulting writings glorified 'the tramp' as well as Gypsies, assuming that being in the countryside and taking part in 'simple' activities such as walking and caravanning automatically brought one closer to nature.[4]

At the same time another body of people was becoming increasingly interested in the lives, habits and origins of Gypsies and others who lived on the road. A strong theme in descriptions of Gypsies had always been their foreignness: not simply their appearance, but their lifestyle, religion and morals. The Magdeburg chronicle of 1417 had described the Gypsy acrobats as 'black and hideous', with countless subsequent accounts linking their appearance with deviant behaviour, typically including theft, sorcery, promiscuity, child stealing and even cannibalism. The Enlightenment did not remove this thinking, but brought a new sense that all members of the human race had the capacity for improvement, but by the nineteenth century this had become increasingly overlaid with new ideas of 'race'. Emerging ideas of evolution combined with attempts to justify social inequalities, colonialism and the differences between nations to produce what became known as social Darwinism. Here 'survival of the fittest' was used to explain the 'naturalness' of European imperialism, the superior nature of northern Europeans over the 'Latin races' and even the dominance of the upper and middle classes over the working class. And indeed, at the very bottom of the social hierarchy was a shifting mass of deviants, threatening to social order and untouched by progress. Such attitudes also found their roots in early-modern concerns about 'sturdy beggars' and the vagrant poor that had combined with suspicion of 'foreigners' to penalize and often expel outsiders. With changing ideas over the purpose and possibilities of the state brought about by the Enlightenment, expulsion was increasingly replaced by attempts at reform and assimilation. In certain parts of Europe from the late eighteenth century, added to these concerns were anxieties over national identity, with the emerging German state in particular seeking increasingly to define who constituted an 'undesirable' individual within its borders.

So, in contrast to romantics who were concerned with the inevitable loss of Gypsies in the face of modernity, those who saw Gypsies as unwholesome deviants were united in their concern that they would *not* disappear unless there was concerted action. Where they differed was in what measures were necessary to make this happen. Missionaries saw the Bible and conversion to Christianity as the answer; educationalists saw literacy; reformers, civil servants and communists saw regulation, settlement and assimilation; and eugenicists saw sterilization or even extermination. Crucially, however, what united both the 'romantics' and the reformers were two things: how they depicted Gypsies; and an urge to distinguish between the 'true' Gypsy and the 'counterfeit Egyptian'. The desire to see Gypsies as representatives of an earlier, easier world, as much as reformers' concerns that this earlier world was rather too attractive to maligners, led to depictions of Gypsies as childlike, closer to nature, even as animals. This equation of Gypsies to part of the natural world set them in automatic opposition to civilization:

> Why . . . are we setting ourselves the impossible task of
> spoiling the Gypsies?. . . they stand for the will of freedom,
> for friendship with nature, for the open air, for change
> and the sight of many lands; for all of us that is in protest
> against progress . . . The Gypsies represent nature before
> civilisation . . . He is the last romance left in the world.[5]

The idea that Gypsies lived at one with nature was taken as given.
Descriptions of them and their camps firmly located them in rural
settings, using imagery stressing their similarity to the animal
kingdom:

> In summer time, these dusky wanderers might be seen
> encamped upon the commons, or on the sprawling borders
> of some quiet road, beneath a sheltering hedge . . . as free
> as the wild bird . . . gliding about the solitudes of the land,
> like half-tamed panthers.[6]

While these quotations were written by nominal supporters of
Gypsies, there was a very fine – indeed sometimes invisible – line
between this and the writings of those wishing to remove the
'Gypsy problem' from society:

> The Gypsies (who are on the lowest scale of culture) should
> be looked upon as a community of children of nature who as
> yet have but a superficial knowledge of civilisation and who
> will long defer its adoption . . . Their volatile nature and in-
> ability to consider the future, their instability and restlessness,
> make any approach to even the lower forms of civilisation im-
> possible . . . they have everywhere either remained untouched
> by civilisation or have adopted merely its worst forms.[7]

In this Gypsies were treated in a similar manner to Europe's colonial
subjects, where relations between colonizers and colonized were
governed by two beliefs: firstly that with help and guidance those
from less advanced civilizations could be brought up to the standard of the Christian West, and secondly the idea of a permanent
physical difference between races, often emphasized by describing
the colonized as animal-like and close to nature.

As we shall see, there was a jagged divide between these ideas and reality: Gypsy lifestyles differed widely across Europe, and could include long-term settlement rather than nomadism, everyday interactions with the wider population and involvement in mundane economic occupations, as well as ongoing adaptations to deal with the demands of state bureaucracies. In order to make sense of the disjuncture between the idea of 'the Gypsy' and reality, the racialization of Gypsies was given an extra twist. Fitting within the broader emergence of social Darwinist theories, the later nineteenth century saw the construction of a theory of the decline in the racial purity of Gypsies linked to their increased mixing and marrying with 'degenerate' members of the settled population. Gypsiologists developed a racial hierarchy that placed 'pure-blooded' Gypsies, who were believed to speak the best Romani, at the top; groups with varying proportions of Gypsy blood depending on which source one reads (*didikais* in England, *Zigeunermischling* in Germany) in the middle; and vagrants with no Romani ancestry at the bottom. This implied that while Gypsies were somehow racially suited to nomadism and so were capable of maintaining traditional codes of conduct, for vagrant dropouts and those of mixed blood this capacity was diminished or absent.[8] So, from the mid-nineteenth century we see a number of gypsiologists and anthropologists using comparative anthropometric surveys – essentially measuring skulls and bodily proportions – in order to provide evidence for theories of the origins of Gypsies. The most systematic of these were the work of the anthropologist Eugene Pittard and, of course, that of the Nazis, led by Robert Ritter. Pittard, using the Gypsies of the Balkans as his base group, sought to find 'les vrais Tziganes' where:

> Very fine men and very beautiful women are often found among them. Their swarthy complexion, jet-black hair, straight well-formed nose, white teeth, dark-brown wide open eyes, whether lively or languid in expression, the general suppleness of their deportment, and the harmony of their movements, place them high above many European peoples as regards physical beauty.[9]

For gypsiologists anxious to discover a Golden Age and a pure Gypsy culture, this outlook allowed them to pursue their pet theories, with any contradictory findings dismissed as the result of cultural pollution and miscegenation.[10] Such scapegoating enabled gypsiologists to distance themselves from the squalid, urban encampments that existed around major cities, as well as any other elements that impinged on romantic notions of a rural Gypsy idyll. It was also useful to detractors of Gypsies, who could argue that they were simply dealing with racially less evolved groups, or 'degenerate' members of mainstream society, who needed to be dealt with firmly via new legislation, education, settlement programmes or perhaps the gospel. This idea of the dangers of mixed ancestry would support Nazi justifications for genocide, and also later twentieth-century refusals to acknowledge the place of nomadic lifestyles in modern Europe.

So, where does this leave us as historians in our search to understand our sources and the 'right' word to use? Firstly, we need to acknowledge our debt to the gypsiologists in terms of the sheer amount of sources they have made available to us over the past 150 years or so. Both in painstaking archival work and in meticulous accounts of Gypsy life and culture across Europe and sometimes beyond, we have a legacy of sources that is rich and valuable, and from which I have drawn repeatedly in writing this book. But we also have the legacy of their perspective: the assertions that the particular group recorded by 'X' were 'true' Gypsies; the dismissal of less picturesque groups as 'half-breeds'; the often tortuous attempts to construct theories of how one particular Indian tribe migrated to Europe over centuries while remaining untouched by any of the societies through which they passed. Similarly reformers, in all their different guises, left a deep paper trail of schemes, theories and plans redolent with ideas of the racial difficulties presented in trying to settle down 'nature's nomads'.

Within all this debate it is now broadly accepted that early Romani groups originated in north-western India. From here they migrated westwards into Persia, intermixing and intermarrying and thereby loosely forming into a people known as the Dom, before moving further west within the expanding Ottoman and Byzantine empires and then into Europe in the medieval period.[11] Within Europe migrations of Gypsies and Roma followed three major streams: whereas the majority settled within the Balkan provinces of the Ottoman Empire, some headed to the autonomous principalities of Wallachia and Moldavia, north of the Danube (in present-day Romania), while others gradually continued to migrate north and west. Ottoman tax registries suggest that early numbers were small, while fifteenth-century historical records from western Europe invariably describe Gypsies arriving in groups of between 50 and 300 individuals. Further mixing with pre-existing peripatetic groups within Europe even more complicated the pattern while, as we shall see, the practice of transportation to New World colonies and parts of Africa, as well as later voluntary migrations, ensured their further migration beyond Europe and across the Atlantic. Later, the early settled Roma population south of the Danube were superimposed upon by migrations from Wallachia and Moldavia of groups of runaway slaves during the seventeenth and eighteenth centuries. Further population churning resulted from the abolition of Gypsy slavery, the mass migrations from southeastern Europe across the Atlantic during the late nineteenth century, while the twentieth century saw movements in response to the crises of the Second World War and the collapse of communism after 1989.[12]

Throughout all this it was rarely possible to decide with any certainty whether someone was a 'Gypsy'. We know when others *thought* someone was a Gypsy, or perhaps a Sinti, Manouche, Irish Traveller or Romanian Roma, and we know what people thought *about* them. But all too often we have no way of knowing what they themselves thought, or how they would like to have been described. Consequently, with hesitations and caveats, when using historical material, I generally use the word 'Gypsy' in this book. Along with 'Egyptian' this was certainly the word most often used for the first few hundred years of their presence in Europe, so it seems most historically, if not socially, accurate. For more recent periods, and when I look in more detail at particular national contexts, where it is possible to be more specific I use the word that is most appropriate for that country at that time. When I write about the most recent, and particularly political, developments within Europe I use Roma, as the most currently acceptable term. But here, as elsewhere when writing about history, we need to be aware that there is no one right answer.

Where to Begin?

It was scholars in the eighteenth century who made the links between Romani and the Indian group of languages, and this led to much effort being expended in the following century and a half to pinpoint exactly which tribe or from which region Gypsies originated. However, it should already be clear by now that the truth is rather more complex: to put it crudely, there was no one group of people who woke up one day in the sixth century in India and said, 'Right, let's start moving north and west. If we keep at it we should hit the Scottish coast by the early sixteenth century.'

While it is now accepted that the Romani people formed out-side rather than inside India, what is rather less clear is the point at which we might meaningfully think of the people we are writing about as being 'Gypsies' rather than 'people who might have had a similar lifestyle to and spoken a language connected to Romani'. Donald Kenrick, who has done more work than most on the subject, has described how constructing 'the early history of the Romanies is like putting together a jigsaw puzzle, when some of the pieces are missing and parts of another puzzle have been put in the same box'.[13]

This naturally presents historians, who are used to dealing with documentary evidence, with the challenges of using a combination of genetic and linguistic evidence in order to piece together the different routes taken by founder Romani groups in the migration from India to Anatolia and the Balkans. It is only after this point that we pick up the first certain documentary evidence of Gypsies.

Developments in DNA sampling have confirmed that proto-Gypsy groups originated in what is now north-western India and Pakistan, probably migrating from this region around 1,500 years ago, with movement to Anatolia and then the Balkans being relatively rapid.[14] Further genetic work, backed up by linguistics and written sources, indicates that it was at this point, rather than before, that proto-Gypsy groups split: travelling through the Balkans and then spreading out relatively rapidly into northern and eastern Europe, and westwards through Germany, France and the Iberian peninsula. We find, for example, higher genetic mixing between Roma and non-Roma populations in the Balkans than in other parts of Europe, so that in Bulgaria 45 per cent of Roma show non-Romani genetic heritage, in contrast to 11 per cent in Lithuania. This supports the general documentary and historical evidence that Romani peoples have been present in the Balkans for far longer and consequently mixed more with local populations, whereas groups present further west have mixed less with surrounding peoples. In turn this contradicts the stereotype of Gypsies and Roma being a closed, 'secret people', only interacting and marrying within their own kind. Rather, genetics, as well as linguistics and, as we shall see over the course of this book, history indicate that social rules and practice by the Roma varied across time and space according to different social constraints and opportunities.[15]

If this is the broad genetic evidence, what of comparative linguistics? Linguists use evidence of the number of shared or 'loan' words, as well as grammatical structure, as a guide to determining the relationship between different language groups, as well as suggesting how long different populations might have been in contact. Put simply, the greater the social contact and the longer the period of contact, the more shared words and grammatical structure there will be. However, it is vital to remember that at the same time as accepting how linguistics might provide insights into the migration paths, we must make no simplistic connection between genetic history and the specific language one speaks. After all a random sample of Americans, to take an example, might contain people with German, Czech, African, Asian and Native American ancestry who are all native English speakers.[16]

This is not the place to go into the possible linguistic roots of Romani within India itself, which remains a complex and contested area.[17] Greek, Welsh and Kalderash Romani all exhibit strong links with Sanskrit and Hindi, sharing more than 500 basic words, and experts have concluded that Romani does not exhibit any of the changes that took place in Indian languages after circa 1000. This suggests that Romani as a broad language formed either within the Indian subcontinent or in the early period of migration.[18] However, after this point matters rapidly dissolve into uncertainty: it is possible to point to a number of loan words from Persia, as well as a far larger number from Armenian, suggesting that early Gypsy groups were located for a significant period of time in the Armenian Empire that sat between the Caspian, Black and Mediterranean seas.[19] There is no direct evidence to explain how or why groups entered Armenia, nor why they may have left, although migration from there into present-day Turkey is likely to have been prompted by the decline of the Persian Empire and the expansion of the Seljuks from the east in the late tenth century. It was their continuous raiding of the Armenian population that created a flow of migrants westwards into the Byzantine Empire, resulting in the creation of a far smaller Armenian kingdom in Cicilia, in modern-day southern Turkey, at the end of the eleventh century.[20]

Reaching the Mediterranean

While we know that a movement of early Romani peoples from India must have taken place, there remains no definitive evidence of a distinctive 'Gypsy' identity – coalescing around language and possibly also nomadism – until Anatolia under the control of first the Seljuks and then the Byzantines. Even after this it is hard to be certain what we are looking at: 'Too often the assumption has been made, in looking for traces of Gypsies, that any reference to a migrant group pursuing a Gypsy-like occupation can for that reason be equated with them.'[21] So, while by the time we enter the Byzantine Empire towards the end of the first millenium we are on slightly firmer ground when it comes to considering the early history of Gypsies, we still need to be wary of early documents that apparently refer to them and their economic activities.

The ambiguity centres around the translation of the word 'Atsingani/Atsinganos' (derived from the Greek $ατσίγγανοι$/ $atsinganoi$), which became the word used by the Byzantines to describe heathens, after the name of a heretical iconoclastic sect that had a reputation for fortune telling and magic and which practised a number of cleanliness taboos.[22] The generally accepted theory is that this word forms the base of a number of European words for Gypsies – $Tsigani$ (Croatian), $Tsiganes$ (French), $Zigeuner$ (Dutch, German) – and consequently references to 'Atsingani' are taken by most scholars as reference to early Romani groups within Byzantium.[23] The difficulty with this is distinguishing between references to ancestors of Gypsies and those simply relating to the original Atsingani. So, for example, in 803 a group referred to as Atsingani apparently used magic in order to quell a riot and were rewarded with permission to move freely throughout the empire.[24]

We have no way of knowing whether or not this refers to ancestral Gypsies, as with an eleventh-century account stemming from Constantinople. There, in 1050 Emperor Constantine Monomachus wanted to exterminate all the wild animals that had invaded the imperial park and were eating its game. In order to carry this out the emperor employed 'a Sarmatian people, descendants of Simon the Magician, named Adsincani, who were renowned sorcerers and villains'.[25] They destroyed the beasts by leaving pieces of meat 'in places frequented by them endowed with magical properties, which, when eaten, killed them instantly'. It is tempting both to attribute the 'magic' to poison, and also to see this as the first confirmed recording of Gypsies in Constantinople. However, there are no other contemporary accounts referring to Adsincani or Astingani, and in fact we need to wait more than 150 years, until the early twelfth century, in order to have consistent and reliable evidence.

Referring to Athinganoi (Atsingani) in a general text discussing the excommunication of people accused of showing animals for entertainment or telling fortunes to the naive, canonist Theodore Balsamon noted that they 'would have snakes wound around them, and they would tell one person that he was born under an evil star, and the other under a lucky star; and they would also prophesy about forthcoming good and ill-fortunes'.[26] He also wrote about them in relation to ventriloquism: 'Ventriloquists and wizards are all those who are inspired satanically and pretend to predict the unknown [such] as . . . the Athinganoi, the false prophets, the "hermits" and others.' As there is no evidence of the iconoclastic Athinganoi surviving beyond the persecutions of the early tenth century, it is reasonable to believe that the 'Athinganoi' referred to here may be Gypsies. And if we accept that references to Athinganoi, Adsincani or Atsingani in Byzantine documents from the eleventh century onwards relate to Gypsy groups, then it becomes possible to chart something, if not of their lives, then at least of their livelihoods. Late thirteenth-century directions to the parishioners of Constantinople forbade them to associate with fortune tellers, bear keepers and snake charmers and 'especially not to allow the Gypsies to enter their homes, because they teach devilish things'. Writings from the following century and a half also place Gypsies in the same bracket as fortune tellers – with the women being particularly singled out for mention – and also magicians, or those engaged in sorcery, as well as acrobats and jugglers.

By the fourteenth century evidence from popular culture, in the form of surviving folk stories from Constantinople, provides the first insight into how they were perceived by the general population, rather than simply by the elite. The surviving stories show how they were considered 'dark', and give evidence that they were sieve makers and bear keepers. The tales also reveal more broadly the contemptuous attitude held by the Byzantines towards them, and one satirical poem – 'A Jocular Tale about the Quadrupeds' – has the protagonist, a wolf, insulting a bear, calling it a 'reservoir of filth, an amusement of the foolish Gypsies'. Later in the poem 'Gypsy' is used as an insult, when a creature is accused of being 'a liar, a thief and a Gypsy', a theme that emerges in another poem of the same period. This suggests that Gypsies were familiar enough to the general population that they would have understood and appreciated the references. However, we should also remember that, despite such contemptuous attitudes, Gypsies *were* able to make a living from providing forms of entertainment and certain services, so that they cannot have been such pariahs as to be unable to garner any audience or custom.

If we can assume that by the fourteenth century Gypsies had become a normal part of Byzantine society, we cannot make any similar assumptions about how they moved into the Balkans and became established in Thrace (modern-day European Turkey). While it is tempting to tie the first recording of Gypsies in Serbia (1348) to the rapid movement of the Black Death from the Middle East into Europe in that year, in fact most of this first wave of the plague followed a route through Italy rather than the Balkans. As with the migration from India westwards, the gradual migration of Gypsies north and west is attributable to a combination of factors, including moving within existing trading routes and responding to small-scale and short-term opportunities and difficulties by moving on. Certainly by 1362 they had reached Ragusan in southern Croatia – a document from then instructed a local goldsmith to return eight silver coins to two Gypsies named Vlachus and Vitanus – and by 1378 they were present in Zagreb. We also have evidence that Gypsies had already become serfs of the ruling princes, monasteries or nobles in Moldavia and Wallachia (present-day

Romania), so that in 1385, for instance, 40 Gypsy families were granted to the Monastery of St Anthony at Vodita. By 1445–6 there are detailed records of Gypsies living in villages in the Sofia region: one of these, Dabijiv, contained fifteen full Gypsy households and three of widows. Comparing the chief's low income from tax here with others in the area we can see how Gypsies in this district were on the lowest part of the social scale. Taken together, these documents demonstrate how Gypsies fully integrated into the feudal system by the early fourteenth century and probably participated in agriculture on a full-time basis.[27]

At the same time that Gypsies were establishing themselves in what was by now a disintegrating Byzantine Empire they were also spreading beyond its boundaries, pushed by the shifting geopolitical realities of the region. By the late fourteenth and early fifteenth centuries they were well established in the areas of the Peloponnese under Venetian control. Given the relatively stability of these provinces, which did not at this time suffer attack from the expanding Ottoman Empire (in contrast to the rest of the Peloponnese), this is no surprise. Traveller writings from the Greek mainland and islands show that 'Egyptians' were well established within these areas, that they had their own language and that they were numerous enough to be seen as one of the most 'notable' presences in the region. In this they were just one part of the mixed Mediterranean societies in the late medieval period, and although they were seen as distinctive, they were not exceptional in the eyes of others. A Franciscan friar who visited Crete in 1323 described some Greek Orthodox Gypsies living on the outskirts of the city of Candia as 'not stopping at all, or rarely, in one place longer than thirty days; they live in tents like Arabs, little oblong black tents'.[28] While this account compared them to nomadic Arabs, tax records from late thirteenth-century Corfu show that they were sufficiently numerous to be counted as an independent fief – the *feudum acinganorum* – and consequently integrated into the island's feudal system. Here they lived under an overlord who held the right to extract money and in-kind taxes, and bring to trial and punish his Gypsy serfs, with the power to imprison and exile them or make them galley slaves. Some decades later, evidence from Crete shows how some Gypsies had become absorbed within the lower ranks of Venetian imperial social structures: a letter argued for John the Gypsy

(*Johannes cinganus*) to be reinstated as head of a company of soldiers, 'under the same terms of law, rank, title and position as before the said deprivation took place'.[29] It may well be that, owing to the increasingly uncertain landscape created by the expansion of the Ottoman Empire, the Venetians acted expediently to ensure that the loyalty of all groups living under their control could be counted on. Granting rights and privileges was one way of ensuring this. It is also clear that, within the context of the ethnically mixed Peloponnese region, a range of different lifestyles, languages and beliefs were common, and in that sense Gypsies could be seen simply as one of a number of peoples rather than as 'the outsiders'.

Probably the most important place for Gypsy settlements in the Venetian Empire in this period was the city of Modon (Methoni) on the west coast of the Peloponnese. Its location on the route to Jerusalem meant it hosted many pilgrims, and surviving accounts from the 1380s onward reveal the existence of a Gypsy settlement located outside the city. An Italian, Lionardo di Niccolo Frescobaldi, visiting in 1384, described a number of *Romniti*, whom he believed were living outside the walls in order to do penance for their sins. The most detailed account, from nearly a century later stated that 'there are many hovels outside the town, about three hundred in number, in which dwell certain folk like the Ethiopians, black and ungainly' and that these people were called Saracens in Germany and that they had 'falsely claimed to have come from Egypt'.[30] Just over a century later the pilgrim Arnold von Harff in 1491, gave an insight into their livelihoods and an explanation of their presence in the city:

> They are called Gypsies: we call them heathen people from Egypt who travel about in our countries. These people follow all kinds of trade, such as shoemaking, cobbling and smithery. It was strange to see the anvil on the ground at which a man sat like a tailor in our country. By him, also on the ground, sat his housewife spinning . . . these people come from a country called Gyppe, which lies about forty miles from the town of Modon. The Turkish emperor took it sixty years ago, but many lords and counts would not serve under the Turkish emperor and fled.[31]

As here, many Traveller accounts from Modon refer to the settlement as 'Gyppe' or 'Little Egypt', in a manner 'paralleled by the
"Little Jewry" of some English towns'. When Gypsies entered
western Europe in the fifteenth century they claimed to be from
Egypt or 'Little Egypt', and more than one gypsiologist traced this
back to this Modon settlement.[32] The timings make this unlikely
as 'Egyptians' began arriving in western Europe from the early
fifteenth century, while the settlement at Modon was still in existence 150 years later. What, however, is certainly the case is that,
just as the successive movements of early Gypsy groups were tied
to the expansions of the Persian, Seljuk and then Byzantine
empires, the fall of Constantinople to the Ottomans in 1453, which
consolidated their domination of the Balkans, was central to the
establishment of Roma communities in what was to become one
of their heartlands in Europe.

We have already seen how although Gypsies in the Byzantine
and Venetian empires were of low status, they were not completely
separate from wider society, but were integrated into the feudal tax
system and provided services – smithing and entertainment – to
the wider population, as well as being tied to the land as serfs. The
Corfu tax records also reveal that they kept poultry, while evidence
from Nauplion shows that it was not impossible for them to enter
the Byzantine hierarchy, albeit at a lowly level. And in this part of
the eastern Mediterranean they existed as simply one ethnic and
linguistic group among many others who settled or moved around
the region as opportunities or difficulties arose. As part of their
daily lives, therefore, they would have come into contact with
feudal officials, pilgrims, traders and travellers as well as the wider
population they served. Consequently, although different and
distinguishable from other communities, they do not appear
particularly exceptional.

In this sense at least, the expansion of the Ottomans into the
Balkans reaffirmed and continued these features of Gypsy life.
However, the Ottomans brought with them some new features too,
not least the active settlement of sparsely populated areas of Thrace
and Bulgaria, and the methodical expansion of their taxation
system across their new territories. Significantly, the Ottomans did
not insist upon conversion to Islam but rather operated the *millet*
system. This term, stemming from the Arabic for 'nation', referred

to the separate confessional communities of the empire that were granted control over matters of 'personal law'. In essence, this meant that Muslim Sharia, Christian canon law and Jewish Halakha existed in parallel across the empire, with communities collecting their own taxes and setting their own laws within a context of swearing loyalty to the empire. This system of government was to have as much impact on Gypsies as it did on the rest of the population of the Balkans.

However, within this we must take into account the way in which the different histories of conquest played into local structures of rule and autonomy, particularly the difference between the southern Balkans, which were ruled directly as part of the Ottoman Empire, and the principalities of Wallachia, Moldavia and Transylvania (present-day Romania), which, along with Hungary, by the sixteenth century represented the furthest reaches of the Ottoman Empire. Rather than being ruled directly by Istanbul they existed as loose vassal client states, and consequently had far more autonomy. So while in 1393 Bulgaria was annexed outright, Serbia retained more independence via its vassal status from 1389, as did Bosnia, Wallachia and Moldavia. This reminds us of the importance of understanding the complex nature of empires; that conquered territories might not only be drawn in, settled and accommodated into empire, but could equally remain separate and largely independent.[33] Crucially, for the Gypsies of Wallachia and Moldavia (and of Transylvania for a short period), the autonomy of these Christian principalities meant that a system of enslavement of the Gypsy populations was able to develop.

In fact, from the first records of Gypsies Wallachia and Moldavia in the 1380s, unlike in other parts of the Balkans, they appear as slaves. Slavery here needs to be understood within the broader context of an evolving feudal system, with its meaning shifting gradually from something closer to serf status in the late medieval period to outright slavery by the time of its abolition in the nineteenth century. In this period, eastern and south eastern Europe, in sharp contrast to western Europe, saw the general expansion of serfdom, where conditions deteriorated for peasants as feudalism and serfdom became the primary means of social organization. Across the region it was often difficult to distinguish in practice between a slave and a serf: in Russia for example, a noble's wealth was measured by how many 'souls' he owned.[34] In the Balkans changes within feudalism need to be tied to shifting economic fortunes across the region, particularly as trade routes moved as a result of the expansion of the Ottoman Empire, turning Wallachia and Moldavia into something of a backwater. At the same time their vassal status required them to pay a sizeable yearly tribute to Istanbul and to supply the Empire with certain foodstuffs. As these financial obligations were passed down the social hierarchy the position of the peasantry worsened so that by the fifteenth century they had descended in semi-serf status. From then matters deteriorated further and from the sixteenth century 'it is impossible to speak of the enslaved Gypsies without mentioning at the same time the enslaved peasants'.[35]

With no firm evidence of when Gypsies reached this northern part of the Balkans or of their economic status at this time we can only extrapolate from what we know of their lives in the Byzantine Empire, and of how serfdom expanded in this region generally to fashion an explanation for the phenomenon. They were likely to have been travelling craftspeople, (horse) traders and casual labourers who, possibly through debt or poverty, had to settle in one place as serfs of the local landlord, who might have been a voivode (prince), bishop or noble.[36] Some Gypsies were able to evade this status, and maintained a nomadic way of life. In some respects these nomadic Gypsies were better off, as although technically classed as slaves of the voivode, they still had considerable freedom (including that to move around in their family groups), as long as they paid an annual tribute.[37] The position of enslaved Gypsies in this period may have been little different to that of the serfs, whose allegiance was transferred along with any change in ownership of the land. So although a 1385 document confirming the transfer of the rights of feudal ownership of 40 Gypsy families to the monastery of St Anthony at Vodita shows they existed within the Wallachian feudal system as serfs, it is not necessarily a record of their slave status. At this time, when donations of Gypsy families were being made, what was being transferred was the right to exact tribute (of work, money or goods) rather than the physical exchange of individuals. So transferrals of Gypsies to the ownership of monasteries – such as the gift of 300 families to the newly established Cozia monastery in 1388 – were probably in this vein, and it was only over time that this tribute became more formally tied to rights over Gypsies as individuals. What is also notable about the practice of slavery in the region is how, against the backdrop of an over-pressurized feudal economy, Gypsies acquired an increasing financial importance. They typically occupied a position between peasants and the growing number of agricultural serfs and the upper orders, and were valued for their artisan skills, particularly as smiths, with entire estates being dependent on their skills to function.

The position of Gypsies in Rumelia (the southern Balkans, directly ruled from Istanbul) was rather different. The expansion of the Ottomans into the region quickly resulted in the entry of more Gypsies, whose presence was documented through the extension of the empire's extensive taxation system. Two key sources exist from this period: a tax register specifically relating to the Gypsy population of Rumelia from 1523; and a general tax register from eastern Rumelia, which is thought to have been compiled in 1530 and included Gypsies within its remit.[38] Taken together these registers allow us an insight both into the nature of the early Gypsy population of the Balkans and how they fitted into broader society. The picture that emerges from the early period of Ottoman rule of the Balkans in the fifteenth and sixteenth centuries is one in which Gypsies were integrated into the emerging society and hierarchies, albeit typically at the lowest level.

The two different types of tax register present different faces of the place of the Roma within the administrative structure of towns and villages in the Ottoman Empire. We need to remember that one of the key roles of the registers was, like England's Domesday Book, to provide an idea about the demographic, productive and taxation potential of the communities under scrutiny. Notably, the Gypsy register of 1523 is very clear that although Gypsies were considered by the Ottomans to be nomadic, they largely travelled in relatively circumscribed areas and so were thought to be controllable by the authorities for taxation or military purposes.

The register shows the Gypsies as groups of independent communities (*cemaats*) that may or may not have been tied to a particular settlement, but were certainly associated with a broader district or territory within which they were based and travelled. In some cases members of the community might have been settled in a town or village in a given district while others from the same group were more nomadic, returning periodically and almost certainly for the winter season. The figures from 1523 show that there were 382 *cemaats* spread across 88 districts, together holding 16,000 Gypsies. These were not geographically evenly distributed: most Gypsies were concentrated in northern Rumelia and in the areas south of Sofia that had been settled before the capture of the city by the Ottomans in 1382. By 1530 there were 17,191 households (possibly 66,000 people) making up around 1 to 1.2 per cent of the total population of Rumelia. Mapping their locations onto present-day state boundaries, a majority of them were based in Bulgaria (5,701), with the former Yugoslav states having the next highest population (4,382), followed by Greece (2,512), with only 374 living in Albania.[39]

The spread of the Ottoman Empire northwards meant that pre-existing Gypsy communities, which were by this time identifiably Christian and took Slavic names, were added to by incoming Muslim Gypsy groups, who came as part of the process of imperial expansion and consolidation. Gypsies are recorded as having taken part in the military campaigns of the Ottomans in the Balkans, before forming part of the waves of settlement as part of the process of Ottoman-Turkish colonization. During the winter preparations for the attack on Constantinople in 1452–3, for example, Mehmed II brought together a large group of blacksmiths and craftsmen that included a number of Gypsies in order to make the cannons. This military use of their skills was something that continued, with particular communities of Gypsies being tied to forts and military settlements such as the town of Vidin and along the Danube crossings.[40] As much as it was possible, the Ottoman rule aimed at facilitating settlement in the sparsely populated parts of Thrace. This simultaneously enabled the establishment of a sound taxation base for the new territories and ensured that the population was not hostile. The groups most favoured for this scheme were in fact nomads, primarily *Yürüks* and Tatars, and also Gypsies, since their mobility made resttlement easier. Initially this occurred relatively spontaneously but then became a specific policy of the imperial power.

By 1530 the balance of religious allegiance was already changing, with records showing that 40 per cent of Gypsies were now Muslim. This shift was less a result of continuing in-migration and more part of the process of Islamicization encouraged by financial incentives. Fairly rapidly then – the fall of Constantinople had only occurred some 70 years previously – not only did the Ottomans manage to create what appears to be a relatively accurate picture of their new dominions, but they had also started having a profound impact on the population of the Balkans. These tax registers also give us a useful insight into how the Gypsy populations related to the wider communities in which they lived and through which they travelled. The evidence strongly suggests that as well as being present in both the countryside and towns, Gypsies at this time were not living particularly separately from other communities: there were no settlements with a predominantly Gypsy population, although they may have been living in particular quarters of larger settlements. Over time these did develop into distinct areas of towns, but in the first decades of Ottoman rule it appears that the situation was far more fluid. In 1530, for example, there were a number of documented examples of Gypsy households, both Christian and Muslim, which were not included in a *cemaat* but rather were dispersed among other residents.[41]

The tax registers also recorded the occupations of the Gypsies. In the register of 1523 they were most often recorded as musicians while, despite the long-standing link between Gypsies and various forms of metalworking, very few are shown as working in this field: only one blacksmith is registered, and only four ironworkers. However, if we cast the net more broadly, we can see that there were also tinsmiths, farriers, sword makers, stove and clout nail makers and ironmongers listed. If anything, what emerges is a remarkable diversity of occupations pursued by Gypsies. The lists mention a range of craft occupations, including shoe and slipper makers, leatherworkers, tailors, carpet makers, dyers; food-related occupations, such as halva, kebab and cheese makers and butchers; as well as sundry occupations ranging from gardeners, monkeybreeders, well-diggers, prison guards, servants and muleteers. There is also evidence of Gypsies working in positions higher up the social scale and within positions of authority: the 1523 returns include army officers, janissaries, policemen, doctors, surgeons and monks.[42]

Recent research has opened up the possibility that many of the nomadic Gypsies at this time were participating in seasonal agricultural work, suggesting a reciprocal relationship between them and the wider population.[43] Similarly close ties seem to have developed as a result of the various military obligations they held as *muselem* towards the state.[44] These were often discharged via employment as military blacksmiths, but sometimes also through engagement in military road construction and repair work during military campaigns, as well as the provision of food and the positioning of cannons during battle. In return for these services, as with other craftsmen, *muselem* received either a salary or tax concessions, and the position became hereditary in nature.[45] As they were tied to what were anyway fairly mobile military forces, we cannot make an easy equation between their presence in a fort and a sedentary lifestyle. Indeed, this suggests a blurring of boundaries between Gypsies and other auxiliary workers tied to the military: mobility was part of life in the Ottoman Empire where craft positions were often fulfilled by immigrant groups.

The Ottoman tax system does not simply provide us with a description of the emerging society of the Balkans under its control, it was also central to *creating* the new society. By developing distinct tax obligations for different social groups the Ottomans both tapped into pre-existing community structures and formalized them. Crucially, unlike in western Europe where a nomadic lifestyle was typically assumed to be intrinsically resistant to state intervention, within the Ottoman Empire it was regarded as simply another way of life, whose adherents were deemed to owe certain obligations to the state. Such an attitude towards nomadism meant that, rather than being seen as practically and socially outside the Ottoman community, they were treated as a distinct but intrinsic part of it. Consequently, while both legislation and bureaucratic practices set certain limitations and regulated nomadic lifestyles they were not specifically designed to force either settlement or integration.[46] Essentially, within Ottoman territory all the lands were deemed property of the Empire and, while some parts of it were owned personally by the sultan or religious institutions, the greater part was divided into fiefdoms shared out among members of the military officer class. Within this feudal system responsibility for collecting taxes was devolved to key individuals in each area or community, including nomadic groups. Such groups were divided into communities of roughly 50 tax payers with a designated head who was required to deliver the taxes each year. Being nomadic no more excluded Gypsies from the Ottoman tax system than it did other nomadic ethnic groups such as the cattle-herding *Yürüks* or the Tatars.

In 1530 a crucial decree was enacted. The 'Law for Gypsies in the Rumelia' set out the obligations of Gypsies to the state, and shows how this was intimately bound up with religion. Its importance lies in demonstrating how, as with all Ottoman subjects, a central distinction was made between Muslims and Christians, and how a further distinction was made between Gypsies and the rest of the population. Throughout the Ottoman Empire Muslims were taxed more lightly than non-Muslims, who were required to pay the *cizye*, a tax exclusively imposed on them 'to demonstrate their inferiority'.[47] Uniquely, Gypsy communities fell outside of both these categories, with both Muslim and Christian Gypsies obliged to pay Gypsies the *cizye*. This shows how they were seen as separate from the broader Muslim community and consequently, as far as tax and social status was concerned, there was no sharp distinction in the official mind between Muslim and Christian Gypsies. And yet, while both had to pay the *cizye*, they did not pay at the same rates: the decree of 1530 set the rate for Muslim Gypsies at 22 *akçes* and that for non-Muslim Gypsies at 25 *akçes*.[48]

The law also gives us an insight into the way in which, for Gypsies, the *sancak* (community) functioned as a political and administrative unit encompassing Muslim and non-Muslim Gypsies and both settled and nomadic households. It was headed by the *çingene beği*, or 'Gypsy *sancak* chief', who collected taxes from the community on behalf of the Sultan and was responsible for relations between the community and the state.[49] In effect he acted as the tax collector, magistrate and intermediary between the community and the authorities:

> The Gypsies who stray from their judicial district and hide in other districts as well as in backyards, are to be found, admonished, strictly punished and brought back to their district. The finding and returning of Gypsies who stray from their community is entrusted to the leaders of their companies and to their village mayors . . . [so that] they are present and do not hide their whereabouts when taxes are due to the Sultan or special taxes have to be paid.[50]

Any fines imposed by the Gypsy *sancak* on his community could be kept by him, consequently giving him a strong incentive to implement the laws of the Empire. As well as being drawn into the Ottoman state through the implementation of its tax requirements and the judicial process, the *sancak* leaders were expected to fulfil certain military obligations. The 1530 law details how the leaders from the Nikopol and Nish regions were required to serve in the Nikopol and Smederevo regions respectively, with the other leaders serving in the Pasha region. The resulting mix of obligation and privilege bestowed on the *sancak* leaders which emerges from this document demonstrates very well the ways in which the Ottomans adapted their feudal institutions in order to draw in even the most marginal communities within their territories.

THIS IS A GOOD MOMENT to step back and reflect not only on the emerging position of Gypsies in the societies in which they lived, but the nature of those societies themselves. Already we can see how, far from being separate from society, the migration of early Gypsy groups from India, and indeed their formation as an ethnic group as far as we can tell, was intimately tied to the expansion and contraction of empires: Persian, Seljuk, Byzantine, Venetian and Ottoman. Even strong empires have to work with their peripheries, local elites and frontier groups to maintain compliance, resources, tribute and military cooperation and ensure political coherence and stability. Imperial structures manipulated local elites, drawing them into their bureaucratic structures in order to maintain control in the furthest reaches of their empires. In this vein the Ottoman Empire, through how it dealt both generally with nomadic groups and Gypsies specifically, demonstrated an ability to absorb diverse populations and to create new institutions:

> Ottomans negotiated between the contradictory, yet also complementary, visions and organisational forms of urban and rural; nomadic and settled; Islamic and non-Muslim; Sunni Muslims, Shi'ites and Sufi sects; scribes and poets; artisans and merchants; peasants and peddlers; and bandits and bureaucrats.[51]

Within such a diverse society, through using the *millet*, ethnic, racial and religious categories were deployed in order to make administrative tasks easier for the authorities. At the same time this system allowed the separate communities the space to develop distinctive identities. This entailed a very different world view to the one we will encounter in the emerging nation states of Europe in the early modern and modern periods. This is not to argue that these communities were all seen as equal: as the tax system demonstrated, across the empire Muslims were given preference, while both Muslim and Christian Gypsies were accorded low status. Nevertheless, the everyday practicalities of ruling vast territories meant that compromises had to be reached that allowed different communities to negotiate space for themselves.[52] Such freedom was not always liberatory, and could cause specific local practices of oppression to emerge, such as slavery and deep forms of serfdom.

So far the picture we have of Gypsies under both the Ottoman and the Venetian empires suggests that, while they were perceived as different, they were not seen as exceptional. They were fully integrated into their administrative structures, and undertook a wide range of economic activities from metalworking and seasonal agricultural labour to military functions and even petty official roles. They were present in the countryside and towns, often living alongside the wider population, with no clear division between nomadic and settled ways of life. Sometimes mobile and present in forts, ports and trading towns as well as remote areas they were perhaps better placed than many to understand that life was larger than was often apparent to the average inhabitant of the late medieval world. As we move now into western Europe on the cusp of the early modern period what is perhaps most striking is how rapidly this diversity of Gypsy experience and lifestyle became condensed into one stereotype: that of the wandering nomad.

ONE

Out of the Medieval World

THE ESTABLISHMENT OF GYPSIES across the Balkans by the late fourteenth century created one of the long-standing centres of Romani culture. More than this, it also laid the foundations for an understanding of European cultures: the Balkans already contained a mix of Christians, Muslims and Jews; those living in Modon, and other parts of the eastern Mediterranean, would have been familiar with pilgrims on their way to and from Jerusalem; and through everyday economic and social interactions Gypsies communicated with different populations and had an understanding of how other cultures worked. It is worth emphasizing these points because so much of the evidence of the first interactions of Gypsies with European cultures seemingly focuses on their separateness, their foreignness and their inherent ungovernability.

We do not know why in the first decades of the fifteenth century Gypsies started being recorded in central and western Europe. While the expansion of the Ottoman Empire into the Balkans, as well as the population changes caused by the plague in the mid-fourteenth century, formed something of the backdrop to their movements, we need to be aware of the effect of Gypsies extending their migratory routes further north and west, finding new opportunities and economic niches on the way. The reality is that, despite centuries of speculation, there is no hard evidence. But what we do know from their lives under the Ottomans and Venetians is that Gypsies had a number of strategies at their disposal with which to negotiate the new territories they were entering. Key to their success in any new place was to make themselves explicable to the populations they encountered. However, while the tools and strategies they developed under the Ottomans may well have been translatable into the world of late medieval Europe, Gypsies had the misfortune of arriving at a time when these ways were becoming out of date and being replaced by a rather harsher climate. Coming from the multi-ethnic and flexible practices of the eastern Mediterranean they entered a world that was increasingly inclined to construct boundaries between places, people and religious groups.

Although no period of history is static, the arrival of Gypsies into western Europe in the fifteenth and early sixteenth centuries coincided with a period of profound uncertainty and change. The medieval world had been fundamentally centred on a universal church and religious view that regulated and ordered life on earth as much as it propagated a particular approach to heaven. However, this gradually dissolved and with it institutions, attitudes, under-standings and practices all changed profoundly over the fifteenth and particularly the sixteenth centuries. The process of religious fragmentation through the Reformation after 1517 and then the reassertion of Catholicism after the Council of Trent (1545–63) via the Counter-Reformation interplayed with the emergence of nation states. Britain, France and Spain consolidated their internal terri-tories at the same time as embarking on new overseas empires in the Americas; Protestant cities and states – most notably the Netherlands in its Eighty Years War (1568–1648) against Spain – fought for religious and political freedom from Catholic influence; while the process of creating Protestant churches and congrega-tions shifted balances of power and allegiances at local as much as national and international levels. To add to the political and reli-gious uncertainties of the period the sixteenth and first half of the seventeenth centuries saw population growth, rising prices and falling wages and agrarian dislocation, all of which fed into increas-ing migration and urbanization. It is no surprise then that the early modern period contained a number of complex and protracted conflicts – the French wars of religion, the revolt of the Nether-lands, the Thirty Years War – as well as new ideas about and responses to poverty, vagrants, outsiders and belonging.[1]

And into this contested material and spiritual terrain arrived the Gypsies. Not en masse, but rather in dribs and drabs over the course of the fifteenth century: first recorded in Germany in 1417, France in 1419, Switzerland and parts of Italy in 1422, Spain in 1425 and the Low Countries by 1429. They did not cross the North Sea or English Channel until far later, with the first definite record of their presence in Scotland dating from 1505 and in England not until 1514.[2] So how were these strangers received? What did people make of them, and how did the societies of early modern Europe understand their way of life and presence in their towns and countryside?

To begin to understand how they were received both initially and over the subsequent decades we need to place the multitude of arrival stories recorded by contemporaries in the context of the messy and contested world of early modern Europe. Arriving when they did, the ways in which they were assimilated into, or marginalized from, the European societies through which they travelled has to be seen as a process: they were not encountering state and social systems set in stone, but rather interacting with the emerging societies and mechanisms of early modern states. Arguably what we can see over the first century after Gypsies appeared in western Europe is a profound shift in thinking in which medieval understandings of outsiders were replaced by harsher early modern ones.

At first glance it appears that the appearance of groups of Gypsies, with their dark skin and silver earrings, in towns across western Europe in the fifteenth century, presented a spectacle of utter foreignness. And indeed, contemporary accounts emphasized their exotic appearance and strange practices, as in the case of the reactions of the Parisians who came to see the group of around 100 Gypsies who arrived in August 1427 and were accommodated at St Denis.[3] Their visit was recorded by a 'Parisian Bourgeois', who reported people coming from all over the city to see people he described thus:

> The men were very dark, with curly hair; the women were the ugliest you ever saw and darkest, all with scarred faces and hair as black as a horse's tail, and their clothes were very poor . . . an old coarse piece of blanket tied at the shoulder . . . [with a] wretched smock or shift. . . . I must say I went there three or four times to talk to them and could never see that I lost a penny, nor did I see them looking into anyone's hands, but everyone said they did . . . [and this palmistry] brought trouble into many marriages.[4]

And yet, while clearly novel in many ways, rather than seeing these early groups of Gypsies as utterly incomprehensible to the populations of Paris and the other centres they visited, we can rather see them as part of a continuum of strangers encountered by the people of early modern cities. Despite the long-standing image of late-medieval Europe as essentially static, with individuals tied throughout their lives to one particular place, in fact for many movement and migration were an intrinsic part of everyday experience.[5] Between the commercial revival of the thirteenth century and the end of the middle ages, the transport of goods became quicker and easier and generally safer, with trains of pack animals being replaced by two-wheeled and then four-wheeled wagons run by professional carriers organized from a network of inns that provided warehousing and packing facilities. While this was perhaps most noticeable in northern Italy, where works were often undertaken by the expanding city states, it was also a feature in more remote areas, and was driven by expanding trade that made improvements in the widths and surfaces of the roads and the building of countless bridges economically attractive.[6] Improved travel networks, while mainly pushed by trade, benefited other travellers too, so that alongside merchants and traders on the road were a medley of what the Germans termed *fahrende Leute* (moving people), who included wandering scholars, minstrels and travelling entertainers, knife grinders, travelling healers, hawkers and tinkers. And of course travelling alongside – and sometimes with – these groups were pilgrims following well-trodden national and international routes to sites of religious importance.

And so, faced with novelty, those encountering Gypsies for the first time sought to make them explicable. Consequently, whether or not the Gypsies recorded in Paris in 1427 in fact read palms, the people they encountered believed that they did: this was clearly the kind of activity, along with low-level criminality, that populations expected of certain kinds of stranger visiting their town. And crucially, as far as the sources allow us to interpret their actions, it appears that for their part Gypsies sought to make themselves explicable to the strangers they encountered. The best surviving account of a number of affiliated groups of Gypsies travelling through northern Germany and the Hanseatic towns in 1417 describes how they

Had chieftains among them, that is a Duke [*Ducem*] and a Count [*Comitem*], who administered justice over them and whose orders they obeyed. They were however, great thieves, especially their women, and several of them in various places were seized and put to death. They also carried letters of recommendation from princes and especially from Sigismund, King of the Romans, according to which they were to be admitted and kindly treated by states, princes, fortified places, towns, bishops and prelates to whom they turned. Certain among them were on horseback, while others went on foot. The reason for their wandering and travelling in foreign lands was said to have been their abandoning of the faith and their apostasy after conversion to paganism. They were committed to continue these wanderings in foreign lands for seven years as a penance laid upon them by their bishops.[7]

Here we see the mixed reception they received in some places, alongside mention of their organizational structure – the use of noble titles and self-policing – and letters of protection linked to the need to make a redemptive pilgrimage. While varying in form, these letters were a consistent feature of the early accounts of the presence of Gypsies in western Europe. The image of organized communities led by 'dukes' or 'counts', loyal to its own customs even when they were at odds with the norms of fifteenth-century French or German society, is an intriguing one.[8] Unpicking the meaning behind this phenomenon throws up the first case of something we will come across time and again in trying to explore the relationship between Gypsies and mainstream society: we have evidence of how they presented themselves to the wider world; what we don't know, and probably can never know, is what they themselves actually believed. In essence, was it 'true' or was it a convenient front or, indeed, something in between?

The form of organization recorded here closely mirrors that of the Ottoman system of *sancak* leaders, although chronology works against a simple translation of this practice, for the first Gypsy groups were in western Europe well before the fall of Constantinople. However, leaving this to one side, travelling as a group of extended family members with the nominal head being the eldest male is one of the commonest forms of organization for nomadic people. When we combine this with the need of marginal groups and people to make themselves explicable to the authorities, the use of terms such as 'count' or 'lord' becomes understandable.

We can see this through looking at the contemporary world of vagrants, beggars and 'masterless men', who were a growing feature of the period. It was not uncommon for such people, when arrested or challenged by the authorities, to claim that they were 'Lord of the Rogues'. Claiming some kind of lordly status might improve a vagrant's chances when dealing with the authorities as well as making explicable what otherwise might be seen as a threatening, amorphous social group. In no way can we assume from the fact that vagrants used the term 'kingdom' that they organized themselves into formal 'kingdoms'. In fact court records show that vagrants were commonly arrested in very small groups, which were less likely to attract attention than large bands.[9] Given the importance of hierarchy in early modern Europe, that socially marginal people presented themselves via a language of ranks and degrees is not surprising, and it is no less unsurprising that Gypsies did the same, as evidence from Spain suggests. There, Gypsies arriving in the 1520s passed themselves off as pilgrims with their leaders seeking to ensure safe passage for their kin by presenting themselves as *condes* (counts). Historian David Pym has described this as 'a deftly camouflaged and temporarily effective translation of their own role within the Gypsies' patriarchal clan system to the new social formation through which they were moving'. As occurred in other parts of Europe, letters of safe conduct were duly issued to the new arrivals, who initially at least enjoyed a cordial welcome.[10]

The use of letters of penance and the explanation of enforced pilgrimage played directly into the world experiences of late medieval Europe. Of all the reasons for travel there was nothing as socially sanctioned and universally explicable as pilgrimage and penance. While it was often the wealthy who undertook pilgrimages, this was by no means exclusively the case, and the combination of begging for alms and undertaking a journey of penance had been long-sanctioned by the Church: St Francis had taught that beggars were holy and that the holy should live as beggars, and mendicants were a common feature of the medieval landscape.[11] So while Gypsies, on one level, may have appeared foreign and inexplicable, their stories of pilgrimage in combination with papal and imperial letters of protection set them firmly in the camp of legitimate passers-through. Sometimes welcomed in royal and noble courts, often given food and money, and even exempted from punishment for crimes, it seems that for the first years of their time in western Europe they were able to make their presence explicable and acceptable enough for authorities and communities to accept their presence, albeit sometimes grudgingly.

Evidence from the town accounts books of these early visits of Gypsies to German cities shows how they were routinely given alms in their capacity as pilgrims and accredited travellers: accounts from Hamburg, for example, show that they were given £6 in 1441, two years later they received £4, and over the next decades whenever they visited the town they were given similar sums of money. Likewise, their first visit to Frankfurt in 1418 saw them well received; when they returned in 1434 they were given money to buy bread, meat and straw for their animals and in 1446 a Gypsy was even given citizen status.[12] Perhaps one of the most striking details of this period comes from a chronicle of 1417 from Augsburg that states that they had letters giving them permission to steal from those who refused them alms.[13]

The letters of protection Gypsies carried in this period varied in content and provenance, and there has been much inconclusive debate over their authenticity. The most commonly recorded letter of protection was a document apparently issued by Holy Roman Emperor Sigismund during his stay in Constance in 1417–18.[14] In line with the medieval practice of issuing letters of safe conduct for individual travellers and their followers (the forerunner of passports), Sigismund apparently authorized the document giving the bearers free passage through his land. It was this – or variations of this – which many Gypsy groups, including those discussed above travelling around northern Germany and the ports of the Baltic, carried with them.[15] Versions carried by Andrew 'duke of Little Egypt' in France named the pope rather than the emperor as the signatory. These told how his group had first been conquered by Christians, whereupon they converted, but shortly thereafter were attacked by the Saracens: 'enduring but a brief attack and making but little attempt to do their duty and defend their country, surrendered', renouncing Christ. For this, the pope allegedly decreed that 'for seven years they should go to and fro about the world without ever sleeping in a bed', and that they would receive a 'good and fertile land' once they had fulfilled their penance.[16]

The advantage of the letters ostensibly granted by the pope over that of Sigismund's is that they had universal application across Christian lands, while the emperor's only held good for the Holy Roman Empire. One writer on the subject believes that these documents were entirely counterfeit:

> the Gypsies could always assert they had made [the pilgrim-age] and produce vouchers for the truth of their assertion; for the manufacture of false passports and other forgeries was a flourishing industry in those days and when their old letters (perhaps also forgeries) were out, or lost their virtue, or neared their time limit, they could easily have been replaced by other more efficacious. It is scarcely credible that a horde of four hundred disorderly Pagans could visit Rome, interview the Pope, and occasion a great debate in council, without leaving in the archives some record of their passage.[17]

This legitimately raises the question of the exact mechanics by which groups of Gypsies might have obtained the letters, were they to be genuine. In *The Gypsies* (1995) Angus Fraser speculates that Sigismund would have been willing to grant them an audience 'for the sake of news from his Hungarian kingdom'.[18] How likely such a meeting was is open to doubt, and as with the fabled visit to Rome, there is no independent surviving evidence of such an event. All we do have is the reports of the chroniclers testifying to the existence of such documents, and one surviving copy. What is certain, however, is that taking together the letters of protection for pilgrims, the use of noble titles and the tendency of varying authorities to respond to the presence of Gypsies by giving them alms, it seems reasonable to suggest that Gypsies were success-ful in presenting themselves in ways that were acceptable and explicable to late medieval audiences.

But as the world of Europe began to fracture and change rapidly, so too did the reception of Gypsies. Even in the early days Gypsies might be treated with suspicion: their first visit to Paris, for example, saw them camping outside, rather than being welcomed within, the city walls. And if we look closely at records from Germany, even as early as the mid-fifteenth century, we can see how precarious their initial welcome had actually been. By the third visit of Gypsies to Frankfurt in 1499 they were kept outside the city gates, and in following years, having managed to gain entry, were forcibly removed. Indeed throughout German city states from the late fifteenth century the policy was to keep them outside the walls. When entry was allowed it was in exceptional circumstances, such as in Cologne in 1539 and 1599 when a Gypsy woman was granted entry in order to cure a sick noblewoman.[19] Where we do see continued evidence of alms-giving it seems increasingly to be motivated by a desire to pay them to go away and to protect the town and its inhabitants from their presence. So, for example, the records from Siegburg, although showing frequent gifts to Gypsies after their first arrival in 1439, also have recorded next to the amounts comments such as *um der Stadt schaden zu verhüten* ('to prevent harm to the city') and *von der Hand zu weisen* ('dismissed out of hand').[20] By 1504 the king of France had ordered an enquiry into the existence of Gypsies in the country, and decreed that if they were presented there, they should be 'hunted, robbed and thrown out'.[21] In fact the late fifteenth century saw a proliferation of decrees ordering the banishment and punishment of Gypsies, something that was to become a standard feature of European life right up to the end of the eighteenth century.

What then caused this further hardening in attitudes? The intellectual curiosity stimulated by the Renaissance, an increase of travel in the early modern period and the opening up of the New World to Europeans was not, as we might expect, mirrored by a similar openness to strangers. Historians have shown how the Reformation in the sixteenth century heightened ideas of foreignness and revealed how it was a contest over space as much as it was over theology. Through the desecration of religious buildings, the destruction of pilgrimage routes and through positioning Rome and the pope as 'foreign', Protestants shaped a new geography of Europe with new boundaries, both physical and imaginary. Even apart from the arrival and appearance of Gypsies across Germany in particular, 'a new urban mentality emerged, pitting insiders against outsiders'.[22]

This was the period when western Europeans had to come to terms with the discovery of peoples untouched by monotheistic religion. Beginning with Marco Polo's travels eastwards, Europe's encounters with and colonization of the Canary Islands, the Caribbean and the two American continents threw up questions over 'race' and difference. Although not finding full expression until the late nineteenth century, by the 1600s writers were positioning peoples according to their level of 'civilization' and relationship with nature. The essayist and humanist thinker Montaigne reflected, 'These nations . . . seem to me barbarous in the sense that they have received very little moulding from human intelligence and are still very close to their original simplicity.'[23] Europeans had had contact with other cultures before this, most notably via trade, pilgrimage and crusade routes across the Mediterranean, but

> For the merchant it was a matter of little immediate importance whom the Arab married. To the colonist and the missionary, however, it could be crucial. It was colonisation which forced the 'savage' and the 'barbarian', and with them the intelligibility of other worlds, fully upon European consciousness.[24]

Not only did this train of thinking profoundly influence relations between colonizers and indigenous peoples but spilled over into treatment of 'outsiders' within Europe. Consequently in this period we see the increasingly rigorous definition and treatment of minority groups including the Sephardic Jews and the *mudejar* Muslims in Spain and the Jewish communities across the Holy Roman Empire. In this time of uncertainty there was a powerful temptation to fit previously unknown peoples into already known categories, and the Gypsies were no exception.[25]

If we look in depth at one particular city we can gain some insight into how attitudes towards strangers and minorities, including Gypsies, changed from the mid-fifteenth century onwards. Frankfurt was a free imperial German city, with strong national and international trade links and vibrant semi-annual fairs, and which hosted the election of Holy Roman Emperors. All this meant that there was a relatively high proportion of foreign merchants and other outsiders, and there had been, for example, a sizeable Jewish population since the twelfth century. Like most German cities it was contained by walls that, while having been originally defensive in function, had also developed other uses too. Walls acted as financial regulators, in the form of customs barriers or 'murage'. They also marked the area of special urban law, distinguishing the city from the 'lordly order outside the town' and denoted the area covered by the imperial charter that guaranteed anyone, regardless of place of origin and social standing, who lived in the city for a year, the status of free person. This was often encapsulated in the phrase *Stadtluft macht frei* ('city air brings freedom'). City states have unsurprisingly been depicted as heralding modernity, with their walls being seen as the visible symbol of the 'strife for independence and freedom'.[26]

Jews had long been the archetypical outsiders in European society, and in common with their experiences in other parts of Germany their presence in Frankfurt had been punctuated by periodic pogroms as well as expulsion following the arrival of plague. By the early fifteenth century they had once again been allowed back in the city, and had become integrated into its trading life and political culture, being able, for example, to be granted the status of burgher (citizen). But their new position did not last and the second half of the fifteenth century saw them being expelled from almost all German cities, and from many of the German territories of the Holy Roman Empire.[27] Frankfurt took a slightly different approach, requiring them from 1462 to live in a designated part of the city, in essence a ghetto – the Judengasse – that was surrounded by a wall, the three gates of which were locked at night, on Sundays and on holidays. Only those who had business in the town were allowed to leave the Judengasse, indicating how the city wanted the benefits of their skills while not wanting to face the reality of their presence. These actions were part of a wider trend of marking Jews as outsiders: they were required to wear yellow rings on their clothes, and their stay in the Judengasse was conditional on making payments to the municipality. By 1480 Jews were no longer recognized as burghers, but were rather referred to as *Fremdlinge* (foreigners). Over the next century their marginalization was further entrenched, so that by the time of the Fettmilch Uprising of 1614 the guilds of the town insisted on the expulsion of all Jews, something that was physically enforced by the town's populace. Expulsions right across Germany's towns meant that Jews were increasingly forced to travel so, by the mid-sixteenth century, this had translated into the relatively new justification for their plight – the myth of the eternally wandering Jew – which had bound up with it more general negative connotations of permanent travel and travellers.[28]

This period also saw the hardening of attitudes towards and physical exclusion of other groups across German cities including Frankfurt. There, during the uprising of 1614, one of the town's grievances was that too many masterless maids had been allowed to settle in the city: not only were they accused of bringing down wages, but also of bringing vice and dishonour to the city. This was the culmination of nearly 150 years of marginalization of self-supporting women generally and prostitutes in particular, and was by no means peculiar to Frankfurt. Lyon's city gates were installed to keep out, among others, 'old women or widows with children', while in Munich 'masterless women' who returned three times to the town were pilloried and then expelled.[29] In the light of the treatment of Jews and certain types of women then, the exclusion of Gypsies from city boundaries and decrees expelling them from certain territories – such as the general order to remove them from the Holy Roman Empire following the Diet of Freiburg in 1498 – appear as part of a broader trend. Consequently, when we think about the exclusion of Gypsies from cities across western Europe we need to see this not as something exceptional, visited solely on Gypsies *as Gypsies*, but rather as part of a broader story of how an emerging early modern Europe struggled to deal with groups who were seen as sitting outside social norms.[30]

And yet we need to guard against making easy comparisons between different groups of outsiders. The shifting climate of the sixteenth century also saw the emergence of witchcraft trials across Europe, as states sought to impose discipline and uniformity on plebeian popular culture via religious uniformity. As well as official moves to stamp out local religious traditions and extend their authority, local communities also used accusations of witchcraft as a means of managing inter-communal tensions in a time of rapid social change.[31] While we might expect that Gypsies would have been prime targets for the hunts, which reached their peak in south and west Germany between 1561 and 1670, in fact they appear to have been untouched by the phenomenon. Although Gypsies were both outsiders and strongly associated with fortune telling and sorcery, the move against witches was actually driven by a fear of malevolent magic posing a threat from *within* a community rather than outside: an analysis of trials shows how most accusations stemmed from close neighbours who were only marginally differentiated by social class and standing within a community from those they accused.[32] An understanding of this is useful for reinforcing the importance of being sensitive to the different social meanings 'outsiders' could carry within different communities and historical contexts and is a theme to which we will return, most notably in relation to the Second World War.

While it is tempting to see the processes of tighter state control combined with the suppression of potentially unruly elements as somehow historically inevitable, it is important to remember the contingent, messy and uncertain nature of this shift. For those living through these times the changes were by no means inevitable, and outcomes at the local or individual level could as easily run counter to as reinforce the general picture. We need to remember that the state was emerging simultaneously with the problems it was trying to tackle, working out the extent of its own remit: there was no set 'state' and at this time the main concern of central governments was the issue of security, both domestic and international.[33] We can see this if we look at evidence from Hereford council following a proclamation in June 1530 which had been published and sent out across England 'for the punishing of vagabonds and sturdy beggars' through stripping them naked and whipping them.[34] This was just two months before a group of Gypsies arrived in the Hereford area, and resulted in this document:

> 1530, AUG. 17. – CERTIFCATE OF THE DELIVERY OF CERTAIN GIPSIES TO A JUSTICE.
>
> This indenture made the XVII day of Auguste in the XXII yere of the reigne of Kyng Henry the VIII. bétwene John Cantourcelly, meyre of the citie of Hereford on the one partie, and Roger Millewarde, gentilman, on the other partie, witnessith, that the seid meyre hath delyvered to the seid Roger Milleward one Antony Stephen of the countrey of lytyll Egipte as hedde and capytayne of XIX persons of

men, women and chylderyn named them selfes pilgrims,
the whiche came to the seid citie of Hereford the VIIIth day
of Auguste the seid XXII yere of the reigne of Kyng Henry
the VIIIth, and soo taryed there by the space of IX dayes and
IX nyghtes, and in the seid citie dydde no hurte as I can
perceve as yet, savyng only there was persute made after
them by one Thomas Phelipes of Ludlow for a certeyne
sume of money to the sume of IIIIl. VIIs. VId. taken by
certeyne of them owte of the house and chambre of the seid
Phelips contrary to the Kynges lawes. And soo I the seid
meyre have delyvered to the seid Roger Milleward the seid
capytene with all his compeny, to the nombre in all with
the seid capytyne, as men, women, and chylderyn, of XIX
persones, with bagge and baggayge, and the seid Roger to
use them after the Kynges commaundement. In witnesse
wherof I the seid Meyre and Roger Millewarde to this present indenture entyerchangeably have put to our seales the
day and yere above seid.

[*Signed*] Per me Rogar Mylleward.[35]

Unlike most similar surviving documents, this indenture does not
closely mirror the Latin standard form. Essentially, what we have
here is a glimpse of the English state making itself up, albeit within
existing legal parameters, in this case the indenture and the idea
of obligation that it carries. Generally the mayor's court used a standard form for indentures that were written in Latin and conveyed
commercial debts, so this document is unusual because on the one
hand it is in English, and a different format, and on the other the
'goods' being exchanged are people. There are three further points
of interest that set it apart from normal legal rhetoric. Firstly, the
Gypsies identifying themselves as pilgrims was a local example of
what we know to be a Europe-wide phenomenon. Secondly, that
the document states they have done 'no hurt *as yet*' simultaneously
suggests a presumption of suspicion towards strangers while also
acknowledging, in all fairness, that they did nothing wrong during
their stay in the city. Finally, the phrase 'the king's laws' is quite
unusual. Generally the term used was 'the King's Peace' (as in, for
example, 'Tom committed trespass against the King's Peace') or 'the
common law' (as in 'Becky can find no remedy within the common

law'). This is thus interesting because it potentially implies that the Gypsies did not live within, or did not normally abide by, the jurisdiction of the king. This fits with the wider evidence from across Europe from this period that shows Gypsies being exempted from local laws, either because of their letters of safe conduct or because it was accepted that they had a right to some degree of internal self-government. The other thing that this phrase signalled, from a legal perspective, is that it removed the problem from the mayor's jurisdiction and placed it in the hands of the Crown.

Just as the provenance of the document is murky, its overall purpose is not entirely clear. On the one hand the indenture was one way for the Mayor to demonstrate how he was obeying the king's proclamation, while on the other enabling him to distance himself from the situation. In the normal course of events he would have to detain the suspects and keep them until September under surety (bail), but in this case he bypassed this procedure, in all probability because he did not want to fill up his prison primarily with women and children. He thus gave them up straight to Roger Millward, who was probably a Justice of the Peace. But it is not at all obvious whether all the Gypsies were physically detained, only the 'captain' or in fact none of them. From a legal perspective, the document is rather unclear about what sort of crime the Gypsies might have committed. The sum of money taken – £4 7s 6d – was very large, and would count as grand larceny (a capital crime), while the fact it was taken 'out of his chamber' would also imply burglary (another capital crime). Certainly it was a serious offence; but it is important to remember that, in practice, relatively few people hung for robbery, and that the person 'pursuing' them may have been more interested in getting his money back than having them convicted. If so, he might have sued them for trespass (in which case, if he had won, he would have been awarded damages of the same amount or more), rather than had them charged.

Interestingly this document does not imply an automatic assumption of guilt, or indeed that punishment might follow from the indenture. What we have here then, is not only a glimpse of Gypsies staying in Hereford for nine days in 1530, but an insight into how a newly arrived group to England interacted with an emerging, and fluid, legal system. What is perhaps most telling about this document, apart from revealing something of the ambiguous documents with which historians of the early modern period must work, is how it shows that the Tudor state was making a claim to govern everyone in the realm, even if it was not always successful in doing so.

One of the key areas into which the Tudor state, and indeed states right across Europe, extended itself was that of the increasingly intractable problem of the poor, and the vagrant poor in particular. While recent research has shown that there are continuities between the late medieval period and the early modern era, and therefore we need to be careful about overemphasizing the speed and nature of change, it is clear that the world for the poor was different in 1600 than it had been in 1400.[36] From the late fourteenth century until the early sixteenth century structural poverty – that is, poverty caused by factors beyond that of the individual or the family – declined. The massive population loss following the Black Death meant that landholding sizes increased, and employment opportunities in agriculture and in the towns also widened, resulting in higher real wages. These were combined with climatic improvements that meant that bad harvests were infrequent, and the second half of the fifteenth century saw the tax burden reduced.[37] However, by the early sixteenth century the balance had shifted away from favouring the poor: a combination of declining real incomes, population growth and bad harvests, with consequent food shortages, acute poverty and unusual amounts of migration led to social disruption that was manifested as much in changes in established marriage patterns as it was in outbreaks of violent unrest right across Europe.[38]

At the same time we can detect a sea change in attitude between ideas of poverty in the early modern period compared with the medieval era. Again, while we need to be wary of overstating the discontinuities, historians are in broad agreement that this period saw a general hardening of attitudes towards the poor at the same time as a number of long-term trends including a move from religious to secular priorities, from private alms to public measures, from charity to welfare and from voluntary contributions to compulsory levies.[39] Up until the Reformation poor relief had largely been concentrated in the hands of the Church. The giving of alms not only provided the poor with material support but bestowed them with a status in society by interpreting poverty as religiously sanctioned. Similarly, begging was seen as an acceptable way of life, central as it was to the medieval practice of charity.[40]

Protestantism has often been credited with changing approaches to the poor, with writers traditionally pointing to the dissolution of religious orders and the introduction of the Protestant work ethic contributing to the harsher climate for those in need of support. In part this was manifested through a gradual process of secularization, so that town authorities rather than the Church increasingly handled the relief of the poor as part of their work, with this being most obvious in the German city states that embraced Protestantism and took over the funds and work of their church foundations as part of the Reformation. It is important, however, to recognize recent evidence that has stressed the broadly comparable shifts in how poverty and the poor were managed across both Protestant and Catholic states, suggesting that the 'ubiquity of disease, crime and crisis' across the Continent prompted similar responses irrespective of the religious makeup of the government in question. Indeed, as early as the fourteenth century there was the beginning of writings suggesting that it was wrong to relieve the wilfully idle, and gradually the 'sin of sloth' came to be defined as including physical as well as spiritual vices. By the beginning of the fifteenth century many humanists believed that some types of poverty, far from leading to holiness, caused social disorder and should be supressed. In this they were part of a wider shift in thinking that can be seen as part of the humanist Renaissance, which celebrated values of activity, success and engagement with the world. This chimed with the increasing clamour for reform of the Church, for although good works and almsgiving continued to be popular, their spiritual value was called into question, while friars and pilgrims were mocked as impious frauds. Broadly then there was a movement towards St Paul's attitude that a good Christian works to pay their way.[41]

The rising number of paupers from the late fifteenth century and an emerging idea of the 'true poor' or deserving poor – orphans, the sick, infirm, aged or widowed – left no room to recognize unemployment per se as a reason for beggary. Essentially, unless someone was seen as physically incapable of earning a living, increasingly all who begged were to be considered as idlers and to be treated severely. To the dominant classes vagabonds were a profound threat to the established social order: they were 'master-less' in a period when the able-bodied poor were supposed to have masters, and they broke conventions of family, economic, religious and political life. Sixteenth- and seventeenth-century vagrancy consequently involved more than simply being poor and rootless. It is difficult to capture the meaning that terms like 'beggar' and 'rogue' held for contemporaries: today's equivalent might be terrorist, extremist or anarchist. Edmund Dudley, writing in England in 1509, stated that they were 'the very mother of all vice . . . and the deadly enemy of the tree of commonwealth'.[42]

Unsurprisingly the focus of state attention was not on effective relief of the poor as such, but rather taking measures to control vagabondage and minimizing the socially disruptive potential of bands of wandering 'masterless men'. While no other piece of legislation of the sixteenth century matched Edward VI's 'infamous' Act of 1547, which prohibited begging and sentenced vagrants to branding and two years' servitude for a first offence and execution for a second offence, it all wrestled with the problem of dividing the deserving and undeserving poor and controlling a potentially dangerous section of the population. Spain and Portugal took similarly repressive approaches. In 1552 Spanish vagabonds were sentenced to the galleys, and over subsequent decades the state repeatedly passed similar legislation reinforcing its terms, sending a strong signal of their deviant status. In Portugal, crowds of beggars and foreign vagrants roaming the capital were accused of refusing to work, 'becoming thieves and getting into other bad habits', and faced increasingly punitive measures. The law of 1544 created a hierarchy of punishment – from imprisonment, to flogging and expulsion – and within this a further hierarchy of expulsion: for the first offence, from the place where they were arrested, for the second from the kingdom, and for a third offence, transportation to Brazil.[43]

These measures were in tune not just with England, but with states right across western Europe, as the first half of the sixteenth century saw the passing of laws restricting access to poor relief aimed at excluding the migrant poor, vagrants and 'sturdy beggars'. Such legislation saw the first genuine efforts to codify and rationalize poor relief through, for example, a move from voluntary to mandatory contributions towards the support of the poor and the formalization of a central coffer in each parish to provide for the upkeep of the locally needy. These developments generally benefited the local poor but only at the expense of excluding and punishing 'outsiders', the sturdy beggars, 'rogues' and vagabonds. Turning back to Frankfurt, as early as 1476 the town authorities divided the poor into residents and outsiders through the local poor being required to identify themselves with a special badge when they were collecting alms. A decade later the guidelines were clarified, so that 'local' paupers were only those who had been burghers for at least eight years, or who had served the city for that length of time. These were the only ones entitled to municipal support and who were allowed to beg, with all others being ejected from the city walls.[44] Not only were such rules common across German cities, but they were also introduced across French and a number of Italian cities at roughly the same time.[45]

In such a context the Gypsies' claim to be pilgrims, deserving of and dependent on alms from those they met, increasingly rang hollow. They were far more likely to be seen as vagabond outsiders making demands on already overstretched parish funds, and marginalized and vilified accordingly. It is no wonder that in the rapidly changing world of sixteenth-century Europe, where migration and vagrancy was on the increase and Gypsies were on the move, that all the different groups travelling and living on the road should become entwined, both in popular imagination and in law. Contemporary writers and legislators in Spain made explicit links between vagabonds and Gypsies. In 1597, in his *Política para Corregidores*, Jerónimo Castillo de Bobadilla stressed how the term *vagamundo* (vagabond) should be understood to include the Gypsies, as well as healthy beggars. For him the word was taken to include 'anyone who is not settled in an area, and with neither property, nor trade, nor a master, nor work, wanders idle and suspect, and liable to steal or commit other crimes'. In using this definition he was simply following contemporary practice and reflecting existing legislation.[46] Similar eliding of categories could be found in England where in 1554 the introduction of the death penalty for 'Egyptians' refusing to leave the country struggled to be implemented owing to the number of Gypsies who stated that they had been born in England. As a result the 1562 version of the Act extended the death penalty to anyone 'in any company or fellowship of vagabonds, commonly called, or calling themselves Egyptians', as well as those 'counterfeiting, transforming or disguising themselves by their apparel, speech or other behaviour' as Egyptians. For contemporaries, then, vagabonds and Gypsies were interchangeable categories in their unwelcome, outcast status.

Alongside the moves against the vagrant poor, the sixteenth century saw the creation of a new social outsider: that of the religious deviant. The western Church had faced reform movements and breakaway sects throughout its history, but nothing on the scale of the Reformation, which swiftly gained momentum, creating divisions within and between states. In part we might attribute its wider success to its conjunction at a historical moment that was also seeing the gradual rise of nation states. The Reformation consequently enabled religious freedom from Rome to combine with political independence, strengthening the authority of national monarchies vis-à-vis Rome. It also ensured that new ways of understanding and defining loyalty – who belonged to a state and who did not – became paramount. Throughout the early modern period Catholics in Protestant states and Protestants in Catholic states were doubly suspect, being traitors as well as heretics. And while there was often only a connection in the minds of suspicious governments, they often became tied up with concerns the vagabond and the Gypsy. We see this in accusations of spying so that, for example, the Tudor state blamed Gypsies for plots against Elizabeth I and of harbouring Spanish spies in their midst.[47] Frankfurt was one of the first German states to pass laws against them on the grounds that they were spies:

> when credible proof exists that they are scouts, traitors, spies and explore Christian countries for the benefit of the Turks and of other enemies of Christendom [it is] strictly forbidden to allow them to travel in or through their states to traffick, to give them safe conducts, escorts or passports.[48]

Similarly, the first general law to be passed against Gypsies in the German territories was in 1498 on the grounds that they had 'betrayed Christian countries to the heathen', that is, the Tartars and Turks who were raiding countries not far from Germany's eastern frontier. Given the fact that Gypsies often presented themselves as having arrived from the Ottoman territories it was by no means an outlandish suspicion that they were spies, even if there was no proof.[49]

Lest we are tempted to see the processes of state formation and the increasing control of its populations as primarily affecting north-western Europe and the emerging Protestant states, a closer look at Spain shows how a similar process was under way there. In fact, the history of early modern Spain's treatment of its minority population groups has been described as a 'chronicle of an obsession', as the most varied and multicultural society in western Europe, produced by the long Muslim and Jewish presence on the peninsula, became obsessed with purity and *pureza de sangre* (purity of blood). Tied with a broader political aim to unite the different kingdoms of Spain under one crown, efforts to remove religious, linguistic and moral difference were central to the reigns of Ferdinand and Isabella in the last part of the fifteenth century as well as their successors in the sixteenth.[50]

While superficially the story of Castile and Spain in the sixteenth century was one of success and imperial expansion, in fact a reliance on the wealth of its New World acquisitions and the drain on its coffers from a number of sources, including of course the war in the Netherlands, meant that its internal economy was weak. To this was added the crippling effects of famine and plague in the late sixteenth century that is estimated to have killed 600,000 of the Castilian population. This was an unpropitious set of circumstances, but when combined with a policy of taxing those least able to pay and the spectacularly inefficient administration of Philip III and his chief minister Lerma, the results were little short of disastrous. The decline of Spanish power is well documented elsewhere; what concerns us here is how this fed into the treatment of Spain's minority populations: the Jews, Moriscos and Gypsies.[51] The expulsion of Jews in 1492, the forced conversion of Muslims in Granada, and the subsequent revolt and repressions of 1499–1501 and the expulsion of Muslims who refused to convert that followed was in fact only the beginning of over a century of attempts to enforce homogeneity on the new Spain. The fact that these actions resulted in the creation of a huge population of *conversos* and Moriscos who were suspected of secretly continuing to practise their faith under the cover of Christianity created a society suspicious of difference and anxious to impose certainty. We can understand the activities of the Inquisition in this light, as well as the final expulsion of Moriscos from the Iberian peninsula between 1609 and 1614.

Within this toxic climate issues of culture and control became central to public policy, with Spain experiencing what has been described as 'the exhilaration and anxiety' of an elite attempting to impose order on a rapidly changing and diverse society. In part this was about trying to consolidate an empire that expanded rapidly over the sixteenth century, both within the Iberian peninsula and across the Atlantic, as well as being an attempt to insulate Spain against the intellectual trends of northern Europe.[52] Through the efforts of the Counter-Reformation, most commonly manifested through the Council of Trent and the Inquisition, a particular form of Catholicism became dominant, one that emphasized obedience to authority and religious and cultural conformity. Central to the Catholic Church's revived mission was the definition and maintenance of the moral boundaries of society, both for God and the monarchy. The world view it developed revolved around the strongly held belief that Christian society had been divinely ordained into a well-ordered hierarchy. However this was defined, it excluded Gypsies on both theological and functional grounds. Not only did Gypsies not fit this hierarchical model, but legends surrounding their provenance only served to reinforce their alienation from Christianity. By this time a popular legend had emerged from the stories of penance, linking Gypsies' perpetual nomadism to their refusal to have granted Christ shelter. On top of this were widely held beliefs that Gypsies did not marry in churches or 6baptize their children, and it is important to understand just how profound a challenge this was to the Church's moral and social authority. Given the fact that the Church was the fundamental pillar of royal absolutism, and one of its key roles was to teach moral obedience to the Crown, the persistant unorthodoxy of Gypsies did not simply have theological implications, but was seen as actively undermining the power of the state.[53]

The first orders against Gypsies were passed in Spain in 1499, and were a reflection of both wider European concerns over this minority and their specific position within Spain. As with similar legislation across Europe it combined threats of expulsion with exhortations to assimilate, while accusing the 'Egyptians' of begging, theft, deceit and sorcery. This first proclamation gave 'Egypcianos' 60 days either to settle and adopt a recognized trade or to find a master to serve, and any found wandering after this date were to be treated as vagabonds and punished accordingly. All these ordinances contained a range of punishments: for a first offence, 100 lashes and banishment for life; for a second, notching of the ears and 60 days in chains followed by banishment; finally, those caught wandering for a third time were to become the property for life of those into whose hands they happened to fall. Subsequent edicts of 1525, 1528 and 1539 reiterated the original legislation, with the latter also adding that any male Gypsy aged between twenty and 50 who was without a trade or a master was to be sent to the galleys for six years, while women were to be flogged.[54] This reflected both a preoccupation with the manpower shortages affecting Spain's Mediterranean galley squadrons, and the fact that not only had the previous edicts failed to make much impact, but that Gypsies were seen to have been joined by large numbers of foreigners and other, home-grown vagabonds. [55]

Contemporary commentators also made explicit connections between Gypsies and Moriscos, particularly in the crisis years around the end of the sixteenth century. Writing in 1619, Sancho de Moncada observed that they were 'much more useless than the *moriscos*, since these latter were at least of some service to the Republic and the Royal revenues'. Others believed that they were actively a threat, not least because they were seen as potential spies, while Cristóbal Pérez de Herrera, Royal Physician to Spain's galleys who was preoccupied with the political and demographic implications of Spain's relatively low 'Old Christian' birth rate, feared that:

> within twenty or thirty years, the greater part of this realm (apart from some people of quality and wealth) will be made up of beggars and Gascons, many of whom are *moriscos* and Gypsies, because they are growing and multiplying rapidly, while we are diminishing in numbers very quickly because of wars and the religious orders.[56]

Herrera was one of many who believed that Gypsies should be expelled alongside the Moriscos, something that was considered but initially rejected in favour of a requirement for them to engage in 'recognized trades'. Essentially this should be viewed as short-hand for working on the land, agriculture having been struggling as a result of losing its Morisco labour force. However, in June 1619, in response to a petition passed by a two-thirds majority of the Cortes of Madrid the year before, Philip III ordered the expulsion within six months of all Gypsies found wandering in Spain, for-bidding them to return on pain of death. Those remaining were required to settle in towns of more than 1,000 households (in order that they could not form a dominant part of the population) and prohibited their distinctive dress and language. The edict even banned the name 'Gypsy', on the grounds that 'that they are not so by birth' and so 'this name and manner of life may be for evermore confounded and forgotten'. Essentially then the choice for Spain's Gypsies was between exile and forced assimilation into a society, simultaneously assigning them pariah status while demanding they abandon their cultural identity.[57]

It is worth here emphasizing how even within a climate of tightening repression across Europe, there were important national differences. So, France for example, presents something of an exception in this period. While injunctions against 'Egyptians' had been passed by Francis I in 1539 these were rather vague and set out neither when they should leave France nor the punishment for failure to comply.[58] More details were forthcoming in a 1561 edict, which ordered the expulsion of all Gypsies within two months under penalty of being sent to the galleys and corporal punish-ment. If any returned after the two months they were to have their hair shaved off, with men being sentenced to three years in the galleys. And yet there is no sign that these measures were enacted, and in fact throughout the sixteenth century leaders, still calling themselves 'count' or increasingly 'captain', presented passports and letters of safe conduct and were only rarely inconvenienced by the authorities.[59] So, in 1597 when the Estates of Languedoc ordered local authorities to ban Gypsies from towns and villages and to no longer issue them with the passports that were required for internal journeys, it seems they were completely ignored.[60]

The internal chaos within France as a result of the wars of reli-gion and subsequent civil unrest meant that across the second half of the sixteenth century and into the seventeenth often heavily armed groups of Gypsies were a regular feature on the roads of France: a certain Jean-Charles was recorded at Loches in 1565 at the head of a company of around 60 people. These bands also often participated in different campaigns of these wars, with, for example, the Duke of Guise, governor of Provence, commissioning 'Captain La Gallere, Egyptian, to gather other Egyptian captains and soldiers who were in the area, in order to send them to Languedoc in the service of the King'.[61] As we shall see for the seventeenth century, as states rarely held a monopoly of power within their borders, what was possible very often differed sharply from what a monarchy might have thought desirable. Consequently, although theoretically marginalized and vulnerable, evidence shows how Gypsies could make use of gaps in power to establish themselves as a significant presence on France's roads and as an active part of the civil war.

If Gypsies were increasingly being expelled and vilified within western Europe, seen as outsiders, vagrants and a threat to public order, was this also the case on the other side of the Continent? The early years of Ottoman rule in the Balkans suggested that Gypsies might face an accepted, if lowly, position in society, and something very different from their place in the rest of Europe. However, as the Gypsy population of the Balkans became more established, so too did Ottoman rule and the cultures and local societies that developed in tandem with it, and consequently regional differences became more entrenched. So in Bosnia, for example, the sixteenth century saw the further extension of the *sancak* system, which was formalized so that each group was made of 50 individuals with a designated leader, who had considerable autonomy, although inevitably this was tied to providing group labour in the mines in lieu of taxes to the state:

> No one was to interfere in his affairs or limit him in any way. If anyone should break the law, they should be detained and, provided that guarantees are given by the community, and by its leader, there should be an oral hearing. It has been decided that [the Gypsies] should work in the pits near Kamengrad and should be provided with means for their existence.[62]

There is also ongoing evidence of Muslim Gypsies engagement in the military, both on the front line and as auxiliary personnel. In common with western Europe, by the mid-sixteenth century there is some evidence of the Ottoman administration making attempts to settle nomadic Gypsies in its territories, as in this regulation from 1551:

> Groups of Gypsies ride fine horses. They do not stay in the same place but move from town to town, from place to place. They plunder and steal, thus troubling the population and causing unrest . . . they have to renounce their nomadic way of life, to settle down and to take up farming. The Gypsies must from now on be forced to sell their horses, and if anyone objects they must be punished with a prison sentence.[63]

As in the rest of Europe, this should be seen more in the vein of a complaint about Gypsies getting above their station than an actual policy that was implemented: a similar regulation was passed in 1574 that also banned the use of horses by Gypsy acrobats in Istanbul. There is no particular evidence that the authorities made any systematic or concerted efforts to settle Gypsies, and paying their taxes was broadly seen as sufficient in the eyes of the state. State intervention may have contributed to the emerging pattern of seasonal nomadism common in the Balkans – of travel during the summer and spending the winter in one place – that grew up in response to the Ottoman insistence of inclusion in tax registers. Here though we need to acknowledge that in other parts of Europe where Gypsies did not face such administrative constraints they also often chose to settle for the winter. Consequently it seems likely both that seasonal nomadism was a preferred option and that it fitted within the regulatory framework in which they found themselves.

In the vassal states of Wallachia, Moldavia and Transylvania feudal slavery continued to predominate, and in fact saw the further erosion of personal rights for Gypsies. Rather than their transferral between nobles or monasteries simply being a matter of changing the master to whom tribute was owed, by the sixteenth century Gypsies had unambiguously become slaves absolutely at the disposal of their masters: they and their children were chattels who could be sold, exchanged or given away. It is from 1480 that we have the first documented open sale of Gypsies. In this year Voivode Stefan the Great of Moldavia bought three families of Gypsies from Petru Braescul of Dragoiu (in Wallachia) for 50 Tartar zloty. From this time onwards it became gradually more common for Gypsy slaves to be sold in open markets, rather than in private transfers between nobles or religious houses. In 1533 a visiting Fugger merchant, Hans Dernschwamm, noted that he saw a group of Gypsies in chains in a slave market. These were nomadic Gypsies who had failed to pay their annual poll tax and were being sold as a consequence.[64]

The worsening position of Gypsies was reinforced in law, so that any non-Gypsy who married or made a Gypsy woman pregnant also became enslaved.[65] And yet records show that the niche Gypsies occupied within these feudal societies was often that of the skilled artisan. As well as living in villages and alongside farming land, the men also worked as barbers, tailors, bakers, masons and servants, while women were employed in fishing, housework, linen bleaching and also as seamstresses and embroiderers.[66] As they would often have occupied key roles in local and manorial communities it is unlikely that they would have been treated in the same way as, for example, the field slaves of plantation regions of the New World. Something of the value Gypsies had to nobles and to the local economy is revealed in a decree from 1560 issued to the rulers of the Danube region. This related to the nomadic Gypsies who paid their taxes to the princes of Moldavia, but were currently being abducted, possibly by border guards and taken out of the region:

> certain classes of Gypsies . . . have been abducted by surprise are then sent to the banks of the Danube where they are put up for sale . . . know that the trafficking of tribute-paying Gypsies (who pay their poll tax) out of Wallachia is not permitted. If you learn, therefore, that these Gypsies after being taken were transported to your town to be sold there, you must prohibit it. You will permit absolutely nobody to be subject to this kind of treatment. If there are recalcitrants, you must give me the names and descriptions. This question demands that it is treated with importance.[67]

I think we can safely assume that the voivode was not motivated by concern for the well-being of the abducted Gypsies, but rather his loss of revenue. This document also points to the importance of borders: Gypsies were not simply abducted across the borders, there is evidence that over the centuries many escaped either north into the mountains, or indeed formed something of a counter migration, moving south into the Ottoman territories proper, where they could leave behind their slave status.

SO, AT THIS STAGE IN GYPSY HISTORY, what can we see? We know that Gypsies initially used letters of safe conduct and the identity of pilgrims in order to ease their passage in Europe, and that to begin with this was a relatively successful strategy. We have seen how, with the changing social, economic, religious and state context of the times, this approach became less successful, and that vagabonds and the poor increasingly became targets for legislation which distinguished between insiders and outsiders, and between the deserving and the undeserving poor. At the same time minority groups, the Jews right across Europe, those of a different Christian denomination and the Moriscos in Spain, all became the focus for measures of marginalization, expulsion or repression. If we need to understand the treatment of Gypsies in the light of how other marginalized groups were viewed at the same time, we also need to acknowledge how concerns over Gypsies were at the confluence of multiple anxieties faced by early modern Europe. It is no surprise then that Gypsies, the archetypical outsider – foreign, rootless, with no clear religious affiliation and carrying with them the taint of spying, criminality and sorcery – consistently faced the extremes of legislation both across time and across the Continent. That their experiences within the Ottoman Empire were so divergent suggests that it was not something inherent in 'Gypsyness', but rather the ways in which Europe dealt with difference that prompted the responses found across western Europe.

TWO

Breaking Bodies, Banishing Bodies

IF IN THE LAST CHAPTER we saw how the move from the medieval to early modern worlds in Europe saw the arrival of Gypsies coincide with a tightening of attitudes towards strangers, the continued emergence of nation states, new forms of government and responses to vagrants, then the seventeenth century was no less dramatic. These years saw some of the harshest legislation against Gypsies right across Europe and into the New World. This was the era of grotesque physical punishments – mutilations, public torture and executions – as well as 'Gypsy hunts' and banishments. It was a time when wars and their consequences wracked much of the Continent, while the Ottoman Empire dominated the Balkans and the Counter-Reformation took hold across Catholic territories. And yet, despite all this, these years saw the acceptance of Gypsies into the everyday worlds of many communities across the Continent, as well as the emergence of distinct Gypsy identities in different parts of the Continent.

Without doubt, the seventeenth century was a period in which legislation against Gypsies across Europe was exceptionally harsh, and often the history of Gypsies in this period reads as nothing less than a litany of persecution. The territories of the Holy Roman Empire passed 133 anti-Gypsy measures in the years 1551–1774; in 1571 Frankfurt am Main passed a decree legalizing the killing of Gypsies, making it explicit that the killer would go unpunished; and as in much of the rest of Europe, persecution, torture, transportation or life in the galleys. And yet, despite the number of remaining records across Germany, for example, 'only one instance of the execution of a Gypsy has come to light' within the first 300 years of their arrival, 'a remarkable circumstance in any country'.[1]

It is timely then to consider exactly what enacting legislation meant in the early modern world, and how the state was able, or not, to put it into effect. Even in France and Britain, which by the end of the seventeenth century probably had the highest capacity for implementing the wishes of the central state on the ground, if they had even come close to achieving the aim of removing Gypsies from their societies, 'by the middle of the seventeenth century there would hardly have remained . . . a footloose Gypsy against whom to legislate'.[2] Consequently right across western Europe at this time we can see something of the tension between the expanding ambitions of early modern states, and their material limitations. Looking for an explanation for the mismatch between intention and action we can point to two main factors: the limitations of state power, and the resilience of Gypsy culture in the face of oppression. Indeed due to a lack of coordinated effort and sustained implementation it is important to remember that 'laws in general are a poor guide to the treatment of Gypsies'.[3] This is not to argue that Gypsies were not persecuted: those forced into the galleys of France or Spain's squadrons; those branded, flogged and exiled right across Europe all experienced these things because they were Gypsies. What we need to be alive to, however, is how the difficulties experienced by the early modern state in translating its theoretical authority into actual exercise of power effectively meant there was a space in which Gypsies could carve out a place for themselves in European society.

Consequently we can see the importance of understanding the limits of the technologies of rule available to states in the early modern period. While a monarch might have believed him- or herself, and been believed, to hold absolute power, in reality they were entirely reliant on actors at the local level for their wishes to be put into effect. Here we come across a phenomenon that we will see played out time and again: the 'state' was and is in fact a patchwork of different organizations and actors, often with competing interests and different priorities, and often demonstrating a 'reluctance, resistance or simple inability to comply'. When we overlay these with 'wrangles over jurisdictional competence, endemic corruption and interminable appeals procedures' the wonder is often how any law was ever translated into action on the ground.[4]

Therefore, as we move into the seventeenth century and view the swathe of legislation passed against Gypsies right across Europe we need to understand not only the intentions of those in power, but what impact it had on the ground. It has been suggested that the Spanish edict of 1619 should be viewed as 'gesture of frustration' in the face of the knowledge that previous anti-Gypsy legislation had never been enforced. The key innovation of this new law was that, through banning the use of the word 'gitano', it aimed to officially erase Gypsy ethnicity simply by denying its existence. But in 1633 yet another sanction was passed, on effectively the same lines, declaring that Gypsy dress, language, separate *barrios* or meetings were banned, on the grounds that 'those who call themselves *Gitanos* are not by origin or by nature but have adopted this form of life for such deleterious purposes as are now experienced'. Again, the use of the word 'gitano' was prohibited, and they were not to be portrayed in dances or performances. Anyone identified as a wandering Gypsy could be taken as a slave, and groups of Gypsies were permitted to be hunted. Given the problems of depopulation across Spain full-scale banishment was no longer seen as an appropriate sanction; while women could be sentenced to flogging and banishment, men were put to the galleys for six years. And yet if these measures were implemented, they were certainly done so patchily, both across time and place, for by 1695 further legislation was felt necessary. This ordered a census of all Gypsies, to include their occupations, weapons and livestock. Once again they were ordered not to live in separate *barrios*, but only in settlements of over 200 inhabitants and to work only in agriculture. They were banned from keeping or using horses or weapons, and from attending fairs and markets.[5] The picture then for Gypsies in Spain at the end of the seventeenth century, despite nearly a century of being denied an existence, was in fact one where they lived in separate districts, pursued a range of occupations including horse trading at fairs and markets, and lived in settlements both large and small.[6]

Perhaps the issue was that the Spanish state was simply too big and poorly served by administrators to be able to enforce its will effectively? What happens if we turn to the other end of the scale and consider the possibilities for close attention afforded by a small state, such as was found in the German territories in this period? Far from being a centralized state, this area consisted of around 300 sovereign powers, all of whom could pass special legislation for their own territory. These were overlain by the Holy Roman Empire, which in theory was united under an emperor elected by seven leading princes, but in practice existed as a patchwork of free cities, principalities and bishoprics. Consistent across German legislation against Gypsies in both the sixteenth and seventeenth centuries was a clause complaining that previous legislation had not been enforced. In-depth study of surviving records suggests that

> Not only do the authorities appear not to have gone out of their way to arrest and execute Gypsies, but when they had arrested them for, or on suspicion of some crime, in no case do they put the extreme law into execution: they simply pass them on, with or without a whipping.[7]

Proximity to other states not only presented the opportunity to move the 'problem' on, it could also undermine attempts at prosecution, something we can see if we look at the use of false passports by Gypsies in 1579 within the principality of Stolberg in the Rhineland:

> Some Gypsies, under pretext of possessing imperial safe-conducts, entered his county, swindled the inhabitants out of several hundred florins and escaped into the jurisdiction of the Lord of Hartenberg who was a vassal of the Principality of Mainz. The Count pursued and arrested the fugitives, but the Lord of Hartenberg, fearing the passports, although they were evidently clumsy counterfeits, would do nothing.

This led the Count of Stolberg to pass an edict making the exhibition of all passports compulsory.[8] For us it reveals not only the longevity of the use of safe-conduct letters, a good century and a half after their first use, but the fractured nature of state action. In this period when borders and boundaries were becoming more important – indeed Boes has observed that the German word for border, *Grenze*, did not come into common usage before the sixteenth century – as well as serving to keep out undesirables, they could also act to the advantage of those fleeing the law, particularly somewhere like the Holy Roman Empire, which seemed constitutionally incapable of acting coherently. This not only made a large number of laws necessary, but crucially it made them less effective, and throughout the seventeenth century Gypsies often resorted to borderlands as one way of surviving in a hostile world.

In France, it was not until the second half of the seventeenth century that legislation against Gypsies became properly active. Before this, the lack of clarity of the legislation, combined with the chaos of the Wars of Religion (1562–98) meant that any repression towards Gypsies was geographically patchy and rarely sustained. The wars had also produced decades of unrest fuelled in part by well-armed groups of (ex-)soldiers roaming the countryside. The eventual emergence of a newly centralized French state from this civil war saw the monarchy and state becoming more powerful, and part of this process was the strengthening of its army, and an attempt to stamp out the legacy of lawlessness.[9] Key to this project was Cardinal Richelieu's centrally appointed 'intendants', who acted as the king's agent in the provinces. This development was coupled with an advance in education and Catholic religious socialization, which were part of a wider project to produce the ideal of a well-ordered society. Within this new vision the vagrant and the wanderer had no place, and indeed was perceived by the state as a threat, in both deed and example. Fixed, regular work was seen as the dividing line between those accepted and those rejected. As was so often the case these images and a desire for social control existed in tension with France's, and indeed Europe's, need for a migrant workforce and the reality of migration in the early modern world. While it was their nomadic behaviour and apparent idleness that saw Gypsies classed as undesirables, in fact at the local level they were often accepted, and even welcomed within communities for the services they provided.[10]

The most important development as far as Gypsies, or Bohemians as they increasingly became known in France, were concerned was the setting up of Europe's first fully centralized police force, the *maréchaussée* (marshalry) in 1687. A major part of their work was to follow up on sightings of vagrants and Bohemians and to enforce the terms of an edict of 1682. This law was directed at 'all those who are called *Bohèmes* or Egyptians', and decreed that all adult men were to be sent to the galleys, boys to houses of correction, while women and girls were to have their heads shaved, and if they persisted in their ways, were to be flogged and banished.

In order to encourage enforcement, rewards were given to the *maréchaussée* for each individual captured, whether vagabond, Bohemian, heathen or otherwise, and right up to the Revolution there are accounts of armed rural police hunting down Gypsies. However, while this was a major innovation, the numbers of marshals was relatively small. Even after reform in the 1760s, there were only 3,882 police in all of provincial France, a country of 25 million people.

While the edict was enforced across France, often the effect was the breaking up of the large majority of the companies numbering up to 200 members. They dispersed into smaller, less conspicuous groups who found it easier to move on before they were apprehended, and in addition many seem to have moved into difficult to access and only recently integrated border regions such as Alsace-Lorraine and the Basque areas of the Pyrenees. In some mountainous areas, such as Alsace-Lorraine, large bands managed to continue for some time longer. Here wild game was plentiful and the area was sufficiently lightly governed for groups to be able to launch heavily armed raids on local villages for supplies and to cross the border in times of danger. Some bands gained much notoriety, such as that of Hannikel Reinhardt, which stole pigs, sheep and poultry, and also robbed Jews and ecclesiasticals. They were reportedly so confident of their position that they would march through villages at night with lighted torches, intimidating residents with quasi-military behaviour.[11] However, recent research has questioned the extent to which this strong association between Gypsies and forest regions is backed up by documentary evidence. Rather than being based on multiple reports, it seems that the *maréchaussée* in fact found few Gypsies in the forests, and the French association between forests and Gypsies came as much from assumptions of their animal and anti-civilizational qualities as from reality.[12] Equally we need to be wary of assuming that the 1682 declaration, with its insistence that Gypsies should be condemned 'without any form of figure of legal process' was implemented any more consistently over time than it was across place. Evidence rather suggests that after a brief period of intense implementation, many judges rapidly returned to treating Gypsies like any other citizen.[13] So overall while it appears that large groups of Gypsies were commonly broken up and geographically dispersed at this time, overall any impact was patchy and inconsistent.

Consequently, it is important that we understand how laws often existed more as a threat than an action, and rather served to keep Gypsies on the margins of society than to remove them completely. And by existing on the margins of society it was possible for them to live a life often ignored by the authorities, except at times when they were seen as too much of an irritant, or too potentially useful to be ignored by the state. This becomes clear if we look at the evolving ways in which the early modern state dealt with lawlessness and criminality. As states expanded their ambitions, both in terms of what a state was seen to be *for* and the level of control they desired over their population, ideas of punishment changed.

In part this was manifested through the realization that rather than removing undesirable elements through banishment, states could use the labour power of prisoners for its own ends. In some places, such as Spain, to this was added the extra incentive of depopulation, which made the traditional responses of expulsion or execution far less logical punishments than sentencing criminals to labour. And so we see a trend of criminals being deployed in the galleys as rowers, and in mercury and other mines where it was hard to recruit free labourers. Galleys had become an established feature of anti-Gypsy edicts in Spain and France by the mid-sixteenth century. This phenomenon can be seen as part of a wider trend of the treatment of criminal elements, rather than as something specific to Gypsies themselves. So, as early as 1564 Charles IX of France forbade the sentencing of prisoners to the galleys for fewer than ten years, while a century later Louis XIV, in order to fulfil his expansionist ambitions, ordered that the courts should sentence men to the galleys as often as possible, even in times of peace.[14] Spain's desire to protect its coasts and its shipping led to the maintenance of a standing galley fleet in the Mediterranean, while both Venice and Genoa also required labour to fulfil their imperial and trading aims.

The seventeenth century saw galleys growing larger in order to accommodate more fighting men and cannon, with the rowing forces expanding proportionally. In 1587 the standard Spanish galley needed 170 rowers; by 1621 this had increased to 260.[15] The second half of the seventeenth century saw an absolute and relative increase in the number of men under arms, both soldiers and rowers in the galleys. This was not simply the result of the war-mongering of Louis XIV between 1672 and 1714, but the product of German princes attempting to consolidate their power and maintain fighting forces. The increased demand for soldiers led to pressures on recruitment, with agents then turning to vagrants and the poor to fill the gap, and it is no surprise therefore that while women and children still faced flogging and banishment, action against adult male criminals, as much as specifically anti-Gypsy legislation, saw them sentenced to the galleys.[16]

We can tie this development in with the practice of 'Gypsy hunts' (*heidenjachten*) that were a feature of seventeenth- and early eighteenth-century Europe. In Germany the centre of the hunts was in the south, reaching from Thüringen and Saxony through Bavaria, Württemberg and Baden to the Palatine while also reaching into the French Lorraine region. It is true that this part of Europe, which was politically fragmented and consisted of inaccessible terrain, was attractive to Gypsies, providing as it did plenty of borders to cross and hiding places in which to avoid the authorities. However, recent research has tied the location of these hunts very specifically to their role in providing labour for the armies and galleys of Europe. After 1675 several German states began to conscript their 'unwanted' as soldiers, while Prussia, Bradenburg and Saxony ordered their sub-districts to round up vagrants in order to supply their recruits.[17] At the same time, but in the south of Europe, the demand from Genoa, Venice and the French Mediterranean was more for galley rowers than soldiers in order to sustain the naval conflict with the Ottoman Empire. While some of this labour was supplied through the prisons of some German states – notably Bavaria, Württemburg and Baden – a large number came from round-ups of vagrants in certain parts of Germany. Given this context the 'outlaw corridor' between the Palatine and Saxony becomes explicable: this was an area far enough from both the Prussian-Bradenburg recruitment district, and owing to the expense of transportation in relation to the amount fetched by a slave, too far from the Mediterranean. Consequently this became an area attractive to vagrants, Gypsies and others avoiding conscription. The states in this corridor hosted higher numbers of vagrants, some of whom banded together in large groups in order to further defend themselves, and in order to pillage more effectively. States responded with ever more severe measures outlawing vagrants, and Gypsies, the end result of which were the 'Gypsy hunts'.[18]

Not all the European states had the option of transportation, or even the capacity to translate law into action. It was no coincidence that it was the emerging nations of Britain, France, Spain and Portugal, with their developing national governments and increasing capacity to impose central will on their peripheries, which expanded their empires in this period. But what of other European nations, many of which in the seventeenth and eighteenth centuries were overrun by war and religious conflict? It is hard to underestimate how the political and religious chaos of the late sixteenth and seventeenth centuries very directly tied into the treatment of Gypsies. This was indeed a time when, try as they might, states did not have the monopoly on violence – they may have had increasing ambitions to hold absolute power over their subjects, but in practice this was often limited and contested.

We can see this in Germany in the seventeenth century, which was thrown into turmoil by the consequences of the Thirty Years War (1618–48). By 1648 it was in a desolate state, having lost an estimated third of its population, and for decades armies had been crossing its territories, surviving through plunder, and often supporting a huge troop of women, children and hangers-on, which included families of Gypsies. For example, Wallenstein's army towards the end of the war had around 40,000 troops and 130,000 camp followers. These included disparate family groups of Gypsies whom he employed as spies and soldiers. Similarly, the Gypsy Rosenberg family from Groningen had a long history of serving the Dukes of Sachsen-Lauenberg and Brandenberg as mercenaries, with their extended families travelling alongside the armies during campaigns. In July 1664 a 'large, well-armed and mounted band' of them appeared in Saxony, on their way to entering the service of the Swedish army, while another group of them came through, having already been refused entry into the emperor's army due to the number of women and children in their ranks.[19] All this supports the view that by the end of the conflict Gypsies' experience as 'privileged raiders when attached to armies would tend to make them bolder and more organized in their methods of raiding', something they would carry through into the post-war years.[20]

While writers have agreed over the role of the Thirty Years War in worsening the position of Gypsies across the German states, they have disagreed over the amount of responsibility Gypsies themselves should take for this. In doing this they are reflecting a more general split in writings about Gypsies right through history and up to the present. Essentially the difference hinges around the extent to which the actions of Gypsies themselves are taken in isolation (often resulting in more negative portrayals) or set in the wider context of prejudice and actions of states and wider society (often resulting in more sympathetic portrayals). It is worth here looking in some depth at the writings of two different members of the Gypsy Lore Society from the 1930s, Miss Hall and Eric Winstedt, both of whom looked at Gypsies in Germany in the seventeenth century. Not only does their work give us an insight into the lives of Gypsies in this period, but it also shows us how authors can put different interpretations on similar evidence. Miss Hall emphasized 'the increasing rigour of the laws instituted against them by the authorities themselves':[21]

One is tempted to surmise that Gypsy 'crimes' were in the beginning merely of their customary variety: petty pilfering, mendacity, fortune-telling, and a little sorcery accompanying the wanderers' drifting progress through the country. But it is also easy to understand how the sedentary, agricultural population grew to dread the Gypsies' approach: their very appearance – the strange attire, swarthy skins, coarse black hair, and eloquent eyes – made them objects of mistrust and fear. Their intimate customs, bearing all the alien quality of the East, were branded as immorality . . . Matters grew even worse as war conditions and the waxing ambition of Frederick William I of Prussia sent bands of 'recruiters' (described by Baron von Trenck as 'the very refuse of the human race') scouring through central Europe seizing able-bodied men of all nations . . . rebellion from this incredibly brutal military discipline made of [Gypsies] dangerous deserters, with a knowledge of firearms and a craving for vengeance of their captors. The bands were occasionally joined by other outlaws and deserters, not of their own race.[22]

Here she stresses the behaviour of the 'recruiters', the dehumaniz-
ing effect of military life and the presence of 'outsiders' in the
bands, while attributing negative feelings about Gypsies to prejudice over their foreign appearance, rather than actions they may
have taken. In contrast Winstedt sees Gypsies themselves as far
more accountable for their crimes, and marshalled evidence of
large bands engaging in persistent raiding. In 1674 a group of 600
Gypsies made a surprise attack on a Silesian village, overcoming
the resistance of its inhabitants, beating them and threatening
them with death. They then billeted themselves, ten to fifteen per
house from the Tuesday evening to the Thursday, 'exacting food
and all other necessities and stealing what they could lay their
hands on'. Records from this period also indicate that Gypsies were
well armed, to the extent of travelling with small field pieces. In
addition the archives show that the law did not always work against
them. In 1675 Gypsy Rosenberg appeared again in Saxony and
accused a nobleman of attacking his band and taking their arms
and horses. On showing a pass from the Brandenburg general,
Friedrich von Hessen, the nobleman was ordered to restore his
goods. At the same time a company of up to 100 Gypsies under the
leadership of Johann von Reinhardt appeared at Stolpen with 'fine
hunting rifles and greyhounds, and stole fodder and cattle':[23]

> Gypsies had yielded to the temptation to continue their
> war-time careers as raiders, becoming naturally bolder and
> more criminal owing to the comparative immunity they
> enjoyed during the weakened state of Germany for some
> generations. They had become a real menace to the country,
> and brought upon themselves the severe measures.[24]

However Miss Hall argued that they had little choice given the
conditions they faced:

> Gypsies were arrested on sight and branded, being ban-
> ished after a flogging, and in the event of their return, put
> to death without mercy. Under such bitter provocation the
> Gypsies had no other course than to withdraw into the
> wilder parts of the country, where, banded under leaders,
> fifty or a hundred strong, armed and defiant, they stole for

their sustenance and skirmished with the soldier-police to expel them . . . From the lists of goods stolen on these occasions, it is evident that the Gypsies' main objects were food and decent clothing – butter, cheeses, fowls, flour, and bacon; coats, gowns, and cloaks.[25]

Both Hall and Winstedt agree that the punishments meted out to Gypsies were harsh, although the latter argued that the 'charge of especial severity seems to me to have been exaggerated'.[26] Evidence from the period shows that alongside the Gypsy hunts – which saw at least 100 people being killed across Germany – following capture, states attempted to assert control through highly ritualized and public floggings, maimings and executions.[27] Details of three Gypsy women arrested in Saxony in 1715 give a sense of the physical impact of such 'severe measures'. One of the women had already been arrested twice, the others once. They carried the legacy of these arrests in the loss of an ear each, with the first woman additionally missing two fingers. Whippings and banishment were also common punishments: one case recorded a Gypsy woman flogged with her child tied to her front, in the hope of being able to carry it away with her into exile.[28]

Here it is useful to take a moment to consider the insights offered by Michel Foucault's *Discipline and Punish* (1975), which famously opens with a grisly account of an execution, complete with the difficulties of tearing away flesh with pincers and a botched attempt to quarter the condemned by pulling him apart with four horses. Foucault reflects on the body as a subject of political power, and how in the early modern period the power of the state was limited and contested, and so was forced to use violence as a means of exerting its control.[29] Certainly it is the case that in the seventeenth and early eighteenth centuries the punishments faced by Gypsies were comparable to those given out to vagabonds, bandits and other criminals. If we look in detail at the torture and execution of Johannes la Fortun, known as Hemperla, the 'great Galant', his brother, Anton Alexander (the 'little Galant') and the rest of their Gypsy robber band in the winter of 1726–7, we can see the material and physical efforts put into creating what were deemed appropriate punishments and the importance of the ritualistic nature of these punishments in asserting the authority of the state.[30] After capture Hemperla and the other leaders denied their guilt, were placed in solitary confinement and condemned to torture *in extremis* and under the public gaze.

One of the less important band members, Lorentz Lampert, was the first to be called. He was 'ushered into the icy-clammy "rackchamber" at 4am, undressed by the hangman's vassals and seated in the "Pein-Stuhl". He apparently paid little regard to the "thumb-screw" (an instrument with small serrated jaws that close down upon the lower thumb joint), and so the torturers moved onto the "Spanish Boot" (leg vice), that was "firmly screwed together". Under 'writhing agony, and tempted with the promise of relief and warmth, he gave way and confessed the guilt of the band', after which he 'was allowed to be unscrewed and taken to a warm room'. Next was Hemperla himself, who resisted both 'the pains of the thumb-screw and "boot"':

> Having searched his whole body in vain for some concealed charm, the Inquisitors' men cropped his hair – a thing which disturbed him curiously – afterwards applying the 'boot' yet more excruciatingly, so that under the crushing of muscle and bone he at least broke down and made the confession they required.

At this stage, 'as a final touch of artistry to the torment', the officials brought forward Hemperla's mother, so 'she might share the spectacle of her son broken by the extremity of agony'. At this point he broke down and confessed, which then resulted in a blanket guilty verdict: the leaders were to be 'broken on the wheel', nine others to be hanged, and thirteen (mostly women) beheaded, an event that was watched by 'many thousands of onlookers', and recorded by a contemporary artist in a woodcut.[31]

If this account is revealing of the physical suffering imposed as part of early modern justice, the contemporaneous imprisonment, trial and execution of a group of Gypsies in Bohemia gives an insight into how law and order was constrained by material factors and contested and acted out at the local level.[32] Initial laws banishing Gypsies from Bohemia had simply ordered them to be deprived of weapons, exiling them without harm. As this and subsequent legislation was not enforced, despite there being 'such large bands of Gypsies found pillaging that the military had to be sent against them', by 1689 banishment backed up by hanging. In 1697, this was further strengthened so that Gypsies were proclaimed outlaws, with men being condemned to death and women to flogging and having their right ear cut off. These measures were followed by a period of severe persecution, which 'soon passed over', with the fact that the laws were repeated in both 1721 and 1726 suggesting that they were not fully enforced.[33] But what did this mean at the local level, both for individual Gypsies and for those expected to carry out the measures?

Following their capture in eastern Bohemia, owing to a shortage of cells, a group of Gypsies was distributed across a number of towns in the region, whereupon the town of Netschetin, which received two of the prisoners, promptly complained of 'the expense to their poor community and of the unfitness of their prison'. The subsequent escape of one prisoner may have been more attributable to the limited prison facilities and reluctance of the town authorities to mount an adequate guard than to the officially cited reason, which was witchcraft. Pressed by Prague, the town reluctantly sent out 28 citizens to capture the escapee, a process that took three weeks and 'the assistance of some local peasants'. The escapee was sentenced to be hanged, the women to having their right ears cut off and to being 'flogged with rods round the gallows, and banished from the country after giving a bond not to return on pain of death'. What we see next is a further insight into the inconveniences and benefits visited on local communities who were required to enact punishments on behalf of a distant state: the 'execution of this sentence involved the town in more expense and trouble, but provided it with considerable entertainment'. Part of the trouble lay in the fact that Netschetin had no functioning gallows, so every citizen was required to provide three oxen and to help with hauling wood in order to construct new ones. When this had been done and the gallows made, 'the whole company were treated with beer and the carpenters, masons and *Dorfrichter* [town judge] to bread as well'.

As well as being revealing about the mechanics of the early modern state, this account allows us to reflect on the importance of distinguishing between the impact of laws on individuals and that on Gypsies as a group. While we may point generally to the failure of the legislation at a broad level to remove Gypsies from European, or even German, society, this is not the same as it having no effect. The physical brutality of imprisonment, torture and punishment, the practical and emotional difficulties of losing husbands and other family members, as well as the impact of banishment, would have all been manifestly devastating for any in-dividual or family group. Indeed, records of a number of women involved in one group punishment demonstrated a high number of double surnames alongside 'the mention of two husbands [of one woman] who had been shot, [which] shows how frequent violent deaths were among these people'.[34]

In the sense raised by Foucault, brutal punishments were a way of drawing Gypsies and other criminals into the body politic: using their bodies as a way of inscribing and demonstrating the power of emerging states. Although apparently living outside the law and social norms, through such public displays of institutionalized violence their punishment served to provide an example to the wider popu-lation of the dangers of criminality and deviance. At a time when the authorities could not hope to catch everyone engaged in lawless activities, it was deemed important that those who were caught were punished in such a way as to act as a deterrent to the wider popula-tion: 'Men are not hanged for stealing horses, but that horses may not be stolen.'[35] In this sense then, although manifestly brutal, the treatment of Gypsies has to be seen as part of the normal continuum of behaviour of early modern states rather than as an aberration.

While we might argue that one profound difference for Gypsies was that they were outlawed and hunted purely on the basis of their identity rather than behaviour, a close reading of the evidence suggests that this distinction was far from clear cut. If we take, for example the pronouncement made on 18 August 1722, by Charles VI of Austria, we can see that he complained how his decree of 1 July 1720 had been ignored. With the death penalty as sanction, it had aimed for

> the complete banishment of the gipsies wandering about the country along with their wives and children and the other rabble of thieves, robbers and murderers who have joined themselves to them . . . for the general quiet and security of the country.

Here we get the sense that the target was in fact the large bands roaming the countryside engaged in criminal activities, who though made up of people from a range of backgrounds (including Gypsies), had for convenience's sake been lumped together as 'Gypsies'. Interestingly, the reason cited for the failure of this legislation to work was not simply that it had not been properly implemented, but rather that it had been actively thwarted: 'Certain of our subjects have had the audacity to give the forbidden lodgements and shelter to this gipsy rabble, pests of the country, both within and after the most carefully arranged time allotted for their departure.'[36] This suggests that, far from being complete outlaws, certainly some Gypsies were seen enough as part of a local community to be given protection and a place to stay.

Other evidence from this period also points to the mixing of Gypsies with wider society. Just because many of those who seem to have travelled and lived alongside Gypsies came from the dispossessed this does not mean we can or should underplay the importance of this contact. Given the chaos produced by conflict in central Europe in the seventeenth century, the vagrant poor would have included peasants forced from the land, those migrating for work between cities and states, as well as ex-soldiers and longer-term vagabonds and people of the road. Evidence from Nuremberg suggests that this mixing was of particular cause for concern to legislators. In 1732 when more severe legislation was being discussed, the fact that 'deserters and other undesirables had joined the Gypsies to escape detection' was cited as a reason for tightening the law, as was evidence that a farmer's son had joined a band of Gypsies. There was also concern that the Gypsies were trading with metal dealers and others in order to make their living, suggesting that they had normalized contact with the wider population based around trading and artisanal activities.[37]

Evidence of the place Gypsies were making for themselves in European economies and societies does not simply come from the German lands. Complaints from the French crown in 1682 over the failures of previous legislation demonstrated that

it is impossible to entirely hunt these thieves from the kingdom due to the protection which they have always found, and which they still find daily with gentlemen and judicial lords, who give them sanctuary in their castles and houses, despite the orders of parliament, who expressly defend them under pain of privation from their status as judges, and of arbitrary fines, this disorder which is common in the majority of the provinces of our kingdom.[38]

Taken with the evidence from Germany and the Spanish edict of 1695 this document gives us something of an insight into the lives of Gypsies of the period. It allows us to look beyond the writings and laws that stressed the lawlessness and foreignness of Gypsies and see that at the local level in France, in some places at least, they were able to evade the galleys and punishments set out in law. More than this, such evasions were made possible through the complicity of local elites and the wider community who actively sought to protect them. Similarly, in Royal Hungary decrees for expulsion were only very patchily enforced by the nobles who implemented the laws in this frontier land. Some lords implemented the decrees of banishment on pain of mutilation and execution, but others were anxious to keep their Gypsy populations *in situ*, as they valued their work as smiths, soldiers and musicians. So, for example, György Thurzó, the Count Palatine of Hungary, in direct contradiction to imperial policy, issued safe conduct to a company of Gypsies who were 'performing military services'.[39]

By the beginning of the eighteenth century then, Gypsies had undoubtedly established themselves in niches in the local economies. This could include music, dancing and general entertainment, as well as fortune telling, which had been part of Gypsy work since the first accounts from the early fifteenth century, and was often carried out alongside begging and asking for alms. Overall, evidence of the period stresses the versatility of Gypsy livelihoods, with the varied activities of Antoine Delon in Bourbonnais being a case in point. From the age of eight he worked as a valet, going on to sell remedies, play the tambourine and violin and performing as a Harlequin before moving onto producing and selling remedies and balm. Accounts from the seventeenth and early eighteenth centuries also show how Gypsies worked as regular soldiers, mercenaries and as military musicians, with evidence from Spain suggesting most Gypsies lived as blacksmiths, butchers, shearers, basket weavers, horse traders and agricultural workers, and were settled in villages and towns.[40]

Occasionally we find contemporary evidence giving an insight into the realities of everyday life. György Thurzó in the early seventeenth century issued a document urging authorities to allow Gypsies to settle in their lands, pitch their tents and practise smithery, and is notable for showing some sympathy for the harsh reality of nomadic life:

> In accordance with their ancient custom they are used to leading a very hard life, in fields and meadows outside the towns, under ragged tents. Thus have young and old, boys and children of this race learned, unprotected by walls, to bear with wind and rain, cold and intense heat; they have no inherited goods on this earth . . . with no sure resting place, knowing no riches or ambitions, but, day by day and hour by hour, looking in the open air only for food and clothing but the labour of their hands, using anvils, bellows, hammers and tongs.[41]

This document gets to the heart of the precarious and tough existence often lived by Gypsies, and then raises the question of how Gypsies' lifestyles, apparently so free and 'careless', adapted to deal with this. One way of doing this is revealed in the trend we can see by the seventeenth century of becoming far more closely associated with particular countries and often to particular regions within them. This is in contrast to the early years of their presence in Europe, where groups seem to have travelled extensively right across the Continent. So, in France for instance, between 1607 and 1627 a Captain David de la Grave was reported around twenty times in the same twelve places in Lower Provence.[42] In the context of growing repression, while the ability to leave a place quickly obviously had its advantages, there was also increasing value in developing local knowledge of a place and its people. Becoming a familiar part of a community, perhaps arriving at roughly the same time each year, and providing the same services, or settling down in a discrete area of a town to fulfil niches within a local economy were ways of reducing uncertainty. Evidence from Spain indeed suggests that many Gypsies had fairly fixed annual itineraries determined by labour demands of the changing agrarian seasons.[43] One result of this was that Gypsies began to develop national identities of their own: while continuing to speak variations of Romani, they adopted the languages and surnames of their countries, and adapted their lifestyles to fit with local conditions.

The extent to which Gypsies might become integrated within local state systems, as much as within economies, is demonstrated in how they became affected by vagrancy legislation in the seventeenth century. We have already seen how over the previous century legislation attempting to tackle issues around vagrancy inevitably drew in Gypsies. While this meant 'Egyptians' as well as 'counterfeit Egyptians' were drawn into repressive efforts to control the mobile population, it also had the effect of including them within emerging attempts to provide relief to the country's poor. In England the Old Poor Law – in fact a series of laws in operation from 1601 to 1834 – and the closely related Settlement Act of 1662 created a system of 'miniature welfare states', with each parish collecting poor rates in order to provide relief to its 'impotent' poor, with the able-bodied expected to work in return for their upkeep.[44] Crucially, the vagrancy legislation was discretionary, casting a broad net within which justices and constables were able to discriminate, meaning that not all poor wanderers were punished as vagrants. In fact constables' accounts reveal that fewer than one in ten migrants passing through a parish were whipped, with the rest being given alms – often 3–4d – and sometimes a night's lodging provided they left the parish the next day.[45] Interestingly for us, constables' accounts across the seventeenth century show consistent evidence of parochial expenditure towards Gypsies.[46] The account books for Repton (Derbyshire) in the years 1651–66 recorded ten payments given variously to 'Jepses' or 'a compane of Jipes', with other towns similarly showing evidence of irregular but not uncommon disbursements. The amount given was small, but in line with the averages given to other vagrants, the highest being 2/6d and the lowest 4d. Occasionally more detail is given, so that in Repton between 8 May and 7 July 1655 sixpence was 'giuen to a companie of Jipes that wos sent with a pas frum Ser[geant] Samaill', while another account notes that money was 'given to a companie of gipsses and [for] watching them all night'. An entry from Utoxeter's books in 1647 details the presence of 'forty-six Egyptians . . . with a pass from Parliament to travel for the space of six successive months for relief', who were given 4s before moving on.

These accounts show how, just as occurred in mainland Europe, Gypsies were sometimes paid to go away and that sometimes towns felt they needed to pay someone to keep watch while Gypsies were in the area. They also reveal that they could also be treated as other vagrants, and granted relief money, sometimes given lodging or passes, and that constables conducted them in person or by proxy to the next place. The records are as interesting for what they don't show as much as what they do:

> There is no mention in any of the account-books examined of Gypsies being taken before a justice or to a house of correction, or of their being 'whipped and stocked'; and that says a good deal for the petty constables' humanity, or their lack of courage. Other indications are not wanting that they were lax in their administration of the laws in force against Egyptians and other vagrants; and that their laxity in this respect was often shared by the high constables and justices of the peace.[47]

So that in 1622 the Hertfordshire justices, and those of Berkshire, were reprimanded by Lord Keeper Williams, Bishop of Lincoln in a letter for failing to 'extirpate beggars, rogues, vagabonds, Egyptians, and such lazie and unprofitable members of the commonwealth'. While some of those Gypsies being given payments were supposed to be returning to their place of birth accompanied by a guide,

> one cannot help wondering whether the guides who accompanied two of the parties relieved, one at Ecclesfield and the other at Helmdon, were undertaking a grand tour with their charges. In 1596 a certain William Portyngton set off with 187 of the very large band of Gypsies arrested in Yorkshire in that year, intending, it appears, to return, 'everyone to the place where they were born, or last dwelled, by the space of three years', which task he was to accomplish in seven months.[48]

Fifty years later at the trial in York of five Gypsies, one, Richard Smith, confessed that he and the rest of the group had been arrested in London, that they were 'ordered to bee sent to their severall dwellings or countryes, conducted by one Grey', and that they had been in 'Herefordshire, Stafford, Salop, Cheshire and Lancashire' and were on their way to Northumberland. All this gives us an insight into the working of the early modern state, and allows us a way into squaring the circle of the harsh legislation enacted against Gypsies with the knowledge that already by the seventeenth century they had become an established part of the social landscape across Europe.

Although much of the evidence and discussion around Gypsies and the law is based on what might have been done *to* them, in fact as details from Oxford Quarter Sessions in August 1736 show, it seems that Gypsies might have been comfortable with trying to get the law to work *for* them. Here John Boswell and four family members were recorded as 'Remov'd by Habeas Corpus from Ailsbury and Charged upon the oath of Henry Lovel with Robbing him on the King's highway of one guinea, one half guinea and 10s 6d in silver.' Here it would appear that one family of Gypsies had robbed another, who then took their grievance to court. Given the relatively large sums of money involved on the face of it, it appears strange that the charges do not seem to have gone any further:

> It seems unlikely that gorgios [Gypsies], if they charged them, would have failed to see the case through; whereas it is by no means uncommon for Gypsies nowadays to repent of bringing a charge against one of their kindred, and give their evidence so vaguely and volubly that the bewildered magistrate suggests that they should settle the matter out of court . . . Were the thefts real thefts, or were they . . . revenge for some wrong suffered or some debt unpaid?'[49]

While we are unable to answer these questions, what this does do is open up an understanding of how Gypsies might have felt that the judicial system was there to be used for their own purposes, rather than simply something that was only ever imposed on them. It shows that at least some Gypsies at some times had the confidence and legal insight to draw the law into their own lives and possibly to use it to provide leverage over other Gypsies and strengthen their own standing within their own community. Taking this alongside evidence of how Gypsies were drawn into poor law arrangements, that they could often be seen as contributing to and part of the wider community, and consequently protected from repressive legislation, we can see how the seventeenth century was more than a period of unrelenting repression. When we add to this an understanding of the precarious and incomplete power of early modern states we can see the importance of looking beyond repeated waves of anti-Gypsy decrees. Undoubtedly, individual Gypsies and communities suffered, and many only survived on the physical and geographical margins of society, but at the same time their persistent presence revealed the weakness of early modern states and signalled the permanence of Gypsies place in European society.

THREE

The Dark Enlightenment

THE TENSIONS WE OBSERVED in the seventeenth century over the expanding desires of states to control their populations – which for Gypsies most commonly translated into edicts of banishment or execution – and the limitations in their power continued into the eighteenth century while taking on new characteristics. Overseas European expansion in the previous 150 years had resulted in the creation of colonies in the New World, presenting states not only with opportunities but fresh challenges. At home, states gradually began to expand their notion of what they were for, beyond the control of territory and subjects for the benefit of a monarch and elites. Through the ideas of the Enlightenment as much as the everyday functioning of poor law relief, the state began to be seen as something that might exist for the improvement and benefit of the wider populace. While the idea of the state as a vehicle for social and political change found its most vigorous expression in the French Revolution, the gradual establishment of professional state bureaucrats and the reforms of 'enlightened despots' were equally a response to new ways of thinking. For Gypsies we begin to see periods of concerted action directed at them, not only repression, banishment and execution – although all these continued throughout the century – but transportation to the colonies as well as new attempts at assimilation, settlement and reform.

We will begin with the New World. Just as states were attempting to expand their use of the law in order to consolidate their position at home, this period also saw them attempting to use it to expand their ambitions in their imperial acquisitions in the New World. In part the practice of transportation to the new and emerging

European colonies across the Atlantic can be seen as an extension of this earlier assumption that Gypsies did not belong within the borders of the 'host' nation. And yet while banishment – as in physical removal from a place – was also a symbolic removal from the heart of the realm, penal transportation was more complicated. As with sentencing to the galleys, part of transportation's function was the extraction of labour by the state to further its own agenda. So, for example, along with Spain, as early modern Portugal struggled with depopulation it systematically used the judicial system to provide emergency labour to power its galleys and to populate its colonies. Approximately 50,000 Portuguese subjects were exiled inside and outside mainland Portugal up to 1755.[1] This practice was not unproblematic, for penal colonies were also the vanguard of colonialism, with their garrisons, convicts and ex-convicts forming the kernel of new colonial societies. Yet the bulk of these populations were made up of the socially undesirable – *Moriscos* and blasphemers exiled by the Inquisitions of Spain and Portugal, criminals and vagrants as well as Gypsies – and we have already seen how early modern states struggled to impose their will within their own borders. What we would expect then, is that in the New World colonies, where of necessity the centre had little control over day to day practice, social and ethnic boundaries could be renegotiated and reformed.

Portugal's practice of transportation to Brazil demonstrates how this tension between punishment and opportunity played out for the Gypsies transported both before and during the mass transportation of 1718. Up to the beginning of the eighteenth century edicts against Gypsies in Portugal had been largely ineffective, resulting, as across Europe, in their existing on the margins of society in the face of intermittent community and official hostility. In 1718 João v orchestrated a clampdown on Gypsies with the aim of 'exterminating from the kingdom all Gypsies for their thefts, serious offences, and excesses they frequently commit'. They were to be 'scattered through the separate conquests of Indis, Angola, São Thomé, Ilha do Principe, Benguela and Cabo Verde, Ceara, and Marahão'.[2] This was backed up by the immediate deportation to the Brazilian port of Bahia a community of 50 Gypsy men, 41 women and 43 children. As we will see later with executions, the deportation was carried out in a 'deliberately ceremonial fashion', with the port acting as an 'open stage' for the 'sight of Gypsies leaving in chains'. The message being given was that 'assimilation was no longer an option for Gypsies to escape their criminal status'. This was by no means the first transportation of Gypsies – Inquisition records from the late sixteenth century show Gypsies had been transported following sentences for blasphemy, and magistrates' records from Rio de Janeiro in 1655 detail complaints of theft by Gypsy men and women – but these were the first in which Gypsies were deported as whole communities, simply on the grounds of their identity rather than for a specific crime.

Once in Brazil, the transported Gypsies proved impossible for the local authorities to control, physically, culturally and economically. Although it had been intended that on arrival they be shipped either to Angola or to the plantation areas of Brazil, many managed to remain in and around the port towns where they landed. At the same time prohibitions from speaking Romani and teaching it to their children proved impossible to enforce.[3] Part of this was due to the fact that the authorities had few means of controlling them: while women were supposed to work as maids or in shops and the children were to be apprenticed to a trade, the gold rush and the rapid increase in the colony's population made it very hard to keep a close eye on transportees. While they were barred from mining areas, records show how in fact many migrated to them in groups, so that the governor of Minas Gerais issued a decree in 1723 ordering the arrest of 'every Gypsy man and women together with everyone in their company'. Perhaps inevitably, given the vast frontier, rugged terrain and limited number of troops available, this and other edicts were largely ineffective. In addition, the fact that most of the Gypsies had had long experience of harsh countryside, difficult living conditions and evading the authorities before they were transported, can only have worked to their advantage in this new context. By 1737 colonial authorities had been prosecuting Gypsies for thievery, trading in contraband and murder for a number of years, and their ongoing lawless presence caused the governor of Minas Gerais to complain that 'so many *ciganos* have arrived here since last year and . . . they trek through this backcountry introducing their wretched lifestyle and other habits'.

What is perhaps most interesting about the presence of Gypsies in Brazil is how they negotiated the opportunities and constraints offered by the frontier. They had a reputation for travelling in large companies, such as that led by the da Costa brothers who became notorious across the mining territories for counterfeiting and highway robbery. Yet we need to remember the essentially lawless nature of this place and era: the gold rush territories were so violent that it was said that 'men killed each other like drinking a glass of water', and that the roads and towns were full of fortune hunters, vagabonds, pedlars and fugitive slaves as well as outlaw bands from all backgrounds. So while Gypsies clearly took part in criminal activities, it was also the case that they often took the blame for the actions of others. As one governor accepted, 'complaints about Gypsies are only made because they are Gypsies, without anyone being able to point out guilty individuals'. And many Gypsies took part in other economic activities, notably horse dealing and petty goods trading across the frontier towns.

Most notable in their trading activities was the way in which they acted as intermediaries in the slave trade, which was central to Brazil's mining and plantation economies. Already travelling widely across the country and engaged in general trading, they used their networks to operate as middlemen between the plantation owners of the interior and slaving agents along the coast. Their presence was so important that by the early nineteenth century reports from travellers detailed how they dominated the southern inter-provincial slave trade:

> At the time of my voyage it was principally the Gypsies who, in Rio de Janeiro, sold slaves second-hand, having among them some who thus became quite wealthy . . . [in São Paolo there was a large band] all of whom appeared in good circumstances, they owned slaves, and a large number of horses and pack animals.[4]

A report from 1731 from Angola also indicates that Gypsies who had been transported to the colony states were in control of the interior trade in slaves, ivory and honey, suggesting that the Brazilian case was not unique. The colonial slave trade consequently seems to have offered Gypsies a means of legitimizing their nomadic lifestyle, and shifting from a pariah status to that of an accepted, if unpopular, minority. Evidence suggests that the several thousand Gypsies living in Brazil in the decades leading up to independence were able to respond to this changed climate in different ways. Individuals could of course disassociate themselves from the Gypsy community and integrate into wider colonial society, particularly among the poorer 'white' communities. But what is more notable is how Gypsies in both larger towns, such as Rio de Janeiro, and the interior were able simultaneously to maintain a distinctive identity while at the same time throwing off something of their deviant image:

> [They] preserve much of their peculiarity of appearance and character in this their trans-atlantic home . . . but their conformity does not appear to have influenced their moral habits. They employ their slaves in fishing, and part of their families is generally resident at their settlements, but the men rove about the country and are the horse-jockies of this part of Brazil. Some engage in trade, and many are very rich . . . they retain their peculiar dialect.[5]

So by the late colonial era in Brazil Gypsies were well established as slave owners and traders, living in distinctive communities in the country's leading towns, as well as continuing to maintain a distinctive nomadic element to their lives.[6] Part of the context for this was of course the fact that they were operating within a colonial society where 'race' had different meanings and outcomes than at home in Portugal. The preoccupation at home with purity of blood became much diluted on the other side of the Atlantic, in the face of a limited settler population and less social control. Essentially, with the exception of those with obvious African ancestry, the opportunities presented by social mobility in the colonies meant that individuals and their descendants could move beyond their ethnic identity and establish themselves as part of mainstream society.

The experience of Gypsies transported to Brazil feeds into one of the areas of debate among Romani scholars around whether their relocation to the colonies of the New World resulted in the establishing of new Gypsy communities on the other side of the Atlantic (and consequently continuing the diaspora that began in India), or resulted in assimilation into the wider colonial society. Seventeenth-century records confirm that New World colonies received Gypsies transported from Britain and France. In 1665, for example, the Scottish Privy Council granted a warrant and gave power to an Edinburgh merchant George Hitcheson to transport to 'Gemaica and Barbadoes', a number of 'strong and idle beggars' and 'Egyptians'. Some 50 years later nine Gypsies from Jedburgh in Scotland were transported after sentencing by Glasgow magistrates to the plantations of Virginia at a cost of thirteen pounds.[7] Court records from Henrico county, Virginia, in 1685, against a woman named Joane Scot, show her discharge from charge of fornication as she was 'an Egyptian and a non-Christian', while transportation of Gypsies from France around 1700 resulted in the creation of a distinct colony on Biloxi Bay, Louisiana.[8]

For the earlier years of transportation evidence from Brazil as much as from North America suggests that Gypsies tended to be transported as individuals rather than en masse. Consequently the likelihood is that, certainly initially, transportation did little to spread Gypsy communities and culture, even if it did take individuals across the Atlantic. Most Gypsies transported would have travelled alongside 'strong and idle beggars . . . common and notorious thieves, and other dissolute and looss [sic] persons banished and stigmatized for gross crimes'.[9] A 1714 Privy Council permission to British merchants and planters to ship Gypsies to the Caribbean to be used as slaves cannot be taken at face value. According to this document prisoners were sentenced to be transported to the plantations for being by 'habit and repute gipsies',[10] reminding us that throughout this period the legal definition of Gypsy was taken from the Vagabond's Act of 1597. This covered 'all such persons not being Fellons wandering and pretending (i.e., identifying themselves to be Egypcians, or wandering in the Habite, Form or Attyre) counterfayte Egypcians'.[11] As is so often the case we are left with the arbitrary distinctions made by outsiders as to who constituted a 'Gypsy', or even a 'counterfeit Egyptian', rather than any definitive evidence that those transported were Gypsies.

If, for Britain at least, there is some murkiness over the identities of those transported, what is clear is the social conditions faced on arrival. Most of those transported – 80 per cent in the case of Britain – were male,[12] and as we have observed for Brazil, the pragmatism of settler life often outweighed the ideological concerns of the homeland when it came to keeping social or racial boundaries. Early Gypsy settlers in Bahia mixed freely among lower-class whites, with most women working as domestic servants and men as labourers, although there are also records of Gypsies becoming shop owners and gaolers.[13] Although the documentary evidence does not exist, we can reasonably assume that, in this context, relationships between Gypsies and other settlers would have been common, leading to loss of a distinctive Gypsy identity across even one generation. Even where particular Gypsy communities did develop, as in Louisiana, the scanty evidence that exists suggests that creolization was just as likely as the distinct Gypsy districts noted in Brazil. Memories from a planter from Alexandria, Louisiana in the last years of the eighteenth century showed that the inhabitants at the time were 'of mixed nationalities, French, Spanish, *Egyptian*, Indian, Mulattoes and negroes', with the Gypsies speaking 'a language of their own' alongside French and Spanish: 'Though of a dark colour they passed for white folks and frequently intermarried with Mulattoes.'[14]

Without doubt, transportation to the New World moved Gypsies, alongside others who were deemed deviant, across the Atlantic and to the settler colonies that sprang up right across the Americas. The presence of peoples 'more different' than Gypsies to the bulk of Europeans moving in and to the colonies allowed Gypsies to create different spaces for themselves. Either by moving away from their identity, reasserting it through nomadism and trading, or remaking it, as did the slave dealers of Brazil, Gypsies as with so many other settlers were able to use the opportunities presented by the Americas to break away from some of the constraints imposed on them in Europe. However it wasn't until the mass migrations of the late nineteenth century from south-east and eastern Europe that the Roma and Gypsy diaspora fully crossed the Atlantic.

Although existing in a very different context, the Ottoman Empire also continued to offer an example of the way in which distinct populations might exist within one state system. While clearly not privileged, and often living in materially very poor circumstances, Gypsies were enabled by the Empire's acceptance of heterogeneity combined with its flexible bureaucratic system to be seen as different but not separated from the communities in which they lived. So, for example, in Syria, western travellers to Aleppo noted how alongside local Gypsies, who camped on the outskirts of the town and tended to hire themselves out as labourers, every spring there was a larger influx that came to work on the wheat harvest. In other places, as well as living in tents, they lived in caves, but whatever their mode of living, were universally Muslim. They were also recorded as making 'a coarse sort of tapestry or carpet work for housings of saddles, and other uses, and when they are not far from towns, deal much in milch cattle'. One western observer, passing through Aleppo in the 1740s observed how

> [they] have a much better character than their relations in Hungary, or the Gypsies in England, who are thought by some to have been originally from the same tribe. These and the Turcomen, with regard to offences, are under the pasha and cadi . . . but with regard to taxes they are immediately under the grand signor, whose tribute is collected yearly by an officer over each of these people.[15]

Although presumably unintentional, the direct contrasting of the situation in both Hungary and England where Gypsies were seen very much as outsiders, with that under the Ottomans where they were clearly integrated into the legal and taxation systems, is very striking. And yet once again we need to be wary of generalizing too heavily, but rather to point also to the role of local circumstances if we are to understand the position and treatment of Gypsies. So, if we return to Moldavia and Wallachia, we come across what appears at first glance to be a surprising decree from 1726 made by Mihai Racoviță in the last year of his reign. This dealt with the removal of a tax on the Gypsies of the kingdom, a measure that had originally been seen as temporary:

> What with the armies with their devastations and by the capture of slaves and many things of a similar nature which have brought about the impoverishment of the country, leaving it not only weak but also oppressed by heavy debts and therefore not able to raise the necessary amount to pay the taxes and to carry on, the Government has continued the taxation upon the Gypsies, which I have hitherto allowed to continue, not realising it was a bad practice and that there was no shame in following it, for it has been assumed to be a good practice.[16]

Although the decree states that the tax should be 'entirely abolished', in fact it only related to slaves belonging to monasteries and nobles, as 'the Gypsies belonging to the ruler' were still liable for tax.[17] Not only does this document give a flavour of the court of the time – it reads as if the words have been recorded verbatim by a court scribe – it also demonstrates how the situation of the Gypsies in the Balkans was intimately tied up with the wider political situation of the region. This period had seen the extension of direct Ottoman rule over Wallachia and Moldavia under the ethnically Greek Phanariots, who effectively added an extra layer of exploitation onto an already overburdened peasantry.[18] And as the power of the local rulers collapsed in the face of the expansion of external control, their inclination to side with their populations increased. Racoviţă's decree here should be seen in this light, as should the actions of his successor Constantin Mavrocordato who attempted both to reduce the burden of taxation on the peasantry and to outlaw serfdom, and in 1756 sponsored legislation banning Gypsy children from being sold separately to their parents. Lest we get carried away thinking that this signalled a significant change in attitude towards Gypsies, in 1749 Mavrocordato also passed a charter categorically stating that Gypsies were permanently enslaved; while his successor, Grigore Ioan passed a charter in 1753 affirming that any nomadic Gypsy not under a noble or the Church would automatically become the property of the state.[19]

And yet it is worth looking more closely at documents from this period, such as a decree in 1766 against 'mixed' marriages, because they reveal something of the complexities of everyday life. As we know, since the fifteenth century marriages between Gypsies and the wider population had been outlawed, as such unions would result in the non-Gypsy party being consigned to slavery. Even so,

> my princely highness has seen from an evil and wicked deed, that in some parts Gypsies have married Moldavian women and also Moldavian men have taken in marriage Gypsy girls, which is entirely against the Christian faith, for not only have these people bound themselves to spend all their life with the Gypsies but especially that their children remain for ever in unchanged slavery.[20]

This document simultaneously shows us that the authorities had concerns about such marriages – partly, it seems, on the grounds of their lack of religion, but also the implications, as we have seen, of non-Gypsy people becoming subject to slavery – and that such unions were sufficiently common for them to be legislated against. The decree goes on to threaten priests who performed such a 'great and everlasting wicked act' with being 'severely punished', as well as emphasizing how its measures should be 'publically read in all parts of the towns and villages of this district, and in all the cloisters, so that everybody should know exactly the meaning of it'. We are left with two conflicting impressions: first, and most obviously, that the state intended to do everything in its power to ensure that the edict was obeyed; secondly, that it was necessary to adopt such a strident tone precisely because there were many priests who did not object to performing these marriages. Perhaps one reason for the apparent common occurrence of mixed marriages was that, despite their slave status, Gypsies actually fulfilled crucial skilled and artisanal roles in society:

> The Boyard [noble] had everything he needed on his estate: cooks, bakers, postilions, gardeners, masons, shoemakers, blacksmiths, musicians, labourers, other classes of workers – and all of them were Tziganes. The Gypsy women helped the mistress of the house with her work, and they were on such good terms that they were even allowed to assist in the beautiful embroidery done . . . [he] could close his gates and live for months at a time with his family and woman servants and his men – eighty to a hundred [Tziganes] – without having the slightest need of those who lived outside.[21]

Taken together these documents and insights allow us to move away from a rather 'flat' understanding of Gypsy lives under slavery. Without in any way suggesting that slavery was a desirable or acceptable condition, it is obvious that the little surviving evidence we have on the matter reveals how central Gypsies were to the social and economic functioning of feudal Wallachia and Moldavia.

So far as we have been able to construct a picture of the various experiences of Gypsies by the eighteenth century, it seems reasonable to suggest that despite fierce legislation they were by and large able to create an often precarious existence, often, but not exclusively, on the fringes of European society. In this regard, their experiences can be seen in the same light as Jews of eastern and central Europe, whose opportunities were constrained socially by their religious difference, and economically by common prohibitions on landowning. Positioned between the Catholic nobility and peasantry, they emerged as artisans, tradesmen, merchants and estate managers. In Poland, for example, everyone, 'whether nobleman or labourer, peasant or city dweller, turned to the Jew to buy or sell, to borrow or to pay taxes, to travel or to patronise a tavern'.[22] It is perhaps clear to us how states and societies were consequently instrumental in the creation and fulfilment of stereotypes of minorities: Jews were barred from certain livelihoods and then criticized for being, and stereotyped as, money lenders and avaricious merchants. Similarly, Gypsies across Europe were moved on, hunted down, seen as foreigners and regarded with suspicion. No wonder then that they kept to the margins of societies and the borders of countries.

If we can see how stereotypes might become a self-fulfilling prophecy, contemporary writers, thinkers and legislators were grappling with a very different perspective on the place of minorities in European societies. Although our idea of 'the Enlightenment' has become more nuanced as we have moved away from a straightforward narrative of 'history as progress', it is still accepted that the late seventeenth and eighteenth centuries saw a significant shift towards a more secular and 'rational' understanding of society and humanity.[23] As well as being associated with new ways of understanding the relationship between the state and individuals, and hence the function of the state in society, this period also saw the acceptance of the importance of attempts to understand and categorize the world on the basis of observation and evidence. Although appearing to exist in the elite and rarefied world of salons and universities, in fact the shifts in thinking which the Enlightenment engendered are crucial to understanding momentous events of the period – for example the theoretical bases for the French Revolution and American Independence – as well as laying the groundwork for how Europe's Gypsy populations would be understood and treated in the coming centuries.

We saw how by the sixteenth century European societies began to wrestle with ideas of 'race' that were informed by the process of colonial expansion outside Europe. By the eighteenth century these emerging ideas of 'race' intersected with Enlightenment ideas of progress and rationalism so that, to put it crudely, thought, reason and civilization became associated with 'white' people and northern Europe, while unreason and savagery were conveniently located among 'blacks' and 'non-whites' outside Europe.[24] Within Europe we see similar hierarchies of race being set out (a tendency that was to become intensified in the nineteenth century with the ascendancy of social Darwinist thinking), so that those living on the margins of Europe and at the margins of society were positioned as closer to nature, to chaos and to savagery.

Despite the fact that Gypsies were thoroughly entrenched within the different national cultures right across Europe, very often their perceived social deviancy was seen as an expression of their innate foreignness and their position as outsiders. There was consequently a tension between the broad ideas of the Enlightenment stressing the rationality of human existence with its belief that education and reform might raise humanity, and suggestions that differences between 'races' were impermeable to change. We see something of this in that landmark publication of the Enlightenment, Diderot's *Encyclopédie*. While on the one hand the entry for Gypsies might be taken as an objective description – 'Gypsies . . . vagabonds who profess to tell fortunes by examining hands. Their talent is to sing, dance and steal' – the suggestion here is that they have particular, and possibly innate characteristics that are seemingly shared by all of them. Similarly, the *Dictionnaire de l'Academie française* of 1718 focused on how the women were seen as thieves, commonly 'telling fortunes and derobing with skill'.[25]

If we were to look for one Enlightenment text that epitomized the tension between the belief that all humans might be improved and the assumption that some 'races' were innately doomed to inferiority, it would be hard to do better than Heinrich Grellmann's *Dissertation on the Gypsies*. Grellmann, who worked at that seat of the German enlightenment, Göttingen University, was long credited with making the link between Romani languages and an Indian origin for Gypsy peoples. While more recent research has shown how his work was more a synthesis of the insights of his contemporaries, his *Dissertation* nevertheless rapidly became the cornerstone of subsequent scholarly work on Gypsies in both Europe and America.[26] His book set out to be 'equally useful for entertainment, as for the promotion of the knowledge of manners and mankind', and covered the history of Gypsies, their language and their place in European societies.[27] Although the linguistic findings are often seen as the most important part of the work, in fact his descriptions of the position of Gypsies right across Europe became the standard accounts of their lives for well over a century.

As well as being at the forefront of emerging scholarship on Gypsies, Grellmann is particularly interesting in the way in which he struggled to resolve the conflict in his thinking between the roles of 'nature' and 'nurture' in creating 'Gypsy character' as well as designating their place in society:

> Neither time, climate, nor example, have in general, hitherto, made any alteration. For the space of between three and four hundred years, they have gone wandering about, like pilgrims and strangers: they are found in eastern and western countries, as well among the rude as civilised, indolent and active people; yet they remain ever, and every-where, what their fathers were – Gipsies. Africa makes them no blacker, nor Europe whites; they neither learn to be lazy in Spain; nor diligent in Germany: in Turkey Mahomet, and among Christians Christ, remain equally without adoration. Around, on every side they see fixed dwellings, with settled inhabitants, they nevertheless, go on in their own way, and continue, for the most part, unsettled wandering robbers . . . Let us reflect how different they are from Europeans; the one is white, the other black. This clothes himself; the other goes half naked. This shudders at the thought of eating carrion, the other prepares it as dainty . . . Perhaps it may be reserved for our age, in which so much is attempted for the benefit of states and mankind, to humanise a people who, for centuries, have wandered in error and neglect.[28]

Here, in his preface he quite clearly sets out the ways in which Gypsies were fundamentally and irredeemably separate from Europeans. And yet, at the same time, part of the function of his work was to push ideas of reform, to 'humanize' them: while the 'error' of which he writes was clearly that of the Gypsies themselves, the 'neglect' was that of society. Given this preoccupation it is no surprise that a large portion of his work was given over to the actions of the 'enlightened despots' of the Austro-Hungarian Empire, Maria Theresa (1717–1780) and Joseph II (1741–1790), who enacted 'civilizing' reforms within a context of compulsion. Both these monarchs set into motion a number of policies aimed at the Gypsy populations of their territories.

Maria Theresa's edicts centred around attempts to forcibly assimilate Gypsies into the wider population and its perceived norms of behaviour. The first decrees, stemming from 1768, were focused on Hungary, which held a significant Gypsy population, and aimed at regularizing their lifestyles and denying a separate cultural identity or existence:

> [Gypsies were] prohibited from dwelling in huts or tents; from wandering up and down the country; from dealing in horses; from eating animals which died of themselves, and carrion; and from electing their own Wayda [voivode] or Judge. It was intended to extirpate the very name and language of these folks, out of the country. They were no longer to be called Gipsies, but New Boors (Uj Magyar), nor to converse any longer with each other in their own language, but in that of any of the countries in which they chose to reside . . . They were to procure Boors clothing, to commit themselves to the protection of some territorial superior, and live regularly. Such as were fit for soldiers, to be enlisted in the regiments.[29]

In 1773 these orders were made more 'rigid' so that

> no Gipsy should have permission to marry, who could not prove himself in condition, to provide for, and maintain a wife and children. That from such Gipsies who were married and had families, the children should be taken away, by force, removed from their parents, relations or intercourse with the Gipsy race, to have a better education given to them.[30]

And in fact Grellmann gave detailed accounts of how children over the age of five were taken away on two separate raids 'between five and six o'clock in the morning' in December 1773 and April 1774 in order to be rehomed and 'usefully educated':

> Among the former was a girl fourteen years old, who was forced to submit to be carried off in her bridal state. She tore her hair for grief and rage, and was quite beside her-self with agitation, but she has now [1776] recovered a composed state of mind.[31]

And yet, despite Grellmann's whole-hearted endorsement of the measures, overall these new regulations were not enforced either enthusiastically or systematically in the localities as he would have liked, dependent as they were on particular overseers and other officials to see them through. Here we see the emergence of one of the themes which is to become increasingly important in our story: that of the tension between the desires of central governments and informers and the preoccupations of local governments who were usually required to implement the policies. Although as states became more modern and citizens were no longer physically required to set aside days of labour to build scaffolds, central states still required resources from and ultimately the will and support of local authorities in order to implement its desires. And in the context of limited resources, and indeed often without an agreed sense of what the state was *for*, local authorities could prove to be enduringly obdurate in the face of change.

In continuing to push for the assimilation of Gypsies, and a denial of their separate identity, Joseph II built further on his mother's reforms. From the time of his co-regency, but particularly from 1780 when he ruled alone, he put in place a number of measures that again aimed to reduce Gypsies' visible differences and bring them in line with what were perceived as the norms of society. So, they were ordered to send their children to school and receive religious education; they were to ensure their children no longer ran around naked 'to prevent annoyance and disgust in others'; and that chil-dren of the opposite sex should no longer sleep in the same bed. These 'New Magyars' were to work for an employer and stop horse dealing – only gold panners were to own their own horses – and were to labour on the land. And then there was a host of measures aimed at removing any visible signs of their ethnic difference:

> In diet, apparel and language [Gypsies] were required to follow national usage, eat no dead cattle, sport no multicoloured garments, and refrain from speaking their own tongue. They should no longer let themselves be seen in mantles whose only purpose was to cloak stolen goods.[32]

Here we can see how both the material basis for their lives, as well as the outward expressions of their culture and ethnicity were seen as equally important targets for reform: it was not enough that they were to work like Hungarians, they were to eat, speak and dress like them too.

We need to set these attempts to turn Gypsies into 'industrious and useful citizens' and of 'winning this poor and unfortunate people for virtue and the state' in the broader context of the reforms of the period. Far wider in scope than tackling the 'Gypsy problem', Joseph II initiated a range of measures designed to create a workable modern centralized state out of the shambling and highly diverse institutional structures inherited, and only partially reformed, by his mother.[33] Wide ranging in their reach, the reforms included abolishing serfdom, putting limitations on the amount of violence that could be used in the punishment of subordinates, improving educational facilities, regulating poor relief, prohibiting children under nine years from working in factories and improving the employment conditions of servants. While very much inspired by the Enlightenment, this does not mean change took the same form as the *liberté, egalité, fraternité* of the French thinkers of the early revolutionary period. Rather, equality was taken to mean conformity, a conformity that was to be enacted under a monolithic and centralized state. It was driven by expectations that people would abide by certain 'norms', and so although a number of edicts increased toleration for Jews, they went hand in hand with legislation insisting that Jews must bear a German family name, must speak and write German and, in public at least, not speak Yiddish.[34] So, as with Gypsies, assimilation rather than toleration of difference was ideology underpinning the reforms.

Similarly, and given what we have already seen regarding the treatment of the poor and vagrants over the early modern period, there are unsurprising parallels with the measures enacted against beggars and 'loafers'. Joseph's reforms included the creation of a new network of facilities for the poor, with local authorities in combination with parish churches keeping count of the numbers of poor and distributing alms on Sundays to the needy. At the same time as increasing and regularizing access to alms for the 'deserving' poor, there was a significant hardening of attitudes towards those seen as 'undeserving'. Measures enacted under Maria Theresa were hardened by Joseph II, so that both itinerancy and lack of steady employment became punishable offences.[35] All these actions speak of a state that was trying to extend its reach, to use its power to improve the lives of its subjects, but also to control and regulate their behaviour.

While Grellmann was largely in praise of the reforms, his work also demonstrated his ambivalence: there was a very real struggle in him between his rationalist and his racial beliefs. So in relation to two of the regiments of the Hungarian army in which an eighth of the soldiers were newly conscripted Gypsies, he discussed not only the official attempts to assimilate them, but his disquiet:

> In order to prevent either them, or any other person from remembering their descent, it is ordered by the government that as soon as any of them join the regiment, he is no longer to be called a Gipsy. Here he is placed, promiscuously with other men, and by such a wise regulation, may be systematically rendered useful. But whether he would be adequate to a soldier's station . . . is very dubious . . . he can defy hunger, thirst, heat, cold and other inconveniences [which] make him uncommonly qualified for a military life: on the other hand . . . How could a regiment, composed of people, without heart or courage, who would be overcome with fear and dismay, on the least appearance of danger, would give up everything, and only think of saving themselves by flight, ever perform any great action?[36]

Here we see something of his assumptions around racial characteristics – innate cowardice and physical endurance – while also stressing how 'Men may be formed to anything', and how banishment, that time-honoured strategy for dealing with Gypsies, needed to be understood as both ineffectual and wasteful:

> an increased population is more advantageous than a smaller one . . . Every man has taxes to pay, and powers to exert, the Gipsies none of the least; if he does not know how to make use of them, let the state teach him, and keep him in leading strings until the end is attained . . . [for] when he has discontinued his Gipsy life, consider him with his fecundity and numerous family, who being reformed, are made useful citizens, and we shall perceive how great want of economy it was to throw him away as dross.[37]

Attempts to make Gypsies a productive section of the population were perhaps most systematic in the Habsburg lands under Joseph: although his death in 1790 and then the chaos caused by the Napoleonic wars rapidly caused them to fall into disuse. Yet, they are important because they can be seen as the spearhead of similar policies across Europe, so by the late eighteenth century we can track a growing tension in policy towards Gypsies with authorities vacillating between older ideas around banishment and repression and newer policies aiming at reform and assimilation.

Spain here is a case in point, as the eighteenth century saw the use of banishment and forced labour alongside measures aimed at assimilating Gypsies and denying a separate ethnic identity. In part this needs to be tied to the establishment of the Bourbon dynasty in Spain and their subsequent reforms that aimed at a far higher level of centralization, with a consequent reduction in the autonomy of the separate regions.[38] As in the Austro-Hungarian Empire one of the motivating features of the changes was a desire to make unproductive and marginal groups more useful to the state and society in general. This was part of the thinking that lay behind the edict of 1717, which reaffirmed previous restrictions and decreed that Gypsies were only to live in one of 41 specified towns (with sentencing to the galleys for men and flogging for women the punishment for defiance). The limits of its success can be seen in the fact that 1746 saw another 34 towns being included in the list, at a ratio of one Gypsy family per 100 inhabitants, suggesting that up to this point at least Gypsies had largely continued living where they wished, irrespective of the supposed regulations.[39]

Where the efforts of the authorities over the past century and a half had been more effective, however, was in almost completely eradicating nomadism among the Gypsies of the peninsula: it appears by the mid-eighteenth century they were almost completely sedentary. This meant that the next measure targeting Gypsies – the 'great round-up' of 30 July 1749 – was far easier for the state to carry out. The round-up aimed to eliminate Gypsies completely as a separate group, by incarcerating men separately from women and children and setting them to forced labour. Rather than being con-signed to the galleys, which had been abolished in 1748 as a result of improvements in naval technology, labour was to be diverted to the building of ports and arsenals as well as to the Spanish garrisons of North Africa and the notorious mercury mines of Almadén. Boys aged between twelve and fifteen were to be placed in apprentice-ship in order to be initiated into 'useful' trades, or were to be entrusted to the Navy if they showed an aptitude for maritime activities.[40] Overall the aim was to destroy Spanish Gypsies as a separate group: the ex-prime minister, the Marquis de la Ensenada, who was central to the success of the project, had personally declared 'that this category of people will disappear'.

Here it is worth pausing for a moment to think about the implications of both the ambition and actions of the Spanish state, and drawing on the insights of Zygmunt Bauman who conceptual-ized the change from early modern to modern states as a shift from 'game-keeping' to 'gardening'. Gamekeepers, as he saw it, keep a general eye on the land under their care, unable to make more than a few broad-brush interventions to affect the populations under their jurisdiction; gardeners on the other hand pay close attention to working both the land and choosing their plants, deciding which are desirable and need cultivating, and which are weeds.[41] This in-sight allowed him to argue that the Nazi regime, rather than being an aberration of modernity, was in fact its most logical expression, and it also allows us to look at the actions of the Spanish state in a broader historical context.

As on the other side of Europe in the Austro-Hungarian Empire, ideas of the Enlightenment were feeding through into state practice: in a whole range of ways states were seeing that they might exist not only to wage war and control territories, but might actively intervene in order to make their populations more prosperous and productive, as well as more taxable and orderly. While these changes may have had many beneficial implications for those in mainstream society, this was at the expense of those on the margins. While superficially banishment of all Gypsies from the kingdom might seem little different from the round-up, there were two crucial differences: by the mid-eighteenth century the capacity of the state to carry out its actions was greatly increased, and so it was not simply an expression of desire, but an order for action; and secondly there is a difference between banishment and incarcerating all Gypsies simultaneously, holding men and women separately with the express aim of breaking and ending Spanish Gypsy ethnicity and culture in all its forms. Consequently, while we will see how for various reasons it failed in its ambitions, and while the word is anachronistic in this context, the 1749 round-up needs to be seen as genocidal in intention if not in outcome.

The surviving documentation makes it clear that it was Gypsies as a whole ethnic group which was the target, rather than 'anti-social' or other elements within it. When discussing the different options for removing the problem of Gypsies from society, the opinion of Ferdinand VI's Jesuit confessor was sought. He replied:

> The means proposed by the governor of the council to root out this bad race, which is hateful to God and pernicious to man, seem good to me. The king will be making a great gift to God, Our Lord, if he manages to get rid of these people.[42]

And yet there was some confusion over who 'these people' might actually be. Documentation from the round-up demonstrates the extent to which mixed marriages between Gypsies and the rest of the Spanish population were relatively common. Debates over what to do in such cases resulted in the central council clarifying the rules and deciding that the husband's background was to take precedence in all cases. Although seen as separate from and outside of Spanish society, the need to construct these rules demonstrates that things were not as clear-cut as Spanish elites would have liked to believe.

What is notable about the round-up is the scale and efficiency of the exercise: while manifestly not laudable, it is nevertheless testament to the growing competence of Spain's state apparatus that in the course of one night 881 Gypsy families were arrested and incarcerated. Overseen by the Marquis de la Ensenada, the operation was planned and executed under strict injunctions of secrecy: centralized records and the insistence that Gypsies were only settled in certain towns made finding them and planning the operation easier; delegation of the bulk of the work to local magistrates and the Captaincy General of Valencia and his troops ensured there was an adequate body of men to enforce the action. Furthermore the whole operation was financed by auctioning the goods of the detainees. The proceeds covered everything from the hiring of the carts and draught animals used for the journey, and the food needed during their journey to the irons, chains and ropes used to prevent them from escaping. Again, the records give us an insight into the lives of Gypsies in Spain in this period: while much of the property was of little value, in some cases Gypsies are shown to have owned or rented housing, animals used in farming, and trade tools, such as those used by blacksmiths; they seem often to have also been property owners.[43]

In fact, the round-up also revealed the limitations of the state. So secret had it been that while the detention of Gypsies had gone relatively smoothly – there is one report of three people being killed trying to escape during the Seville operation but no others – the prisons were not prepared, and rapidly became unworkably overcrowded. Their arrival at the arsenal of La Carraca (Cadiz), for instance, also raised a whole series of problems, including the lack of accommodation for both prisoners and troops guarding them, and how the absence of building skills among the prisoners resulted in unforeseen and prolonged delays in naval construction.

More than the practical difficulties, the round-up also revealed the problematic nature of bureaucratic desires to define and categorize people and how everyday experience contradicted stereotypes and popular understandings of 'Gypsyness'. In this, officials wrestled with some of the issues faced by their counterparts in the Third Reich two centuries later, as they dealt with appeals from people who did not see themselves as Gypsies but had been defined as such. It rapidly became apparent that the round-up had been indiscriminate in nature, as a number of arrestees appealed their incarceration:

> Sir, the new Castilians, who are imprisoned in the arsenal
> at Cartagena bow to Your Majesty's royal feet. [. . .] They
> humbly beg Your Majesty to deign to mercifully attend to
> their humble pleas, and grant them freedom so they can
> remove their abandoned property; and join their poor
> wives, children and families, who are equally dispersed with
> the affliction of being separated from one another, having
> by nature and love such close links as those of blood and
> marriage: Your most unfortunate vassals respectfully hope
> for Your Majesty's royal generous mercy . . .[44]

Soon after the round-up a committee was convened in order to
consider the cases of those who had letters or official documents
proving their non-Gypsy status, sales of property in these cases
were suspended, and by the end of October it was acknowledged
that there had been mistakes. An instruction was then issued
which accepted the existence of Gypsies who, 'out of tiredness,
fear or repentance', observed the pre-existing laws governing
them, and consequently they 'never could, nor should have been
included in that royal decision because, being innocent, they are
exempt from any charge and any punishment'. At this point what
we see is the division of the incarcerated into 'good' Gypsies, who
led relatively assimilated lives and held letters testifying to their
good character and 'bad' non-conformist Gypsies, who were
variously described as delinquent, guilty, disobedient, offending,
pernicious and deviant.

As in the Austro-Hungarian Empire however, we also see a gap
between the desires of central government and the actions of local
authorities. Even those designated as rightly incarcerated and set
to forced labour were sometimes treated leniently by magistrates,
who felt that attempts to escape were 'excusable' on the part of
people so lacking in prospects. And the everyday practicalities of
managing the convict population – which was made up of a significant proportion of the 'old, crippled and valetudinarian' – also
caused complaints from those required to set them to work. So, in
1762, for instance, the authorities of El Ferrol wrote to Madrid
requesting the release of those 'who, absolutely unfit for any form
of work, are constantly in hospital and give rise to costs for their
upkeep and treatment without yielding any profit'.

The combination of the large number of appeals and the often ineffective nature of the workforce contributed to the central government moving towards pardoning and freeing all those caught up in the round-up. Begun as a means of releasing the unproductive workforce, so the state would not have to bear the cost of their upkeep, by 1763 it appeared it would become a general pardon on the decision of Charles III who had ascended the throne four years earlier. Matters were delayed, however, as state prosecutors demanded that the issue of 'unproductive' Gypsies became tied up with the wider question of what to do with them after release, insisting that measures be put in place to regulate their lives and behaviour. It was not until July 1765, sixteen years after their initial arrest, that all the internees were released. The effect of the round-up on Spain's Gypsy population was nothing less than catastrophic: of those who survived most had experienced deportation, internment, been subjected to forced labour, punished and hurt. As a result the community's inner structures had changed completely, and Caló, the distinctive language spoken by Spanish and Portuguese Gypsies, disappeared. This episode has rightly been called the 'dark Age of Enlightenment'.[45]

The debate over their place in Spanish society continued, however, and resulted in two men, Pedro Valiente and Pedro Rodríguez, being given the task of drawing up a report that could be used as the basis for future legislation. Finished in 1772 their work reveals a central truth of the treatment of Gypsies in Spain: while laws had pushed towards assimilating them, popular feeling worked against this, treating Gypsies as outcasts who were only able to exist within a highly circumscribed field. Stressing the importance of education, the report also asked for all economic activities to be open to Gypsies, and to ban the use of the word 'Gitano' or even 'New Castilian'. While their findings were not universally accepted they did form the basis of the legislation of 1783 in which Gypsies were given equal citizenship but denied a separate identity. With most trades made accessible to them and all places except Madrid and the royal palaces now open as places for them to live, this represented something like progress. But, as with the reforms in the Austro-Hungarian Empire, they came with demands for conformity: nomadism and Caló were banned, and certain trades – including some of the mainstays of their community such as innkeeping, trading at fairs, shearing and clipping animals – were closed to them.[46]

These measures continued to be enforced vigorously for the rest of Charles III's reign, but more patchily after his death in 1788. Here, as elsewhere in mainland Europe, we can see the fragility of these emergent states, with policies being very much tied to the will of individual ministers or monarchs, as well as the acquiescence of the localities. So, similarly in France in the final years of the *ancien régime*, banishment also became a less favoured response to Gypsies, as it was noted that it was 'not capable of containing people for whom life is a type of voluntary and perpetual banishment'. By the Revolution the main piece of legislation targeting Gypsies was still the decree of 1682, but as we have seen, its main effect was to break up larger groups into smaller ones, and to push Gypsies to the geographical margins of France. That over a quarter of the Gypsies in the French galleys in the mid-eighteenth century had been born abroad – mainly in the Netherlands, the Rhineland and Switzerland – suggests that opportunities for Gypsies were seen as being better in France than neighbouring parts of Europe.[47]

By the 1770s consideration was being given by central government to sending them to the Americas, possibly Guiana, although we need to be aware of the gap between intention, policy and implementation.[48] Conditions deteriorated rapidly in France from the 1770s, and we need to contextualize treatment of Gypsies within responses to the more general social disorder stemming from the poor harvests and crises of the peasantry and urban poor. This period undoubtedly saw increasingly repressive edicts against vagabonds, beggars and 'disreputable persons' (who were estimated to make up 10 per cent of the population by 1791) and which resulted in nearly a quarter of 'delinquents' condemned to death and around one-fifth sentenced to the galleys in perpetuity. And yet at the parish and local levels, the understanding of priests and officials of the abject poverty of the population and their need to engage in migrant labour in order to survive meant that proclamations from the centre were habitually ignored in the provinces.[49]

AS THE EVENTS OF THE REVOLUTION overtook first France and then the rest of Europe the capacity of all states to deal with their Gypsy, vagrant and marginal populations reduced rapidly. Priorities shifted back to the simple survival of regimes and schemes for the improvement of populations disappeared under the tread of Napoleon's armies. This does not mean, however, that the changes that occurred from the seventeenth century disappeared, rather that they were put on hold. What shifted in this period was not so much that Gypsies were regarded differently by the states and societies in which they lived, for however much they had made their lives within all the different national and cultural contexts of Europe's nations they were still seen as outsiders, still largely mistrusted and marginalized. Rather, what changed was how states saw themselves. The ideas of the Enlightenment suggested that government could exist for the good of its population, and reforms could be put in place to educate, protect and improve the populace. This however, came at a price for those living on the margins of society.

FOUR

Nationalism, Race and Respectability

WITHIN THE BROAD SWEEP of European history, the nineteenth century is often depicted as a time of transition from the early modern world of the *ancien régime* to the post-agrarian and modern nation state. Fuelled in part by population growth and rapid economic change, it was also the product of new ways of conceiving society. So at the same time as large-scale political arguments over the place of monarchs, nation states and democracy were raging across the Continent, industrialization and urbanization – driven by and driving the transport revolution of canals, railways, steam and improved roads – began to rapidly alter how cities and the countryside felt, looked and functioned. People, goods and ideas were able to move between places more easily: social control of the mass of the population by the elites was challenged as much by the emergence of a wealthy and significant middle class as by the explosion of the urban population and an articulate and increasingly organized labour movement. At the same time travel and migration, which had always been a feature of existence, became less daunting, and it is no coincidence that this was the period of mass emigration from Europe to the New World.

Such profound change did not go unchallenged, nor did the world being lost go unmourned. Over the century, elites and their allies developed ways of responding to the altered world they faced: as in the past revolutions were resisted and revolts suppressed, but increasingly it was accepted that resistence and suppression were insufficient tools for social control. And so as well as fledgling democratic systems, technologies of state expanded to increasingly regulate not just the physical environment, but people's lives, their right to cross boundaries and their right to remain. At the same

112

time as these innovations and the creation of now familiar systems of government, there was also a looking back at the world that was being lost. Consequently, the nineteenth century was also a time in which writers, artists and commentators evoked a prelapsarian world of unchanging rural bliss in order to counter the squalor of mushrooming urban life and industrial filth they encountered on a daily basis. As ever, we cannot think of these developments as all marching together at the same rate of change or in the same manner: they were more noticeable in western than eastern Europe, and in cities and industrial areas than the countryside. But sometimes rapidly, sometimes haltingly and patchily, over time what came to be thought of as 'modernity' made its presence felt across the Continent.

And where in all this did the Gypsies fit? If we were to believe the writings of gypsiologists and other contemporary writers, the nineteenth century's relentless modernity represented a decisive attack on their primitive existence. Yet, from what we have seen so far of their history, it would be a surprise if suddenly they were no longer affected by the broader changes and processes felt by wider society. We shall see how from some angles the nineteenth century might be depicted as one of the easiest for Gypsies since their arrival in Europe, as the grotesque punishments of the early modern period fell out of use, while rapid economic change brought new markets and possibilities for livelihoods. But modern ways of articulating bigotry, new forms of regulation on the part of ever expanding states, developments in policing and surveillance systems, as well as new ways of codifying insiders and outsiders by newly formed nation states all meant that we need to be wary of thinking in terms of unproblematic progress.

If the world was changing rapidly, the stereotypes surrounding Gypsies remained consistent, although they did take on a new urgency. Taking their lead from Grellmann, across Europe writers increasingly crafted the image of Gypsies as a pre-civilized race, sensual and unrestricted, existing in stark opposition to modern man with all his self-inflicted limitations and obligations.[1] Depending on one's perspective this was either a positive attribute or something to be stamped out. The Romantic movement saw them as the last refuge against the horrors of the modern world: the writer Paul de Saint-Victor was not alone when he admitted that often the imagination, tired of the chains of social life, takes wing on its dreams to collapse under [Gypsies'] tents and enrol in their bands. The day they disappear, the world will lose not just a virtue, but a poetry.[2]

Within German-speaking Europe Tetzner's *History of the Gypsies* (1835) set the tone, depicting them as the 'sputum of mankind', who had descended on Europe 'like a punishment from god, like a swarm of locusts':

The character of these people is an embodiment of wicked-ness, carelessness, loquaciousness, cowardice – that is why they are bad soldiers – revengefulness, crapulousness, ridicu-lous arrogance, deceitfulness and laziness which creates further vices are the main characteristics of a Gypsy's soul.[3]

His tropes and prejudices were to be taken up and repeated by authors across the following decades, until they had reached the status of indisputable fact. Encyclopedias of the day propagated a mix of these exotic and negative stereotypes: the *Encyclopédie Catholique* (1839–48) asserted that 'it is not rare to see father and daughter, uncle and niece, brother and sister living together and mixed-up in the manner of animals'; while *La Grande Encyclopédie* (1886–1902) noted how their 'demeanour is, in spite of the wild air of them, and often remarkable character of native elegance'. Almost inevitably, it was commonly asserted that Gypsy women dabbled in prostitution: the *Encyclopédie Nouvelle* (1835–41) was simply one among many in suggesting how they 'sing, dance, get mixed up in fortune telling, steal occasionally, and do worse again just so long as they get their profit'.[4]

The reality of Gypsies' lives was of course simultaneously far more mundane and diverse, and is a point worth emphasizing. From the Roma factory workers of Sliven in Bulgaria, to the suc-cessful Polish Gypsy voivodes (dukes or governors) noted by Grell-mann, from the long-established Gypsy districts of Spanish cities, to nomadic extended family groups crossing the Continent trading and working as they went, for every example of what 'a Gypsy' might be we can find a counter example. This diversity in part came from the different positions that had been imposed upon them and which Gypsies had established for themselves across the Continent since their arrival in the fifteenth century. It was also the product of the massive disparity in Europe's economies: industrializing and urbanizing Britain, north-eastern France, the Low Countries and the German Ruhr all produced rapidly growing cities driven by mass migration and an increasingly restive proletariat. In contrast, huge areas of rural Europe continued to revolve around the agricultural calendar, peasant culture and governed by firmly embedded feudal hierarchies. Consequently, Gypsies were as much a part of the seemingly unchanging round of peasant life as they were of the flows of migrants between and within districts, cities, regions and countries.

Crucially the improved road system, which gradually extended right across the Continent, meant that from the 1830s onwards the caravan – *vardo* in English Romani – become the practical and attractive, as well as ultimately iconic, mode of dwelling for many Gypsies. Improved communications also began to reshape their relationship with the economy. At the beginning of the century poor transport meant Gypsies and other travelling people were commonly welcomed in remote rural areas, not simply because they supplemented the goods and services available to the population, but because they also provided news, gossip and a diversion from the normal round of life.[5] Over time this role became challenged by improved postal services, wider newspaper circulation, higher levels of literacy and, by the end of the century, the spread of telegraph and telephone networks. However, we also need to remember how geographically patchy these changes were, with Travellers being recorded as still performing this kind of role in the 1930s in parts of upland Scotland, and in the west of Ireland as late as the 1960s. Undoubtedly, however, the areas where they were a central part of the everyday economy became more marginal as the nineteenth century went on.[6]

More generally, the round of Gypsies' nomadic life across the Continent continued, with many of their main staples of work – metalwork; horse trading; basket and sieve making/wickerwork; pilfering and begging; shows and spectacles; and fortune telling – remaining roughly consistent.[7] And at times governments might even recognize the economic role played by them and other ambulant traders: in 1811 an enquiry led to the issuing of more permits for travelling traders across France, while five years later the minister for the interior instructed prefects to fully enforce the law of October 1798 which guaranteed freedom of trade. As in earlier periods, we also see evidence of local elites refusing to comply with orders from above on the grounds that local Gypsies were valued for the contributions they made to the community. In 1820, the mayor of Saint-Jean-de-Luz explicitly asked for their exemption from general surveillance measures ordered in a prefectoral circular of 20 August 1820:

> I must observe in this respect, Mr Under-Prefect, that since time immemorial, several families of the caste of *bohemians* vulgarly called *cascaroits*, live in this town, where they are lodged in houses where they pay the rent to the landlords, in part through days worked. The men of these families are all sailors and pay their levy to the government by serving years as the vassals of the king, and the women work without cease, either on a day-to-day basis [in a house or shop], or by making baskets and ropes.[8]

Here, as in other parts of France, the population of the region was falling at this time, and the authorities were quick to recognize the need for labour during a period that was simultaneously one of economic growth and significant trading opportunities. So, when the Justice of Amou proposed the deportation of Gypsies to America, he was quick to specify that 'the intention is not to depopulate a place of people who have made themselves useful by their work, and who are otherwise of good conduct, much less navigators and their families'.[9] Such protection of 'good' Gypsies, often linked to local economic interest, was a regular theme of contemporary mayoral pronouncements across the region.[10]

The variegated nature both of the laws and their enforcement interacted with pre-existing patterns of settlement and travelling routes so that certain areas, such as the French Midi, became a particular focus of Gypsy populations. In the process, illustrative of a pattern common across Europe, many Gypsies of this region became closely associated with particular routes and towns, such as Perpignan, Elne, Thuir and Béziers, and within specific quarters of these towns. Here Gypsy communities became well established in and wealthy from particular businesses – such as the horse dealers of Perpignan – and in the process more obviously region-alized in their culture, taking on both local dress and dialect if not mainstream religious practices over the course of the century. Similarly Gypsies of Ciboure and Saint-Jean-de-Luz in Labourd became associated with a number of maritime trades, notably as seamen on merchant trade ships and as fishermen.

In Spain the process of regionalization was particularly marked, to the extent that within the Basque country the *Erromintxela* – Kalderashi Roma, a Romani subgroup, who had settled there in the fifteenth century – had become deeply integrated into Basque society, expressing closer affiliation with the settled community than with other Spanish Gypsy groups. By the nineteenth century they had adopted much of the Basque language, as well as certain aspects of local culture including explicit rights for women and im-portant traditions such as *bertsolaritza* (improvised poetic song) and *pelota* (the national Basque ball game). In Andalusia the merg-ing of *Gitano* and local culture was perhaps even more profound, and perhaps best exemplified in the emergence of flamenco as an art form. Although Andalusian rather than *Gitano* in origin, it rap-idly became associated with Gypsy culture to a remarkable degree: both within Spain and then across Europe generally, by the end of the nineteenth century it was taken as the embodiment of authen-tic 'deep' Gypsy culture. In no small part this was due to the writings of George Borrow, a Norfolk-born Bible salesman and writer, who allegedly spent five years travelling through Spain. His most famous work, *The Bible in Spain*, while building on his own experiences in the country also borrowed heavily from Spanish Golden Age sources and philologists to create one of the most influential works of popular gypsiology.

His writing both fed, and was fed by, the growing appetite for picturesque depictions of 'authentic' pre-industrial cultures. As the Grand Tour of Europe's idle classes, emboldened by improved transport links and the romantic's desire for exotic locales, extended their scope to include Spain, encounters with Gypsies became something to be added to the travel experience. Anda-lusia in particular 'was constructed as a dream world where the course of time could be slowed, life savoured to its fullest' and modernity avoided. Central to the Andalusian experience became the spectacle of flamenco, with descriptions of performances in the Triana district of Seville becoming a staple of European travelogues alongside the requisite descriptions of monuments and cathedrals. While many travellers confirmed the attitudes of the French tourist Jean Francois de Peyron that Gypsies were a pack of thieves who 'only seek to rob and injure you', still others saw them as an essential part of 'realistic' local colour. Many of these tourists watching flamenco were blind to the professionalism of these performances, instead choosing to see them as a spontaneous and passionate expression of the exoticism of Gypsy lifestyles.[11]

What we should perhaps pay attention to is less the spectacle of flamenco and more how it was a demonstration of the ways in which Gypsies had become an intrinsic part of local and European culture. While we also see this in other cultural and musical forms across the Continent – most notably in the Gypsy choirs of Russia and the tradition of Hungarian Gypsy violin groups – there are myriad rather more mundane and everyday indications of the close relationship between Gypsies and majority populations right across rural and urban Europe. So, a clergyman from Prussian Lithuania, for example, described how, 'Gypsy men in this region dress exactly like the local Germans do on Sundays.'[12] Other eye witnesses similarly stressed, alongside the poverty of Gypsies, the way in which their lives were intimately bound up with the local peasantry and local economies. Carl von Heister's account of meeting with a Gypsy family living in a Baltic coastal village in 1842 suggests a life closer to the peasantry than that of an 'Indian wanderer'. The village he visited housed around eighteen Gypsy families, totalling 140 people, with the inhabitants mainly working the land. When he was invited into one of the houses, 'in order to find a seat . . . [he] had to expel a sow . . . although the house was dirty, it was well-ordered and the adults were well dressed'. He also noted that Gypsies in this part of East Prussia tended to be Catholic and 'only worked out of necessity',[13] neither of which presumably endeared them to the local Protestant bourgeoisie. Not all the Gypsies of the region were settled: some worked as rag sellers and horse dealers, moving in circuits through the region and taking in the main markets of Wehlau, Tilsit and Labiau. Similarly, accounts from the 1860s detail how along with horse dealing, occupations included wood carving, music and fortune telling.[14] We see similar patterns of living in the 'Gypsy' settlement in Kirk Yetholm, on the English/Scottish border, with Gypsy Travellers living alongside, but largely separate to, other villagers: still recorded as speaking Romani, the 1841 census for the village counted around 100 'Gypsies', and stated that although they were based in the village, they still mainly travelled from the spring to autumn, making a living through making goods, hawking and poaching.[15]

Overall, the nineteenth century saw increasing numbers of Gypsies, as with Europe's population more generally, living not simply outside the walls of cities and settlements, but as an integral part of urban districts. So as Britain and France, for example, became more urbanized, Gypsies, alongside the whole range of people engaged in the travelling economy, moved partly or wholly to cities and towns. Often they based themselves in poorer neighbourhoods over winter, living in tents or vans on wasteland or commons, or moving into houses, huts and temporary shelters, but taking to the road as the weather improved. The work of the French reformer Henri Bunel, which focused on the eighteenth and twentieth arrondisements of Paris, showed how these districts had Bohemians living in an 'agglomerations of shacks, made of planks, cloth and rags'.[16] The mixing of Gypsies with other *zoniers* of the area and the difficulty for authorities (and historians) of distinguishing them shows how well-enmeshed they were within the communities in which they lived.

In London they could be found in the peripheral commons and Forests of Epping, Loughton and Mitcham, as well as the brickfields, wastelands and shanty areas of Crystal Palace, Shoreditch, Battersea and Notting Dale potteries, and poor slum neighbourhoods such as in the East End.[17] The memories of the small-time crook, Arthur Harding, who grew up in the East End at the turn of the century, reveal just how integrated Gypsy Travellers were into the local economy: families based in Bethnal Green exchanged second-hand clothes for plants, ferns and china, hawking around the estates of London, and selling the clothes at markets and at the Exchange in Houndsditch. Many of these families were Gypsies 'living a more settled life', while also qualifying, in Harding's mind anyway, as 'proper cockneys'.[18] Living in the cities, for some of the year at least, did not remove the importance of the seasons for Gypsy Travellers: many went on the road from March to October, punctuating their year with regular stints fruit- and hop-picking, as well as race meetings and fairs. These were important parts of the calendar, not only for the important money-making opportunities they often represented; they were also social highlights, where families met up and, crucially, young people were able to socialize and court.

If this provided an example of an increasingly typical way of organizing their year, the most prominent example of Gypsy settlement in Britain was an indication of how they were able to adapt to the new economic opportunities presented by the nineteenth century. Blackpool had become well established as a coastal resort by the mid-nineteenth century, partly due to the rapidly expanding popularity of seaside daytrips and holidays and the improved rail links of Blackpool to the Lancashire cotton towns of its hinterland. The presence of the 'Gypsy' camp on its South Shore, providing rides, side shows and fortune telling, was aided by the 'endless disputes over the ownership and control of the beach below the high water mark'.[19] Gordon Boswell's childhood coincided with the heyday of the camp, when it contained over 300 stallholders and showmen. His mother ran a palmistry tent and they spent their summers on Blackpool's South Shore:

> She always had good seasons, as our position was a good one – near the old switchback, in the run of the people . . . [I would have] fun and play from morning to night . . . all summer through, when thousands of other children would only get the privilege of one day a year.[20]

While settlement and close affiliation to particular areas was a key feature of Gypsy life, we need also to be aware of the ongoing importance of cross-regional and international movement. This was perhaps best exemplified by the long-established presence of Sinti and Jenische within France. Sinti, who had emerged as a distinctive group within German-speaking territories from the sixteenth century and had also developed a strong presence in northern Italy, by the mid-1800s had also started moving into south-eastern France. As with the wider phenomenon of Italian migration in this period, there were strong economic push factors driving their movements. They rapidly established particular routes, such as along the banks of the Loire, which they then extended as they moved into France's interior. Once they had developed a good economic base within a region, geographic stability often followed: so, for example, the 'interior passports' of one family (the Michelets; given to them as foreigners in France) show that they primarily followed the same pattern of recognized routes across a particular area of western France.[21]

Similarly, groups of Jenische moved from Germany and the Low Countries into Alsace and Lorraine, notably the north Vosges region, where they lived and competed with the more established Sinti by the mid-nineteenth century. At the same time they expanded from this base throughout the east, the north and the Paris region.[22] Their mobility was profoundly affected by the Franco-Prussian War of 1870, with Prussian victory pushing many Gypsies from the annexed territories of Alsace and Lorraine westward: the scattered birthplaces of the seven children of one Jean Winterstein – Reole, Abbeville, Vannes, Castres, Montagnac and Cerilly – are testament to this phenomenon. In other cases families simply shifted the centre of their travelling to another department, such as the Muntz family of basket makers who established themselves in the Yonne area.[23] Choices of route were also tied to economic opportunities – both in terms of markets and access to raw materials – so that the decision to circulate in Burgundy, for instance, was directly related to the presence of wild reeds that were used in wicker-working. Evidence suggests that while they developed a reputation as musicians, Jenische in fact practised a wide range of trades, so that one family group might contain, for example, individuals involved in cabaret, carpentry, remoulding and hatting.[24]

Across the Balkans it appears that the mix of sedentary and nomadic lives, often centred round a particular region, was also a strong feature of Roma experiences in this period. For historians from the early nineteenth century, the absence of comprehensive Ottoman tax records was in part offset, at least in terms of evidence of Roma lifestyles, by an increase in travel writing by European visitors to the Balkans. Many were struck by the large Roma population of the region and left detailed accounts of their impressions. These show that seasonal nomadism had become a common pattern – making it hard to talk of clear-cut distinctions between 'nomadic' and 'settled' Roma – and also how farm work had become an integral part of many Roma livelihoods:

They breed a vast number of buffaloes, the very best in Eoumelia. In early spring they leave the place in great carts drawn by buffaloes, and travelling in the moist valleys continue their march until they have sold all their animals. Their families and culinary implements are all in the carts. They are all Musulmans, and are most of them wealthy. The carts are generally from five to ten in number. In autumn they return to their winter quarters in Hariupol . . . In a village some forty miles from Adrianople . . . are a number of Gypsies, who make sweetmeats which are sold at all the neighbouring fairs. Nearly all the musicians of Eoumelia are Gypsies. They have sweet voices, and are very clever players on the violin. On the farms they are employed at times in mowing and reaping; sometimes they plough, but they are generally weak, and cannot stand at their work as the Bulgarians. They work generally on the farms as basket-makers and ironmongers . . . At Kizanlik, a small town near Adrianople, they employ Gypsy women as servants in the Ladies' Baths.[25]

To this varied, but nevertheless traditional, range of occupations, by the mid-nineteenth century we need to add the 'Gypsy proletariat' of the Sliven textile factories. Largely established to provide cloth for the Ottoman army, in 1836 the Bulgarian entrepreneur Dobry Jeliazkov opened the country's first modern textile mill. Owing to difficulties in recruiting the general local population, he turned to the region's Roma population. Roma men, women and children all worked in, and lived around, the mills, so that by the time of Bulgarian independence they had formed a substantial working class population within the town.[26]

The account of two English residents of the Muslim Roma population living in the Christian village of Derekuoi near the Black Sea port of Varna in 1868 is particularly valuable.[27] In common with other observers they saw the Roma as only nominally Muslim, 'conforming outwardly to the State Religion of the country . . . though they never enter a mosque', while their separation from the wider Bulgarian population was reinforced by the fact that they generally spoke Romani rather than Bulgarian. The Englishmen's observations went well beyond descriptions of Roma economic activities to reveal something of the close and contentious relationship they had with the wider Bulgarian population:

> Our *Chinguines* exercised the universal gipsy trades of begging, basket-making, tinkering, and forging iron, to which the Bulgarians said that they added in an especial degree that of thieving, but . . . as in all our dealings with the gipsies we found them quite as honest (to say the least) as their *Rayah* [non-Muslim] neighbours. Every morning the gipsy women, furnished each with a big sack and a long stick to keep off the dogs, who seem to bear them an especial antipathy, start in couples upon an expedition to beg or buy flour and other food amongst the villagers, who occasionally give it to them without payment, not from any motive of charity, but because they are to a certain extent afraid of them, having a deeply-rooted belief in their power to cast spells, cause rain, and other beneficent or maleficent attributes. The men remain at home mending pots and pans, tinning copper vessels, and doing all the iron-work required by the village, whilst the children blow the bellows, or accompany the cattle to their pasturage.

The authors emphasized how it was the villagers who often went out of their way to cheat the Roma, consistently overcharging them for food and other items, or exacting excessive labour penalties when they could not pay in cash. While allowed to live in the village in the winter when they were 'a positive pecuniary advantage to the villagers', in spring when they had milk and butter to sell the village elders forced them to move on, since they were 'not paying for the privilege' of grazing their cattle on communal land, something which was free for all other villagers. Instead of simply ordering them to leave, the Roma quarter was burned to the ground and its inhabitants forced to vacate it. And yet, the next winter a different group were invited to settle in the village:

> The voluntary or forced migration of a tribe in search of fresh quarters is one of the most picturesque sights to be seen in Bulgaria. A long string of oxen, buffaloes, and horses (which we will hope have not been stolen), transports the

tents and cooking utensils of the voyagers, as well as the very old men and young children . . . The life of the gipsy in Turkey is very much that of a Pariah: disliked and despised by the Turk, hated by the Christian, he yet earns his living by harder labour than that of the latter, whilst his only crime is petty larceny amongst a people with whom roguery is the rule, honesty the exception . . . The gipsies are allowed to settle in their villages by Mussulmans and Christians, but are usually much worse off amongst the latter than with the former.

Even such a brief look at how the economic changes of the nineteenth century affected Gypsies points to the complex way in which what we may broadly characterize as modernity affected their lives. While it is rarely helpful to point to a 'Golden Age' in any people's history, there seems to have been a period in the early to mid-nineteenth century, between the crumbling of *anciens régimes* and the emergence of nation states, when what we might think of the technologies of rule were in flux. Put simply this was a time when the early modern solutions to the 'Gypsy problem' of banishment and extreme physical punishment fell out of use, while modern mechanisms of surveillance and regulation had yet to take hold.

As ever, this was not the same across the Continent, nor, as we shall see, was it a linear process. But it is clear that it was within these gaps, and at the edges, where Gypsies were most able to flourish, taking advantage of places where regulations were lighter or controls were lifted as much as they did new economic opportunities. And it was within the gradual disintegration of the *ancien régimes* and empires under the pressures of economic change and demands for political change and national expression, such gaps might open.

Just as the Enlightenment found expression in the revolutions of France and the United States, so too did it inform the nationalisms emerging as a popular force across Europe. Nationalism, often tied, but not always, to ideas of democracy, became something that challenged autocratic monarchies and the concept of the divine right of kings. Once again, such generalizations hide as much as they reveal: both the Dutch Republic and Britain's constitutional monarchy were well established by the early eighteenth century, while it took the convulsions of the early twentieth century and of the First World War to dislodge the Russian Tsarist and Habsburg empires. While paying attention to such differences across place and time, overall the nineteenth century was to see the idea of the nation state becoming the dominant political ideology in Europe. Central to its success was the way in which the 'nation' was not only depicted as more 'natural' but more modern and power-ful than empires.[28] And yet, the idea of the nation state was far from natural. If France and Britain, both of which had emerged as rela-tively stable nations during the early modern period, still struggled with how to treat their peripheries, how much more was this the case for Germany, riven as it was by countless boundaries, compet-ing histories and religious affiliations? Or the Balkan region, with its history of multi-ethnic and highly diverse communities?

If the 'nation' was a political construction, then, as we shall see, so too were the stories on which it so often relied. Indeed, the nationalism of the modern period was often a carefully constructed bundle of myths deployed by an emerging political class. In this revived, or even invented, folk myths combined with the emotional power of romanticism in order to produce a cultural rationale for a political idea that seemed to offer a powerful alternative to the in-justices of empire. And it was no less powerful for being invented: by the end of the century, the Greek, Serb and Bulgarian wars for independence had become nationalizing projects, in which minor-ities, often Muslims, often also Roma, fell victim to the purifying violence of the Balkan nation-builders.[29] As well as reshaping the political map of the region, these wars were a foretaste of just how destructive the collision of nation and identity might be: a collision which was to be writ large in the twentieth century.

What is perhaps unexpected, given the marginal position of Gypsies in societies across Europe, is the way in which they could form a key part of debates over and constructions of national identity. If we look at the Balkans we can see different ways in which emerging national movements might interact with particular Roma populations. The diversity which was the legacy of 400 years of Ottoman rule ensured that not only was there no one path to nationhood, but that the relationship between Gypsies and the Balkans' other populations could play out very differently depend-ing on the context. We need to remember that by the beginning of the nineteenth century there were between three and four times more Muslim Roma than Christian in the Balkans, and while both contemporaries and historians made attempts to distinguish between settled and nomadic groups, evidence suggests this could be profoundly fluid. And as we shall see, at various points Roma might identify, or be identified, as 'Turkish' or 'Greek' as much as 'Gypsy', 'Bulgarian' or 'Romanian'.

Already by the early nineteenth century the Ottoman Empire was struggling to effectively rule its Balkan territories. A complex process of nation building that began with the Serbian uprisings of 1804–13 and fed into the political outcomes of the Congress of Paris at the end of the Crimean War profoundly challenged the centuries-old Ottoman ideology of disparate territories united under Islam.[30] While the revolutionary 1830s and 1840s awakened a belief in the right and capacity of nations to determine their own fates, what was less clear was how those nations might be defined. Intellectuals across the Balkans, inspired by romantic nationalism, began to look to native traditions of language, religion and ethnic group for cultural inspiration and political solutions.[31] At the same time, they also looked for inspiration beyond the region, particularly to France.

The political instability of the region, as well as the wider intellectual context of the time increasingly produced an atmosphere in which the foundations of serfdom and slavery were challenged. In Bucharest in particular we see how the tentacles of the Enlightenment and of ideas of *liberté, egalité, fraternité* spread via its sizeable French expatriate population. Crucial here were the writings and political activities of two such residents in the 1830s, Jean Vaillant and Félix Colson. Both French language tutors to the emerging national elites of the city, they not only introduced modern educational ideas, but alongside their French language teaching brought its Republican ideas to their charges. They rapidly became preoccupied with the position of Roma slaves within Wallachian and Moldavian society, seeing it as indicative of not only the backward nature of the region as a result of Ottoman imperialism, but as a more general symbol of the need to throw off the yoke of oppression.[32] Vaillant argued that slavery was based on the complicity of the entire social system: 'the state sells them, the private entrepreneurs buy them, and the monks also sit around with their palms exposed'. He wrote vividly of an encounter with some enslaved Gypsies who were chained together at the leg and neck in a river mining sand:

> Who are these beasts I see in the darkening dusk? Walking back and forth on all fours, like rats, when on two legs, like monkeys . . . certainly they're not men; they're animals. My God! They *are* people! Gypsies![33]

Such awareness of the miseries of slavery were also articulated by key liberal reformers and nationalist politicians such as Mihail Kogălniceanu, who compared Roma slaves to the ex-African slaves of the Americas. His graphic descriptions of their circumstances were widely circulated and commented on within the emerging Romanian nationalist movement:

> I saw human beings wearing chains on their arms and legs, others with iron clamps around their foreheads, and still others with metal collars about their necks. Cruel beatings, and other punishments such as starvation, being hung over smoking fires, solitary imprisonment and being thrown naked into the snow or the frozen rivers, such was the fate of the wretched Gypsy.[34]

By the late 1830s attitudes were changing more widely across society, to the extent that some nobles themselves began freeing their slaves: Barbu Ştirbei, who had auctioned 3,000 slaves in order to pay for palace renovations, was so ashamed by the public's reaction that he suggested abolition. This fed into changing state policy, so that in 1837 the governor of Wallachia freed all state slaves, granting them the same status as peasants, and permitting them to speak Romani and practise their customs. In 1842 the ruler of Moldavia followed suit as part of a general efforts to lift the province 'from the slough of primitive stagnation and instil modern ideas of government'. Two years later Moldavia's church slaves were freed, and in 1846 Gheorghe Bibescu, the French-educated nationalist ruler of Wallachia, freed its church slaves.[35] All this formed the context to the 1848 Wallachian revolutionaries' proclamation that included a denouncement against the inhuman 'disgrace' of slavery, setting the tone for the aspirations of a new Romania. While, as with all the European revolutions of 1848, the uprising had no short-term positive consequences, the 1850s saw the increasing independence of Wallachia and Moldavia.[36] One way in which this was manifested was through the gradual acceptance among elites of the unacceptability of slavery within an aspirant modern European nation. Consequently in 1855 the prince of Moldavia banned slavery completely as 'this humiliating vestige of a barbarous society', with Wallachia following in early 1856. At the end of the Crimean War in 1864, the newly united Romania's constitution guaranteed, in principle if not in practice, equal citizenship status for all Romanians, including the Roma.[37]

Ever complex, we need to avoid implying that all those emancipated willingly embraced their new status, let alone used it as means of escape. In fact contemporary documents reveal the unwillingness of considerable numbers of Roma to have their status changed from that of slave to 'free' citizen. Many were financially far better off paying a fixed annual tax than the far higher number of taxes chargeable to citizens, particularly when emancipation left them with no money, possessions or property.[38] The petitions from that period of recently emancipated Roma offer us a more nuanced insight into their situation than the political propaganda writings of reformers and nationalist politicians. While such writers were right to point to the immorality of slavery, that emancipation was not backed up with material support for ex-slaves feeds the suspicion that Roma emancipation simply served a wider political and nationalist agenda. Once national liberation had been achieved, the material state of the Roma ceased to attract attention.

In Bulgaria, which had always had a closer relationship with the Ottoman Empire than the vassal states of Wallachia and Moldavia, the atmosphere of change and reform was manifested differently. Crucial here was the period of *tanzimat* (reorganization) which was exemplified in the 1839 Rescript of the Rose Chamber, a piece of empire-wide legislation which established 'security of life, honour, and property, regardless of faith or ethnic background'. Broadly conceived, these reforms aimed to stem the growing tides of nationalism and external aggression through a process of modernization, and were heavily influenced by the Napoleonic Code and French law under the Second Empire.

Between 1839 and 1876 successive measures were passed covering everything from changes to imperial uniforms to the abolition of slavery and the slave trade (1847), and educational, institutional and legal reforms.

However, both within the empire in general and for Roma in particular, the effects of the reforms were contradictory. While attempts were made to bring the civil status of Gypsies more in line with other subjects of the Empire, they did little to change their position in wider society. And yet, they were affected by the changes, although in perhaps unexpected ways. So, for example, during this period of crisis as local populations stopped carrying out specific roles and obligations these were taken over by local Roma. In Sliven after the *tanzimat* the annual duty to travel to Istanbul to graze the Sultan's horses and mow the Sultan's lawns became the sole duty of the Gypsies. Over the same period the proportion of state-appointed watchmen who were Roma increased significantly, as did recruitment into irregular police contingents. Their duty here was to suppress the growing number of uprisings in the provinces, and in this way they became involved in the looting and burning of Christian villages, which was seen as a legitimate perk for those putting down revolts.[39]

This suggests that unlike in Romania, where as we have seen nationalism dovetailed with the interests of Roma emancipation, in Bulgaria the growing nationalist movement seemed to exist in conflict with its Roma population. And indeed, as their role in the irregular police contingents suggests, this could be manifested in brutal and unpleasant ways. Such tendencies became more pronounced as Bulgarian nationalism swiftly became defined in relation to Orthodoxy, and was articulated both in opposition to Istanbul and to the Greek domination of the church hierarchy within Bulgaria. The granting of an autonomous Bulgarian bishopric in 1870 was viewed as a major triumph within the country, where it was seen as implicitly recognizing Bulgaria as a separate nation with rights to religious and cultural self-determination apart from Greece. And yet, this Bulgarization of the Orthodox Church served to marginalize Muslim Roma from claims of Bulgarian identity, while also providing a new outlet for anti-Roma prejudice. This gives context to the nationalist pronouncements of newly created Bulgarian bishops, who declared it was 'a great sin to give alms to a gipsy or an infidel'. And of course, the large proportion of Roma, who were also Muslim, were doubly damned by such a pronouncement.[40]

The combination of social and economic uncertainty, emancipation and the profound political changes in the region spurred mass emigration within and from the Balkans, leading to one of the largest migrations of the modern period. For Roma it was a trigger for the migrations of Kalderashi, Lovari and other Gypsy populations out of the Balkans, profoundly altering the distribution of Gypsies across the globe. Although this period is often seen as the peak of European imperial ambition, unlike in the seventeenth and eighteenth centuries where the movement of Gypsies across the Atlantic was closely associated with formal imperial projects, by now transatlantic migration was also an expression of the expanded opportunities offered by improved transport technologies and communication links.

Initially many Roma headed for Poland, but conflicts with Polish Gypsies and Tsarist policies spurred them to continue moving westwards, first into Germany and then France.[41] These groups rapidly became closely associated with particular trades: the Kalderashi, coppersmiths from Wallachia and Moldavia, continued to live as metalworkers and cauldron makers after their arrival in France in 1867, while the Bosnian Ursari, as their name suggests, were known as bear trainers.[42] Both these groups initially were seen as a novelty and attracted many curious visitors who were taken with how 'their ragged clothing contrasted with the mass of gold and silver with which they bedecked themselves'.[43] Their visit to Paris in 1872 prompted Emile Zola to write admiringly of their customs, fortune telling and physical qualities, but in more horrified tones of their 'hideous' clothing and living conditions.[44]

Yet for many this was just a small part of a longer journey across the Atlantic to both North and South America, most notably to Argentina. Until restrictions on the entry of paupers were brought in in 1882, which were used to turn back Roma, alongside thousands of others emigrating from the Balkans, thousands also entered the United States.[45] Here emigrants continued peddling, hawking and finding work as musicians, while horse trading was one area where 'some made large sums of money in this trade. They owned sales stables, racehorses, and supplied large contracts . . .

Owing to the great demand in their country for fortune telling, many of the women earned large sums.'[46] Demonstrating how they were able to combine traditional ways of making a living with new opportunities, those who did fortune telling used 'modern methods of advertising'.

As in the Balkans, by the middle of the century in France, too, ideas of the place of Gypsies in relation to the French nation were beginning to emerge, suggesting that even in the land of *liberté, égalité, fraternité*, the relationship between the nation state and its nomads might be problematic. After the nationality law of 3 December 1849, which legalized the deportation of aliens, treatment of Gypsies became entwined with that of foreigners:

> For a long time, the government has occupied itself with guaranteeing the safety of our population against the crimes and the depredations of bands of individual vagabonds and nomads known under the name of *Bohemians* . . . Prefects must thus concentrate themselves with the magistrates . . . [to enable] an energetic application of the police laws concerning vagabonds and dangerous foreigners.[47]

The Bohemians appear, in effect, in one or the other of these categories, often in both at the same time. Added to the sense of their foreignness was the way in which they were positioned as 'nomadic criminals', whose movements had to be controlled in the same manner as those of other criminal elements. The 1851 coup which had preceded the establishment of the Second Empire (1852–70) saw the implementation of emergency measures allowing the transportation of offenders, ranging from Parisian insurrectionists to petty criminals, to Algeria or Guiana for periods of hard labour. At the same time a new, harsher system of surveillance was instigated, which included requiring suspects to remain at an 'assigned residence'.[48] The way this might be mobilized against Gypsies was spelled out by central government to prefects:

> Once placed under legal surveillance, these individuals will find it difficult to escape repression, the government could, in assigning to each one of them a distinct and obligatory

residence, disperse them and in this way break the associations of criminals which live by begging disguised in different forms, when they do not have recourse to marauding
or to stealing. If they break their ban, they will fall under
the decree of 8 December 1851 and could from then on be
deported to Cayenne [in French Guiana].[49]

The tendency to lump together foreigners and Gypsies became
more pronounced over the second half of the century, fuelled by
the influx of foreign migrant workers to France, and the very visible
presence of Balkan Roma groups. And yet the first significant state
initiative to impose order on Gypsies, ambulant tradespeople and
the mobile poor – a census undertaken on 20 March 1895 – in fact
showed the gap between fear and reality. The anxiety of the time is
expressed in the Minister of the Interior's directive to the
maréchaussée that showed that some Gypsy groups, particularly
mobile Manouches, were believed to be acting as German spies:

> Be informed that nomadic bands all over France and abroad
> obey a leader living in Paris. It is of capital interest to dis-
> cover this leader and to know the nature of the links uniting
> the nomads, the orders he gives them and the missions he
> entrusts them.

This was of course pure fantasy, but that fact did not stop the arrest
and questioning of a Russian Gypsy, Petro Boumbay for this very
reason.[50] In fact evidence from the 1895 census suggests that fears
over their disloyalty and their 'foreignness' far outweighed their
actual presence: the itinerant total was put at 400,000, of which
25,000 were 'nomads travelling in groups and in caravans', and the
majority of names returned were Gypsies with French nationality.
Also numerically significant were Manouches, many of whom had
left Alsace-Lorraine after German annexation, along with Pied-
montese Sinti, who were often recorded as basket makers, hawkers
and accordion players and were most numerous in the Auvergne.
In contrast only very small numbers of Gypsies from central or eastern Europe were recorded across France.[51] Debates over the census,
as well as earlier directives over 'nomadic criminals', show how the
presence of Gypsies intersected with issues of national identity and

foreignness, as well as with the perennial question of how to deal with the overlapping criminal and vagrant populations. As with earlier periods, assumptions remained that these categories were natural bedfellows, and that Gypsies represented a challenge to both national and social boundaries.

Although the preoccupation with Gypsies as criminal and foreigners outside the nation state was also a strong presence in Germany, the path it took was rather different. To understand this we need to reflect for a moment on the particularities of Germany's relationship with nationalism and modernization. Germany, as a unified state did not emerge until 1871, and despite rationalization, even at the end of the Napoleonic wars it remained a patchwork of 39 city and regional states. Given impetus by Napoleon's defeat of Prussia in 1806 and then the national War of Liberation (1813–15), the decades leading up to unification were ones in which the idea of Germanness and of nation were intensely debated, with writers articulating, celebrating and politicizing the uniqueness of being German.[52] Yet, unlike some other European countries that were able to construct simple (if inaccurate) narratives linking the dominant peoples in the contemporary nation state with historical ancestors and a particular territory, in Germany this simply was not possible. While the peoples of central Europe may have maintained degrees of distinctiveness, intermixing clearly had taken and continued to take place. Equally, due to patterns of medieval and early modern migration, significant German populations lived outside Prussia, the German Confederation and Austria, most notably in parts of Russia.[53] Put simply, many of those within Germany did not speak German nor identify as German, while there were many well beyond the German heartland who did.

In order to move beyond this difficulty, a narrative was constructed in which the cultural traditions of the *Germania* identified by Tacitus could be shown to be handed down from one people to another through a chain of intercultural exchange. It allowed a seemingly fragile national identity to simultaneously claim a Teutonic heritage while suggesting it was cultural continuity and autonomy, not blood purity that was the guiding principle of German identity. For romantics like Schlegel, adherence to the idea of a German-led modern culture fusing the ancient, medieval and modern, as well as the German, Roman and Christian, lay deep in the nationalist construction of historical consciousness.[54] Within such ideas of a 'natural' and continuous German nation, language was tied to cultural markers, often grounded in peasant culture. Romantic thinkers idealized the natural strength of the peasants, seeing it as a creative force that could be tapped to forge a new social order from within. This stimulated the collection of songs and folk and fairy tales, and it is no accident that the Brothers Grimm's hugely significant collection *Kinder- und Haus-Märchen* (Nursery and Household Tales) was published in this period. The Grimms were strong advocates of German unification as well as disciples of the Enlightenment anthropologist Johann Herder's ideas of the importance of the *Volkspoesie* ('natural' poetry) of the peasantry. Crucially for us, within the stories they collected and reworked, Gypsies were habitually depicted as witches, thieves or devils, with the children described as 'ugly' or 'dirty'. Even their positive images of Gypsies centred around stories of their magical powers as fortune tellers or sorceresses.[55] Early then, in the project of German nationalism, Gypsies were constructed as not simply outside the nation, but as outside humanity itself.

The very artificial nature of the constructed idea of 'modern Germany' meant that perhaps more than elsewhere in Europe, the fraught relationship between growing national identity, increased state ambitions and emerging powers of regulation and control, can be seen in the German states. These, by the middle decades of the century, were struggling to give political and administrative form to nationalist ambitions. And this was given impetus by the socio-economic changes affecting the region, as from the 1830s Germany experienced growing industrialization and population growth. In the rural areas, and with agriculture still based on a pre-industrial economy, this led to food riots, rural unemployment and increasing migration, not simply to the towns, but often with those from the Balkans, across the Atlantic.[56] Consequently, with the emergence of a new middle class there was also increased pauperism as well as a significant migrant population and political turmoil.

More so even than in France, local political identities remained bound up with the historic states, not simply larger ones such as Bavaria and Hannover, but minor principalities like Schwarzburg-Sondershausen. These continued to compete with articulations of a broader Germanness which, it was argued, now needed to be expressed through political, as well as cultural unity, so that Germans could take their proper place in Europe. Although the German Confederation had a federal assembly and was pledged to mutual defence, it was in fact the Prussian Customs Union, or *Zollverein*, in which from its formation in 1818 we might see the first steps towards political unity. Driven by the growing economic power of Prussia, the removal of customs duties enabled a freer flow of goods and people, while also being seen as an essential move towards nationhood:

> The 830 toll barriers in Germany cripple domestic traffic and bring more or less the same results: what if every limb of the human body were bound together, so that blood could not flow from one limb to the other? In order to trade from Hamburg to Austria, from Berlin to the Swiss Cantons, one must cut through the statutes of ten states, study ten tolls and toll barriers, ten times go through the toll barriers, and ten times pay the tolls. Who but the unfortunate has to negotiate such borders? To live with such borders? Where three or four states collide, there one must live his whole life under evil, senseless tolls and toll restrictions. That is no Fatherland![57]

At the same time as these broad-scale developments were taking place, individual states began working more closely, creating bi-lateral agreements on a range of matters. One issue to which states gave attention was that of cross-border vagrancy, something which, in the early modern period, as we have seen, caused officials repeated difficulties. Hesse and Prussia's agreement of 1819 ended the practice of evicting vagabonds and criminals across their bor-ders; instead they were to be transported and delivered directly to the police station in the relevant location. Single vagabonds could travel alone, but only with authorized papers outlining a desig-nated travel route, and unless from the same family, they were to travel in groups no larger than three.[58] Records from two years later show that the authorities were putting some effort into monitoring and controlling the movement of Gypsies across Hesse. Following reports that groups had entered the province – trading particularly in fine tin-glazed pottery – the police coordinated raids on their camps. They found that several families were being accompanied by people without the proper papers and by 'suspicious vagrants' and others involved in 'aggressive begging'. Such 'guilty families' were issued with restrictive travel passes that were valid only in certain administrative districts. These passes also specified that families had to travel singly on their routes, with no moving in larger bands permitted.[59]

Such focus on Gypsies was part of a wider change in attitudes towards migrants and outsiders. The North German Confederation abolished controls on migration in 1867, yet there was still disquiet over the movement of certain groups across internal borders. In this they faced what was to become a persistent dilemma for states: how to allow the free movement of 'desirable' goods and persons, while restricting the 'undesirable'. It is important not to underestimate the diversity of Germany in 1871: differences within and between states ensured that although we can often speak of broad trends we need to be wary of generalizing national mood or opinion.[60] And so the presence of different minority groups held different meanings in different parts of the empire. Prussia, for example – as the state most directly concerned both by the nationality struggle and by immigration from the east – actively pursued a restrictive policy towards Poles and Jews, which was aimed at minimizing the perceived threat of the 'Slavic influx' prompted by rapid industrialization and the promise of work. In contrast, the Ruhr region actively recruited Poles to its mines and factories.[61] To these growing numbers of migrant workers from the late 1860s were the very visible groups of Kalderashi and other Balkan Gypsies, prompting a great deal of popular comment across Germany. The police responded rapidly with circulars aimed at keeping out, or moving on these 'foreign' Gypsies, with Prussia in 1868 legalizing their deportation.[62]

Showing how German Gypsies were increasingly bound up with the issue of foreigners, it was not simply foreign Gypsies who attracted attention: in Baden in 1855 a decree stated how 'Gypsies, especially from Alsace, have frequently been entering again and roaming about with their families, purportedly to trade, but most for the purposes of begging or other illicit pursuits'.[63] Although often visibly different to the Gypsy populations of Germany, the growing popular literature on Gypsies which had begun with Grell-mann consistently reinforced the idea of even German Gypsies being a 'foreign race', implying that wherever they were they were 'outsiders'. Evidence from Bavaria in particular reveals that the low-ranking police there struggled with 'the restriction of the Gypsy label to aliens'.[64]

The issue of identity became more important as it became tied to states' desires to control migration, particularly immigration. In turn this was tied to the principle of *Heimatrecht*, the right of a citizen to settle in a municipality, or return to that municipality, a right that was tied to the ability to claim poor relief.[65] Even Gypsy groups, if they were deemed to be local, had rights to this relief, and it was taken seriously. This period saw states codifying their citizenship qualifications, such as Prussia's Citizenship Law of 1842, which stated that all legitimate children born in Prussia became Prussian citizens. However, it was also the case that the implications for not belonging were made starker, as the consequence of not choosing Prussian citizenship was expulsion.[66]

Already we have seen how nationalism might be articulated in different ways – in Bulgaria the Orthodox Church was central to ideas of belonging; in Germany language was a key marker – but as the nineteenth century went on ideas of 'race', which while having received the intermittent attention of European thinkers since the late medieval period, gained increasing prominence. Finding articulation in the Frenchman Arthur de Gobineau's *The Inequality of the Human Races* (1855), the following decades saw the emergence of a scholastic field intent on explaining and justifying inequalities between nations, within societies and even between individuals. De Gobineau's work was premised upon the idea of the superiority of an 'Aryan race', with other European 'races' and non-Europeans placed within a descending racial hierarchy. Used to explain and justify European colonial expansion as much as the stark inequalities of industrializing societies, what became known as social Darwinism – on the grounds of its crude use of and tenuous links to Darwin's ideas of the 'survival of the fittest' – became a way of articulating the superiority of 'the Teutonic race' over 'Slavs', Jews and Gypsies. This theoretical approach went hand in hand with the rise of physical anthropology, which aimed to distinguish between groups through the 'hard' manifestations of ethnicity – skin pigmentation, cranium size and shape and so on – while also feeding into the emerging discipline of criminology. Key here was Cesare Lombroso's *L'uomo delinquente* (1876), which was heavily based on racialized categorizations, claiming that certain races, such as Gypsies, were heavily predisposed to crime. His ideas were highly influential and found favour right across Europe and North America. The Spanish anthropologist Rafael Salillas, for example, consequently felt qualified to assert that, 'Gypsies by nature and occupation are more akin to the delinquent than the normal element of society.'[67] Now the centuries-old mistrust of Gypsies and presumptions of illegality could find a pseudo-scientific cloak.

Such preoccupations with 'race' were not simply confined to academic or elite circles, but were to become directly translated into how Gypsies, migrants and outsiders were treated and recorded by the police. While having roots reaching back at least to the late seventeenth century, part of this response was the growing professionalization of bureaucracies in general and police forces in particular. And it is here, rather than in schemes specifically directed at Gypsies, that we most often get a glimpse of how German states thought of, and dealt with, Gypsies. From the eighteenth century, *Steckbriefe*, the police journals containing the details of wanted criminals, demonstrate how simply being an itinerant 'could be sufficient to be deemed dangerous' and potentially criminal.[68] From the 1750s these had become more systematic, and prompted by the enthusiasm of Enlightenment-inspired civil servants such as Georg Jakob Schäffer of Württemberg, began to be shared across different cities and regions. Demonstrating clearly the links between improved administration, increased regulation and territorial unification, these administrators were motivated by a desire to create a more efficient cross-border unitary police system in which, initially at least, south German and Swiss states could work together. They saw a direct relationship between the fight against criminality, a thorough reform of government and ultimately increased national unity. Such attempts by individual police forces, and indeed individual officers, to coordinate their activities is one small example of the many administrative processes necessary to support the political construction of a unified German state.

The journals, crucially, not only demonstrate the police's desire to be more effective, but they also chart their shifting focus from 'bandits' in the eighteenth century to 'harmful tramps' by the 1840s and to 'Gypsies' by the 1880s. In the 1840s three-quarters of those recorded were labourers, travelling journeymen, servants and people such as waiters and hairdressers. Over half of the people listed in the books were wanted for begging, vagrancy or simply having no clear identity. Yet, if we look at Hannover as an example, an analysis of the entries from police journals from 1846 to 1870 shows an increasing presence of the label *Zigeuner* (Gypsy) in the classification of travelling people. And what is perhaps most interesting is that it seems a clear case of a change in definition rather than a change in people. The Schwarz and Trollmann families in this period consistently attracted the attention of the police, as they were not from Hannover and failed to produce the correct permits to carry out their itinerant professions. This interest led to an article in one of the journals calling for the police to construct genealogical trees in order to discover their real *Heimat* to where they could be returned and forced to adopt a sedentary lifestyle. Over the following six years a number of such pedigrees were published for some Gypsy families including the Trollmanns. Up to 1857 they were still included in the categorization 'harmful tramps' and it was only after this date, when the police had included the new category of *Zigeuner* in their records, that they were recorded under this heading. This suggests that it was not that there was an increase in the number of Gypsies in the state, but rather that the definition of certain people as 'Gypsies' had become more important to the authorities. And crucially, as time went on, these genealogies became more regularly circulated between different police authorities.[69]

By the 1880s, pronouncements issued by Bismarck against 'the mischief caused by bands of Gypsies travelling about in the Reich and their increasing molestation of the population' suggested that they had become an important target of state attention. The solution proposed was that police were to stop them at national borders, and they were to be sent back if they were 'unable to account for their crossing, if they carry irregular papers, or if they don't possess financial resources'. Overall the police were to adopt a policy of *strengste Handhabung* (the strictest handling) of Gypsies, so that they could be prosecuted for vagrancy if they could prove they had the resources to support themselves but had inadequate travel permits. In part this was based on the expectation that 'a conviction is to be expected due to the fact that a legal acquisition of the goods and decent lifestyle is highly doubtful'. These measures were not specifically confined to a racial understanding of Gypsies, as they were to apply also to all 'people travelling in a Gypsy manner'.[70]

Overall, in Germany then, as in France, we see the growing importance of the idea of 'the Gypsy', with their presumed foreignness – always a key theme in settled society's conception of them – now becoming bound more closely with the idea of the nation state and control of movement. Both the shift in importance of the category *Zigeuner* and the involvement of the police in tracking their genealogies were to be important precursors to the activities of first the Bavarian police bureau, and later the entire German police force in the first half of the twentieth century.

This flags up the importance of understanding the relationship between the growth of the nation state – sometimes, but not always, tied to ideas of nationalism – and the broader trend of state expansion and social change seen across the nineteenth century. It would be a mistake to suggest that the entire focus of regulation and attention on Gypsies was based around notions of nationalism and of race, important though these were. Centred particularly on Britain and France were growing notions of respectability that became intimately entwined with movements for reform, regulation and social control.

In France, by the end of the nineteenth century, the dominant political response to the upheavals in French society had manifested itself through a conservative republicanism which consciously constructed an idea of a France united around shared values of nationalism and responsibility to society. This was a France which brought together the old elite, new middle-class property owners and rural landowners, and put the sanctity of private property at its heart.[71] In Britain, while it was legitimized by the subdued culture of Victoria's court, 'respectability' was most strongly associated with the consolidation of the middle classes, which placed bourgeois values at the centre of cultural and public life. At its best, this trend looked at the slums of Britain's ever-growing towns and cities and decided that it was not acceptable for the working classes to live in such conditions, and pushed for reform of housing and control of unscrupulous landlords and employers. At its worst however, it simply attempted to move problems out of the sight of those offended by the 'nuisance'.

While clearly none of these processes were new – the situation of the poor had long been the recipient of elite attention and Gypsies had, after all, been subject to harassment ever since their arrival – with an ever-growing population, the rapid expansion of urban areas and their increasing regulation by the new municipal and local authorities, they became more fraught. And crucially it was certain *behaviours* rather than *people* that were the subject of the authorities' attention. So, for example, in Britain from the eighteenth century, enclosures removed large areas of common land, drastically reducing the number of stopping places available to Gypsies, with this trend gathering pace through a series of Private Acts between 1834 and 1849. On top of this, road improvements often narrowed wide roadside verges, removing a common source of grazing, used not only by Gypsies but by other wayfarers.[72] Matters were made more difficult following the County Police Act of 1839, which not only formalized rural policing, but in some areas, notably Dorset and Norfolk, resulted in concerted campaigns to remove Gypsy Travellers from the countryside.[73] Similarly, the Commons Act of 1899 allowed local authorities to manage commons and pass by-laws prohibiting camping or lighting fires; while the Housing of the Working Classes Act of 1885 allowed sanitary authorities to promote 'cleanliness in, and the habitable condition of tents, vans, sheds and similar structures'.[74] By-laws linked to these and similar acts created a new patchwork of regulation affecting Gypsies, which had the cumulative effect of outlawing sizeable chunks of Gypsy Travellers' lifestyles in particular areas, while not in themselves targeting Gypsies as a specific group. We have seen how there had always been difficulties defining who exactly constituted a Gypsy – hence the long use of expressions such as 'counterfeit Egyptians', and 'those living in the manner of Gypsies' – yet by focusing simply on behaviour this difficulty was bypassed in one stroke.

We see similar processes at work over the Channel in France, where the evolving nature of the French state – complicated by regime changes which lurched between monarchic and republican models – produced a patchwork of highly localized responses to Gypsies' presence. So, in the *département* of Yvelines and the former Seine-et-Oise the prefect Felix Cottu instituted a by-law allowing the police 'to exercise a specific surveillance on bands of bohemians and vagabonds'.[75] By contrast evidence from the Marne in 1882 shows the mayors being relatively tolerant and supporting Gypsies' rights to use traditional stopping places.[76] As ever, we need to set the treatment of Gypsies in the wider context of moves against vagrants and other mobile workers, and the nineteenth-century tendency to widen the definition of vaga- bondage; previously one had to have no fixed home, no regular work and no resources: a 100 sous piece or evidence of recent work could allow release. But the tightening of regulations and a shift in the burden of proof needed to demonstrate innocence meant a doubling of convictions from just over 20,000 in 1861–5, to 51,404 to 1890. By this time local governments had also started invoking and enforcing both new and existing laws against parking in order to move people on.[77]

This did not mean there were not attempts to target Gypsies specifically: in Britain this was done mostly consistently through the trenchant George Smith of Coalville and his Moveable Dwellings Bills. In many ways a model of a Victorian reformer – a self-educated Primitive Methodist who did not flinch from offering his opinion where he thought it would spur the progress of regula- tion – he had no time for romantic notions of Gypsies as bearers of a more authentic life closer to nature. Indeed, he explicitly rejected 'the example of daisy-bank sentimental backward Gypsy writers, whose special qualification is to flatter the gipsies with showers of misleading twaddle'.[78] His writings consistently suggest that 'Gypsydom' was spreading like a disease to the settled population, as he believed large numbers of the settled population were taking to the road as a way to avoid responsibility, hard work and moral duty. This wasn't just about improving the lot of Gypsies, it was part of a wider vision of ensuring that the world's leading imperial nation lived up to its reputation as a modern Christian country.

Introduced in various forms from the 1880s to the 1930s, the Moveable Dwellings Bills centred around compulsory registration of Gypsy Traveller dwellings (prompting discussions over to how 'boughs of trees with some old cloth fastened over them' might be registered and regulated), insisting on sex-segregated sleeping quarters, requiring the children to attend school at least on a half- time basis, with inspectors being given powers to enter any move- able dwelling to check regulations were being followed.[79] The aim was, in Smith's words, to bring 'gleams of a brighter day . . . that will reflect a credit instead of a disgrace to us as a civilised nation'.[80] In fact, despite his zeal, the bills – of which there were nine different versions between 1885 and 1894 alone – were never passed. Central to the failure of the bills was the way in which they conflicted with central government's idea of itself as impartial. Most crucially, Home Office civil servants resisted any legislation that identified the law with the interests of a particular group, and the idea that Gypsies were being singled out for repression offended their liberal notions of equality before the law.[81]

In this Britain was noticeably different to the gathering mood of Continental Europe. Within Germany and France the culture of social conservatism and its stress on creating social order provided the backdrop to the consolidation of police powers, and went hand in hand with social Darwinist explanations for vagrancy and criminality: 'Vagabondage leads to crime. All errants beg and steal.'[82] Contemporary police memoirs reveal ever more virulent 'conclusions' drawn from their work: Officer Boué described the character of Gypsies as 'wily, cowardly, cruel and vindictive', and discourses of how Gypsies promoted the 'infection' of respectable people and of children by their mere proximity were also common. In 1907 *Le Petit Parisien* wrote a very influential editorial entitled 'On the Road', which positioned Gypsies as a public danger and a menace to order in society, while Deputy Dubief described Gypsies as 'Extra-social parasites . . . incapable of the daily work which everyone is paid for . . . anti-social . . . anti-hygienic and propagators of epidemics . . . potential criminals.'[83] In part the history of social unrest and the limited nature of poor law support in France compared to Britain affected the tone of French writing on the matter; destitution was much more closely tied in people's minds to social disorder, causing fear among the 'respectable classes'. It was this climate which spawned the Waldeck-Rousseau law of May 1885 which made repeated vagrancy punishable by deportation, and the general push to expel foreign Gypsies and Alsace-Lorrainers who hadn't chosen France after the Franco-Prussian war.[84] By 1897 the Minister for the Interior instituted a commission to try to ensure closer surveillance of 'vagabonds and heathens'.[85] Within elite institutions we also see anti-Gypsy attitudes being expressed in this period: the wealthy Society of French Agriculturalists, for example, repeatedly passed motions at their conferences 'in favour of a vigorous repression of vagabondage'.[86] Such entangling of the ideas of Gypsies, vagabonds and foreigners, of course, had a long heritage, yet in the context of the marrying of bourgeois ideas of respectable behaviour with the expansion of state regulation and the police force this was to set the tone for the twentieth century.

IT IS OFTEN TEMPTING to look at the nineteenth century simply as a precursor to the convulsions of the first half of the twentieth century: taking note of how nationalisms, as ideology and political reality began to take hold; charting how states, through expanded bureaucracies and police forces, were able to expand their control over their populations, and indeed defining far more closely who belonged to those populations; observing how the increasing importance of ideas of respectability and patterns of behaviour became regulated by state action as much as social norm. These are all trends that were to come to greater prominence in the following decades, and some of these tendencies at least were to find full expression in the death camps of the 1940s. And yet, while all these things are true, and made their mark on the lives of Gypsies, we also need to take the century on its own terms. For all that harassment continued, the Gypsy hunts of the seventeenth and eighteenth centuries had been left behind; the ending of slavery and serfdom in the Balkans, while not necessarily translating into improved living conditions, represented some form of progress, if only by allowing emigration through Europe and across the Atlantic; expanding economies and cities provided new opportunities for livelihoods and modes of living. While as ever we struggle with the difficulty of generalizing experiences across a century as well as vast geographical reaches, it may be fair to observe that the nineteenth century was a time which held a diminishing number of the unsavoury characteristics of *ancien régimes* while not yet fully exhibiting those of modern states. And it was in this era of change that Gypsies were able to live, if not more freely than they had ever done in Europe, then at least less in fear for their lives.

FIVE

Into the Flames

THE FIRST HALF OF THE TWENTIETH CENTURY is rightly thought of as a crucial period in the history of the Gypsies. Since their arrival in Europe they had faced persecution, attacks on their culture, language and lifestyles and yet this period saw something different. Although not necessarily exhibiting new attitudes – for they had long been seen as outside of society and sometimes even outside the human race – what was different was the capacity of states to carry out their intentions. Incidents such as the Spanish 'round-up' of 1749 showed that early modern states could exhibit determined action although, as we have seen, this was the exception rather than the rule: more often governments had to rely on the power of intermittent brutality to control their subjects. What we have already seen emerging in the nineteenth century, and what was to become such a feature of the twentieth, were new technologies of rule. Seemingly low key and sometimes apparently even benign, the expansion of the functions of the state created a different world in which rules and by-laws seemingly took the place of 'Gypsy hunts', the scaffold and banishment. Regulations covering public health, education, environmental control and the use of particular spaces meant that Europe saw the expansion of state action in ever-widening areas of people's everyday lives. Inevitably such regulations did not simply affect the settled population, but rather spilled over into, and indeed sometimes were directly aimed at, the treatment of Gypsies. And as the capacity of states to act expanded, so too did their ambitions: liberal democracies, as much as either Marxism or fascism, had a clear idea of what the ideal citizen might consist of and enacted measures to try and promote their vision.

Therefore, although the Holocaust hangs heavy over this period, when we think of the death camps, internment camps and genocide, it is perhaps most helpful to think of them as one particular manifestation of modernity rather than simply either as a horrific aberration or the culmination of centuries of persecution. Doing this enables us to see the Roma Holocaust as one of a number of manifestations of deeply engrained prejudices against Roma, Sinti and other Gypsies groups at a particular moment in history.[1] Consequently it also helps us to understand how it was that this prejudice might find other expressions at different places and times. Rather than detracting from the deep significance of the Holocaust, it means we can understand the multitude of ways in which Gypsies faced and experienced persecution, harassment and marginalization within modern Europe.

It is useful then to begin by seeing how the extension of regulation more broadly affected Gypsies in the first decades of the century. As we might expect, the diversity we have seen in Gypsies' living patterns across Europe, in which they took on a wide range of occupations, though often, but not exclusively, at the lower end of the social scale, can similarly be seen in their experiences of education. From the 1870s, but gathering pace from the beginning of the twentieth century, there was a mushrooming of educational initiatives directed both at the mass of the working-class population, and at Gypsies more specifically. The general historical context to this, of course, was the attempt by elites across the Continent to negotiate a rapidly urbanizing world in which various labour, socialist and Marxist movements emerged at a time when democracy was spreading to some parts of Europe, and argued for in other parts. Always seen as something of a double-edged sword, education was seen as a way of taming the revolutionary working classes and bringing them into the fold of (a highly mediated and partial) democratic politics. But at the same time education was feared, for once given the tools of literacy and critical thinking, there was no telling how a newly educated proletariat might behave. Hence universal or mass education often went hand in hand with heavy governmental, religious or nationalist agendas, and it was here that we commonly see the coming together of reform movements and debates over national identity and broader political projects. For Gypsies, the picture was often complicated by stereotyped attitudes held towards them. Sometimes education was part of a wider package of tools aimed at repressing their distinctive culture; yet at other places or times Gypsies were seen as unreachable and beyond the reforming power of literacy; and often the only point of consistency was the poor quality of formal education they received.

While it was logistically easier to bring settled Gypsies into the formal school system than it was nomadic families, this did not automatically mean they experienced education in the same way as children from sedentary society. In Hungary, for example, as part of Maria Theresa and Joseph ɪɪ's legacy, by the end of the nineteenth century nearly 90 per cent of its Roma population was settled, of whom around 40 per cent lived alongside the majority population rather than in separate Roma settlements. The census of 1893 looked at the place of Gypsies in Hungarian society and suggested that overall, although often poorer than the wider population, they lived lives indistinguishable from other peasantry. It found that the majority of the homes of settled Gypsies were 'well managed, clean and do not differ too much from the houses of other inhabitants'; moreover, of the 6,000 villages surveyed, in two-thirds of them it was reported that 'the conduct of the gipsies was blameless'. The figures for education were less promising: the census collectors believed that this was an 'important means of culture and social development', yet only 5.7 per cent of Hungary's Roma were literate, and only 12,000 of its 52,000 settled Roma school-age children went to school. And of the 6,332 settlements in which Roma lived, two-thirds reported that enrolled Roma children never attended school, with only a third stating they attended consistently. Census analysts believed that the intellectual achievements of the Roma population could have been under-represented in their findings, for as they acknowledged, many of those who did acquire an education and a profession often tried to assimilate and therefore chose not to identify themselves as Gypsies.[2]

Rather than assimilation, a different strategy was initially pursued in the newly independent Bulgaria. Building on the Ottoman legacy, which accepted the right of different ethnic communities to maintain a degree of religious, cultural and judicial autonomy, the Bulgarian constitution confirmed the principle of national primary-level education. The law of 1885 required all settlements, 'whatever their size', to have at least one school, while legislation passed in 1891 allowed 'non-Christian children to be educated in their mother tongue'. Although designed to reduce Greek influence in Bulgarian society, it meant that Muslim Roma, but not Christian, in theory might receive an education in Romani. While by 1910 this had resulted in the opening of three Roma primary schools in Bulgaria, the majority of Roma children that went to school did so alongside the majority population. Indeed as the vast majority of Roma spoke Romani as their first language and most struggled to do well at school, with their literacy levels remaining far below those of other minorities: in 1905 it was estimated that Roma literacy stood at 3 per cent, compared to 4 per cent for Pomaks (Slavik Muslims who speak Bulgarian), 6 per cent for Turks and 47 per cent for the majority Bulgarian population.

On the other side of Europe, all but a few Gypsies in Britain also struggled to benefit from the creation of free primary education. Here, it was not language that was to prove to be such a barrier, but rather the belief that their nomadism stood in the way of active participation in schooling. Consequently they, and particularly their perceived perpetual nomadism, raised some interesting questions for the expanding state, as they occupied a space between an expanding desire for regulation and a liberal discomfort with active repression. Gypsy Traveller children had been able, and in fact were meant to, attend school along with all children following the introduction of compulsory education in 1870. In practice this was not enforced and only some families – such as that of Gordon Boswell, whom we met on Blackpool's South Shore (chapter Four) – chose to take advantage of it. State discussions over implementing existing legislation more forcefully was partly in response to the ongoing lobbying of supporters of George Smith's moveable dwellings legislation, and led to proposals to include measures in the Children's Act of 1908. And yet, despite a general climate that increasingly accepted the extension of the power of the state into the lives of families and the treatment of children, draconian proposals to remove all Gypsy children from their parents in order to enforce educational requirements were rejected out of hand.

While Gypsies found few supporters in Whitehall, the developing self-image of civil servants that centred around professional impartiality, liberal values and 'fairness' meant they were unwilling to extend regulations which were seen to disproportionately affect family life. While, as we shall see, civil servants' ideas of impartiality might be deluded or self-serving, they did have the effect of putting a break on the kind of measures which were to become more and more common in Continental Europe over the following decades. The terms of the Children's Act – that if travelling children made 200 attendances between October and March, they were free to travel for the rest of the year – satisfied civil servants who had wanted to promote compulsory education but had objected strongly to interfering with the liberty of people who chose to travel for a living.[3]

If the potential for heavy state interference was rejected by the British central state, this was reinforced by the local authorities whose job it was to implement the legislation. Indeed more common than enforcing school attendance were the actions of the Education Committee who 'authorised managers to exclude from school children of nomads who apply for admission' as a response to complaints from parents who did not wish their children to be schooled alongside Gypsies. In other cases committees were 'reluctant' to enforce the law because of the 'heavy expense' of sending the children to industrial school, while a candid letter from the Home Office in 1918 admitted that 'village schools often refuse to admit gipsy children because they are dirty or otherwise unfit to mix with the other children'.[4]

Matters were generally rather different north of the border in Scotland. Here, because of the longer tradition of working-class education, the provisions of the act were taken seriously. The census of Scottish Travellers of 1917 found that, of the 1,120 Traveller children in Scotland, 200 of them were in industrial schools, having been removed from their parents for non-compliance. In Merkinch, Inverness, commitment to 'Tinker' education was demonstrated through the creation of a special school. This was set up 'in the interest of the vagrant children themselves as well as of the other children', with staff stressing that for public health reasons, 'segregation' should be 'insisted upon'.[5]

> This segregation of the Tinker children enabled the teacher (a) to give more careful supervision, (b) to teach such practical subjects to both boys and girls as might induce

them to acquire a desire for settled occupations, (c) to keep
in touch with them during their journeyings in the country,
and (d) to induce cleanliness among all.[6]

Such an emphasis on practical and supervisory elements of schooling shows how the scheme was designed primarily to socialize and
not to educate: 'careful supervision' could have enabled closer
attention for each individual to improve their literacy and wider
academic education, but instead the focus was on 'practical' skills
and personal hygiene to promote settlement and integration. In its
own terms the Merkinch scheme was a success. Rigid enforcement
of the 200 attendances rule was supported by vigilant checking of
certificates by the local police force. Commentators believed the
project caused parents to stay longer in town, and generated 'a
noticeable wish that their children should get out of the special
class and be drafted into the ordinary school'.[7]

In its willingness to enforce new regulations, Scotland in fact
had more in common with Germany than it did with England. In
Prussia, in particular, new educational requirements were actively
combined with everyday controls on movement and often older
regulations over pedlar licences or identity documents to push
Gypsies towards settlement. In 1899 Gypsy children were required
to attend school or would be removed from their parents, and two
years later this was followed by a measure enabling authorities to
institutionalize children in order to ensure they were schooled.[8] In
fact, Prussia had been expending significant resources for some
time regulating its nomadic Gypsy population with the aim of forc-
ing them to settle through making it almost impossible to obtain
the necessary itinerant trade licence. Applicants were forced to
comply with 'a host of meticulously applied bureaucratic requirements' which included 'proof of domicile, absence of serious convictions, satisfactory educational provision for the children, and
proper accounts for tax purposes'.[9] Local authorities might also
prosecute Gypsies for failing to register with them on arrival in a
district, or for military service.[10]

If education is one area in which Gypsies across Europe were
drawn, albeit often partially and unsuccessfully, into mainstream
regulations, the turn of the century saw more active measures
designed to target them and their lifestyles very specifically. Both

France and Germany – this time led by Bavaria rather than Prussia – began using new developments in policing and surveillance technologies in order to register, monitor and control their Gypsy populations. As ever, these innovations did not take place in isolation, but rather can be seen as part of a continuum in the professionalization of the police and the expansion of state bureaucracy into the everyday life of its citizenry.

In France, the mood of conservative republicanism we noted at the end of the nineteenth century was compounded by intense public debates over the nature of Frenchness and the relationship between the state and citizens. Most apparent in the convulsions accompanying the Dreyfus affair, which itself compounded the questions raised by the French loss of Alsace-Lorraine following the Franco-Prussian war, debates over national identity were also a response to rapid foreign immigration in to newly industrializing centres. Overall, it no surprise then that the years 1870–1914 saw a particular concentration of xenophobic attacks and local fights against foreign workers, with a peak in violence occurring in the years 1893–7. At the same time an intellectual racism based on social Darwinist ideas positioned France's Jews as 'foreigners', and formed one of the contexts of the Dreyfus affair.[11]

All this formed the wider backdrop to harsher anti-Gypsy measures, with a circular in 1898 ordering the continuous expulsion of Gypsies through successive *départements* in order to facilitate deportation.[12] And, in a foretaste of what was to come, the French minister for the interior Clemenceau's 'Tiger brigades' intercepted nomads, and were ordered to identify and record as many details (including taking photographs) as the law would allow. Their first operation against a group of 100 Gypsies saw many Gypsies detained in Tamblade in 1907, with the operation's success slavishly feted in the conservative press.[13] Yet confrontations at provincial borders between gendarmes expelling groups of Gypsies and neighbouring forces attempting to prevent their entry into their jurisdiction show that the state had yet to develop a coherent response.

Growing momentum generated both parliamentary activity and a 'Report on the Repression of Vagabondage and Begging' (1910). This, alongside fixing Gypsies as being distinguishable for having 'black eyes, greasy hair, sallow face', expressed anxieties around the presence of 'foreign nomads': 'Like his father and his grandfather, he'll live as a perpetually foreign vagabond on the soil of France, which he knows only for the purposes of exploitation.'[14] Different remedies were explored, with lessons being drawn from other countries: Deputy Flandin, for instance, noted with approval the creation of a repressive 'depot' for Gypsies at Merxplas in Belgium, which had 'isolation at night, [and] forced work during the day under extremely severe discipline'.[15]

The solution chosen by the French state was 'The law of 16 July 1912 relating to the exercise of ambulant professions and the regulation of the circulation of nomads'. As in Britain, however, despite the fevered climate of the time, the principle of equality before the law prevented the passing of directly racially targeted legislation. The decision to base the law on occupational categories rather than race explicitly signalled the French state's twin intentions to both draw Gypsies into the machinery of state and to deny them an ethnic identity. Its terms separated mobile traders into three categories: travelling salespeople (*marchands ambulants*), traders at markets and fairs (*forains*) and nomads (*nomades*). The first category included either French or foreign people who had a fixed address but followed an itinerant trade; the second was for French nationals with no fixed address who lived by selling at markets and fairs, whom it was decreed should carry an identity card, with a photograph, personal details and last address; while *nomades* included those 'no matter what their nationality, all individuals circulating in France with no fixed abode, and not fitting into any of the above specified categories, even if they have resources or pretend to have an occupation'.[16] While, as with Britain's educational legislation, the law of 1912 targeted a way of life rather than an ethnicity, contemporaries were well aware that this law was explicitly aimed at Gypsies.[17]

Building on the new scientific developments in policing, the law's most important provision for *nomades* was the introduction of a full anthropometric booklet designed by the Parisian policeman Bertillon, one of the pioneers of anthropometry. These contained personal information, included detailed physical characteristics and had to be stamped by the police chief, commander of the gendarmerie or the town hall each time an individual or group of Gypsies entered a *département*.[18] This simultaneously enabled the police to keep track of their movements, and created an offence with progressively harsher punishments if holders failed to fulfil this requirement. Some municipalities used this as a way of preventing Gypsies from stopping: if they refused to grant a stamp, the Gypsies had no choice but to move out of the area.[19] Furthermore, nomads were required to have a special registration plate on their vehicles, and their booklet was to contain details of their vehicle's body, wheels, suspension, axle, brakes, paint and hitch. A sanitary element was added in 1913, with the booklets required to include information on vaccinations, sickness, hospital visits and quarantine, and gave local officials the right to check the health and cleanliness of vehicles.[20]

In its use of both expanded policing and developing surveillance technologies, particularly in recording anthropometric data, France was entirely in step with innovations being used in other countries. Most notable here was the work of the Security Police at the Imperial Police Headquarters in Munich, which established an Information Service on Gypsies under Arthur Dillmann in 1899. From the 1880s, despite the relatively small number of Gypsies, Bavaria had been exhibiting an increasing preoccupation with them. This state was located between the German, Swiss, French and Austrian borders, and so often had groups of Gypsies moving through its territories. On top of this geographical situation there was a prevailing suspicion that it was relatively simple for them to evade the law.[21] Using the latest technology – telegraph, photographs, identification cards and finger printing – Dillmann collected and shared information on the Gypsy families of Bavaria with an aim to register the entire Gypsy population. In 1905 he published his *Zigeunerbuch* (Gypsy Book): this was littered with the word 'plague', with the bulk of the text taken up with the numerous regulations which could be used against Gypsies and the detailed records of individuals and their families.[22]

Despite Dillmann's obsession with collecting and detailing the particulars of Gypsies – the *Zigeunerbuch* held records of 3,350 people, 613 of these being detailed descriptions – it is notable that he explicitly used a 'lifestyle' rather than a 'racial' definition. For him, anyone who travelled around with their family deserved his attention, although he further distinguished between 'Gypsies' and 'people who live like Gypsies'. Even then it is not clear that those who were designated as 'Gypsy' were done so on 'racial' grounds:

ethnographic features such as language or skin colour played a sub-ordinate role to manifestations of a 'disorderly life', such as giving false names or other details.[23] Dillmann's work is significant because it was to form the basis for the genealogical charts of the Nazi period, and yet what we see here is the messy conflation of race and behaviour in the construction of Gypsyness.

Evidence from neighbouring Hesse shows that Bavaria was not alone in its preoccupations. A letter on the 'Gypsy pest' from the Hessian authorities in 1912 urged the state police to apply any meas-ures possible to harass Gypsies in their area, a process 'made easier through the use of the *Zigeunerbuch*'. Hesse's regional prosecutor approved of the fact that Munich's approach allowed the police to verify personal details, including criminal records, enabling them to decide if someone was a persistent vagrant. Here too, however, it was behaviour – vagrancy – that was the focus. This letter reminded officials that it was 'forbidden for Gypsies to *travel in hordes* through the state', and recommended automatic detention and a delayed trial for those picked up for vagrancy as a 'useful method' to keep them out of the Grand Duchy.[24] In Prussia we see a similar extension of the role of the police into social surveillance and welfare tasks relating to behaviours and people who were seen as undesirable or deviant, including alcohol consumption, un-hygienic housing and unregulated mobility. As part of their expanded remit the police 'used every rule and regulation to make matters as difficult as possible for travelling groups'.[25]

And although it was issued by Prussia's Minister for the Interior, rather than the national government, the 1906 directive on 'com-batting the Gypsy nuisance' included nine bilateral international agreements – with Austria–Hungary, Belgium, Denmark, France, Italy, Luxembourg, the Netherlands, Russia and Switzerland – indicating that the preoccupations of individual German states had a Continent-wide resonance.[26] Indeed, this was the period when emigration and movement between national states was beginning to be tightened across the western world: boundaries and rights of belonging which might until recently have existed at the municipal or regional level dissolved as they were superseded by national-level borders and rights. Attempts to control the movement of Gypsies across borders came at the same time as, for example, Britain's Aliens Act of 1905. This, as well as trying to stem Jewish immigration, was used to hound visiting Kalderashi Gypsies out of the country.[27]

Nevertheless, we need to be wary of constructing a story of unremitting persecution and the unrelenting extension of bureaucratic control over Gypsies' lives in this period. We can find evidence of resistance from within bureaucracies, even in Germany, to more regulation, although not necessarily for pro-Gypsy reasons. There, in 1912 the police proposed to create a dedicated anti-Gypsy police force in order to enable a system of constant surveillance. This coincided with attempts by the Munich Gypsy station to expand its work across Germany, and yet other states – notably Prussia – resisted these innovations. In part this was due to the costs they would entail, but there were also disagreements over the definition of 'Gypsy'. A number of states expressed concern over Dillmann's sociological definition which, they feared, would mean that 'decent' itinerant traders could be included within their remit.[28] As was the case with so many things in this period, the chaos brought by the war and its aftermath meant that any plans for further regulation were shelved.

It is no easy task to chart the impact of the First World War on Europe's Gypsy populations, but we would expect that given how closely entwined their lives were with majority society, we would see them both on the war and home fronts. Indeed, it is clear that they fought alongside the wider populations on both sides, particularly although by no means exclusively, as part of the Austro-Hungarian armies which had a long tradition of recruiting Gypsies, and where they served in relatively large numbers.[29] Things were rather different for Gordon Boswell, an English Gypsy, who joined the Veterinary Corps in February 1915 and felt isolated by his experiences:

> I never met any Gypsy boys, nobody belonging to me, I felt a lonely man . . . There was no other Gypsy boy in that [punishment] camp. Nobody to talk to . . . We wasn't men – we was numbers. And it used to dawn on me how one British subject can treat another . . . That is what killed my faith in the army . . . I had come from a free life. And then come under this military discipline. And they treated you not as a child and not as a man. You were a number.

Evidence is patchy, yet inter-war and later descriptions of Gypsies' lives contain enough passing references to men injured, shell-shocked or otherwise damaged by their experiences of combat to suggest that if not universal, war service had been a normal enough experience to pass into commonly accepted memory.[30]

We get something of an understanding of the impact of fighting and war losses on the home front for Gypsy communities through the fact that in 1916 the Hungarian government felt the need to develop a policy dealing with homeless Gypsy children.[31] Similarly, in Scotland by 1916 concerns had begun to be raised by local officials and mission workers over the living conditions of Traveller women and children, who were struggling to continue a nomadic lifestyle in the face of the absence of most men. In one case a group of Traveller women and children from Caithness was reduced to living in a section of dug-out peat bog, leading to the death of a newborn baby.[32] Right across Britain, lives were made more difficult through assiduous implementation of the Defence of the Realm Act of 1914:[33]

> [The] prohibition, in many areas, to camp out and light fires; the ration system; separation allowances to be drawn; absence of men folk to take their share of the tent-life with its duties (for even tents have their tasks, e.g., they have to be put up and to be carried); stricter enforcement (at long last) of education of the children; the constant need to be near a Post Office for the eagerly-expected news from India, Mesopotamia, Egypt, France; the advantage of a fixed place to welcome the boys to when they come home on leave.[34]

All these factors pushed for a more settled lifestyle, and we have evidence, for example, of an increase in the number of semi-permanent encampments in the New Forest, which rapidly became the target of the mission efforts of the YMCA.[35] Similarly, in Perthshire, a Central Committee on the Welfare of Tinkers began organizing regular 'Saturday meetings', Sunday services, small loans and 'friendly visitations' to the Traveller households of the city.[36] We cannot, however, assume that this work was necessarily conducted out of any sympathetic desire to improve their lives, with one volunteer admitting her motivation was 'to advance the

Kingdom of God amongst the tinkers . . . she was driven entirely against her will into the work. She hated it'.[37]

If most Gypsies in Europe found life harder simply because their already difficult life was worsened by the conflict and the conditions it imposed, in France this was compounded by active persecution on the part of the authorities. France's preoccupation with issues of identity and loyalty were further heightened by the crises of the war, and the state of siege declared on 2 August 1914 created sweeping internment powers targeting marginal and foreign populations. Previously such legislation had been applied only to immediately threatened border areas, but now modern total war saw the authorities make use of a much wider reach, while the 1912 law made it easier to identify *nomades*.[38] Alsatians living throughout France were interned alongside 'foreigners', other suspect individuals and Gypsies. In total 70 internee camps were created, of which at least eleven contained Gypsies, and one of which (in Crest) was specifically for Gypsies born after 1871 in Alsace-Lorraine. Admission records reveal how ideas of the foreignness and dubious loyalty of Gypsies combined with assumptions of criminality and general lawlessness to justify internment. Rationales for internment included statements such as 'as a general measure', 'no fixed abode, no profession', 'stealing', 'foreigner resident in the army's zone' and 'moving around at night without the army's authorization'. Nine months into the war, it was decided to revive the law of 9 August 1849, giving military authorities the power to 'expel from the army's zone all nomads to be found there or who try to gain entry'.[39]

The camp at Crest opened in July 1915 with 112 'Alsatian romanichels', a number that rose to 159 by December. Following the spirit of the law of 1912, the authorities' sights were on *nomades* in the broadest sense, and internees included Gypsies, Jenische, fairground people as well as vagabonds and itinerant artists.[40] Men who were conscripted into the French army from the camps could see their families released, but many found themselves locked up for the duration of the conflict and beyond. The experience of the Friemann family from Alsace-Lorraine is illustrative both of the difficulties faced by the interned and of their resistance. After some time in detention in Nevers, the Friemanns complained to the prefect of the *département* of the difficult conditions in which they were being forced to live. They were backed up by a Franco-Swiss medical team that on visiting the camps noted how inmates suffered from 'disabilities, wounds, sickness, lesions'. The complaints did not make the family popular: records note Nicolas Friemann had 'an intelligent indiscipline which provokes his comrades to continual revolt' and advised that he be 'very closely watched'. Their appeal failed, causing the family to attack a guard and attempt to escape. As rumours of the imminent end of the war spread, discontent followed and a 'revolt' was recorded on 27 July 1918, with inmates refusing to obey camp orders. Nicolas was blamed for this, which resulted in a recommendation to send him to a high-security camp. Finally, he and his family were liberated along with the remainder of the camp in July 1919, with the local newspaper *Le Crestois* expressing satisfaction at being rid of 'these undesirable guests'.[41] No doubt the feeling was mutual.

The landscape into which not only the Friemanns, but Europe, emerged after 1918 was very different to that of four years previously. Both the Austro-Hungarian and Ottoman empires were in tatters; the Russian Tsarist Empire had been overthrown by the Bolsheviks, who also had their sights on the ruins of imperial Germany; France, while not experiencing revolution, struggled with the challenge of absorbing three million disabled veterans on top of the deaths of 1.4 million men; while across the Continent economic dislocation and political uncertainty caused mass unemployment, inflation and strikes. Politically the Treaty of Versailles redrew Europe's boundaries to Germany's loss and France's gain, created a number of independent countries from the old empires and expanded British and French imperial holdings in the Middle East and Africa. As ever, for Gypsies, appearing at the margins of these events, these changes had significant implications.

In the nations formed from the old empires, new constitutions commonly guaranteed rights to all citizens irrespective of their ethnic background. This was frequently more the product of a concern to make viable national entities out of often disparate groups than it was a reflection of the desire to genuinely support the needs of different ethnicities. So, for example, the new Czechoslovakian constitution contained a Bill of Rights for National Minorities that guaranteed 'the same civil and political rights without distinction of race, language or religion', as well as full economic and employment rights and the right to the 'free use of any language'. There was also provision for education in a minority language where the minority made up more than 20 per cent of the population, which in reality meant only the country's German population. Despite these guarantees, as in Bulgaria in the late nineteenth century, the impact for the country's Roma population was rather different. Too small anywhere to make up a fifth of the population (overall the Roma population was around 31,000 in 1930 against a national population of nearly 14.5 million), they received no special attention from the state, and if they made any gains at all it was as Slovakian peasants rather than as Roma. Contemporary reports of the period suggested that it 'often happens that a Gypsy without resources commits a crime only to escape the pangs of hunger' through imprisonment.[42]

And yet there were some positive developments, such as the Gypsy school in the Slovakian town of Užhorod, which seemingly was a joint state and Gypsy initiative. Unlike British Gypsy schools, where the focus was on assimilation and low-level educational achievement, this school emphasized academic learning: 'Their knowledge of arithmetic and the principles of general science is truly amazing. They answer questions clearly and straightforwardly, and are obviously accustomed to school life.' The adults had shown their active support of the project from the outset, carrying out the building work themselves and supplying the materials, and also becoming involved in a theatre group and forming a football team. A visitor to the school thought that the success of the project came from the fact that the motto and underlying principle of the institution was, 'the Gypsy is also human' and that it was motivated by a 'principle of equality'.[43]

While there were countries in Europe which, if not promoting equality, did not make moves against their Gypsy populations in the inter-war period – in both Poland, and perhaps more surprisingly Mussolini's Italy Gypsies remained largely ignored by the state – for any more evidence of proactive measures we must turn to Soviet Russia. As with the wider population, the turmoil of the Civil War, economic collapse and social change prompted by the Bolshevik revolution resulted in rapid impoverishment and the deterioration their position. As a response to this chaos many Roma who had become more settled in towns took up itinerant lifestyles as a way of coping with the difficulties. By the mid-1920s, however, as the Communist Party was able to establish its hold on Russian society it was able to turn its attention to drawing Roma into its revolutionary project.[44]

Gypsies were seen as a separate national group within Russian society, and one that needed particular support in order to engage more fully in Communism. This was part of a far wider Leninist policy of *korenizatsiia*: avoiding antagonizing the still-potent force of separatist nationalism through the mass recruitment of non-Russians as cadres within the Communist Party and bestowing of material benefits. This policy informed all Party dealings with ethnic minority groups from 1923 until it was scaled back and then reversed by Stalin's 'Friendship of the People' approach from 1932–5 onwards.[45] Consequently the All-Russian Union of Gypsies was established in order to unite them, to draw them into socially useful labour through creating cooperatives and communes and encouraging itinerant Roma to settle. Under its auspices these years saw the flowering of state-sponsored Gypsy cultural activities: Communist-funded organizations such as Nikolai Kruchinin's Gypsy Choir, the Romen Gypsy Theatre and the Touring Gypsy Theatre rapidly assimilated the Gypsy musical elites of Moscow and Leningrad, thereby drawing them into local Party hierarchies. In addition the Union put on evening classes and Sunday Schools, ran clubs and libraries, created Romani-language newspapers, books, textbooks and propaganda material. These developments went hand in hand with attempts to draw Gypsies into formal education, through actively training Gypsy teachers, creating designated schools and classes and running educational programmes for adults.

By the later 1920s cultural approaches to assimilation were combined with measures promoting settlement. In order to attract those willing to farm, Gypsy families were given up to 1,000 roubles and given priority by land allocation committees. At the same time the authorities moved ahead with the creation of Gypsy *kolkhozes* (cooperative farms), which saw 500 Roma families in Ukraine being settled on nine farms in 1927. Soviet propaganda directed both at mainstream society and Gypsies themselves presented the process of settlement and collectivization as a voluntary, natural process, emerging from their enthusiastic embracing of Communism. The reality was rather more complex. Surviving evidence shows Roma accepting funding and disappearing, or beginning the settlement process, receiving credit, farming machinery and stock, but then selling up and moving to a different region. By 1938 there were only 52 co-operative Gypsy farms, housing around 3 per cent of the total Roma population.

The *kolkhozes* were part of a wider policy of drawing Gypsies into collectivization: the 4 April 1936 decree on 'Measures for employment of itinerant [Gypsies] and improvement of the economic and cultural and living standards of working Gypsies' set out a plan for their inclusion in state farms and industrial enterprises. The largest of these was in Leningrad and employed around 200 people in metalworking, but most were little more than family workshops that were established as part of local settlement programmes. Stalingrad's Flame of the Revolution Gypsy collective enterprise attracted 464 roubles in free assistance and loans, suggesting that it could be profitable to cooperate with the state. However, as with the collective farms, records show that the numbers of Gypsies drawn into such schemes were small, both absolutely and as a proportion of their total population.

While early Soviet policies towards Gypsies may have had only a limited impact, it is worth reflecting on exactly how revolutionary state attitudes were when compared to either the historical record towards Gypsies, or the actions of their contemporaries in other parts of Europe. The Communist commitment to improving the position of minorities within the Soviet Union, while often grounded in assimilationist ideas and crude propaganda, was based on a presumption that marginalization was caused by material factors rather than innate racial or 'group' characteristics. For the first time in their history Gypsies throughout the Soviet Union benefited from their long-standing marginal position in society: they were seen as victims of Tsarism, deserving of proactive Communist attention, a measure of understanding and extra resources. In the poisonous atmosphere of the 1930s purges this meant they were free of the taint of privilege that caused the murder or imprisonment of so many. While there are records of 52 individual Gypsies being executed in the anti-Soviet campaign of 1937–8, the new Roma elite largely escaped the mass purges, unlike other peoples in the USSR, who saw almost an entire class of intelligentsia and party activists wiped out.

The Soviet's dual emphasis on material disadvantage and the possibility of progress stood in stark contrast to the developing climate across other parts of mainland Europe, where growing intolerance was increasingly expressed in ever-tightening state control. France moved forward with photographing, recording details and distributing anthropometric notebooks to any families who had so far evaded registration. Local authorities not prioritizing this were directed by a circular in 1920 to institute a 'nomad register' to improve surveillance. This drive had a number of different consequences: some families chose to settle down, others applied for the more liberal, less demanding *forains* or *marchands ambulants* permits instead.[46] Miguel Sausa, who applied for the latter in 1922, explained how with the 'anthropometric notebooks I wasted a lot of time getting it signed in each locality; I only stay sometimes five or six hours in these localities and this loss of time is very onerous for my business'.[47] Czechoslovakia, prompted by a high-profile and entirely unfounded prosecution of Roma for cannibalism, instigated a similar 'nomad pass' in 1927. All Roma over fourteen years of age had to carry an identity card which included copies of their fingerprints; families needed a licence to travel and required the explicit permission of the mayor to remain in a settlement, and even then leave was rarely granted for longer than a week. The legislation further prohibited Gypsies from entering certain specific communities and regions, particularly spa and holiday resorts. Those who did not register were subject to arrest, and over the next thirteen years nearly 40,000 identity cards were issued.[48]

Right across Europe we see further moves to build on pre-First World War attempts at international cooperation controlling the cross-border movement of Gypsies. While the dominance of Germany and Austria in this process was crucial, it is worth reflecting on how this was part of a phenomenon that reached far beyond either Gypsies or the increasingly racial preoccupations of these nations. This was an era in which the League of Nations and other international organizations not based on empires started to emerge on the world stage. The foundation of the International Criminal Police Commission (later Interpol) was part of this trend. A strong theme of its work in this period, pushed very much by the Munich Gypsy police, was the control of Gypsies between countries.[49] In this it was building on the legacy of the bilateral agreements of the pre-war era, but the creation of a formal international structure meant that, following pressure from Munich and Austria, it was able to establish an International Gypsy Central Bureau based in Vienna. This collected information on those who passed between states, as part of a wider plan to compile a 'genealogical tree' of 'international Gypsies' which would act as 'an excellent weapon in the fight against Gypsies'.[50] By 1936 the Central Bureau had sent each country an outline identification form to be filled in by immigration officials upon the entry or exit of a Gypsy. As well as basic biographical information it asked for the names, nicknames and aliases of individual family members and companions, along with details of all crimes committed. Revealing of its preoccupations, it asked for information regarding the 'gait' and 'carriage' of the person, the 'shape of face . . . eyebrows . . . forehead . . . chin . . . teeth'.[51]

The central role of Austria and Germany – particularly Bavaria – in pushing the work of the ICPC was indicative of the growing preoccupation in this part of Europe with the 'Gypsy problem'. The turmoil of Germany in the aftermath of the First World War is well known and not to be underestimated: Germany went from being an expanding, dominant world force, supported by a rapidly industrializing economy, sophisticated education system and cultural innovation, to the brink of collapse in a few short years. Surrender and the Treaty of Versailles were followed by waves of unrest, revolutionary movements and coup attempts from both the left and the right. These reactions were intensified by an economic crisis of hyperinflation, currency collapse, crushing unemployment and endemic food shortages. Unemployment became one of the central features of the inter-war years, reaching an official total of six million by the time the Nazis gained power in 1933.[52]

As early as August 1918 the myth of the 'stab in the back', which asserted that domestic enemies – primarily Jews and 'Bolsheviks' – had caused Germany's defeat, had gained popular currency. While Gypsies were largely excluded from this particular form of xenophobic hostility – although there were claims that they had profiteered as currency dealers and horse traders – the turbulence of the period ensured that in common with other minorities within Germany, these years saw the intensification of publically articulated suspicion against them. A not untypical newspaper article, in language reminiscent of Tetzner's 'locusts', described Gypsies as descending like a 'plague' on villages, going from door to door asking for money. It closed with advice to its reader to 'give them nothing and show no sympathy', as that way they would leave the area faster.[53] The 1920s also saw circulars being issued within states alerting civil servants and the police of current 'Gypsy tricks' by horse traders and the 'charlatanism of Gypsy women'.[54]

Across Germany, matters were to move very rapidly from circulars of this kind to more explicit physical restrictions on both movement and settlement. However, as the Weimar Republic continued to be federally organized, crucial pieces of legislation affecting Gypsies and *Landfahrer* (Travellers) were enacted at state rather than national level. This led to important regional differences, and makes it hard to talk of national policy in this period. As early as 1922 Baden introduced something similar to France's pre-war anthropometric identity cards.[55] In many states camping became permitted only in areas approved by the police, where it was generally limited to 24 hours, with authorities continuing the pre-war Prussian tactic of heavily restricting the all-crucial *Wandergewerbeschein* (pedlar travel licence). In Hesse officials were instructed not to issue them to any 'foreign Gypsies', and were reminded that 'usually there will be a reason to deny domestic Gypsies the licence'. Such reasons might include 'dubious personality', being unable to provide a permanent address, proof of the means to support children or evidence of the education of children.[56]

Bavaria, which continued to lead the way in these matters, in 1926 passed the Law for the Combating of Gypsies, Travellers and the Workshy. Fundamentally this aimed to make nomadism impossible: it forbade movement without police permission; children could only travel with their parents if 'adequate schooling' could be proved to be taking place; people were forbidden to travel or camp in 'bands', which was taken to be in any group beyond that of immediate family members; Gypsies might only camp in specially designated sites; while those over the age of sixteen who could not prove 'regular employment' could be sent to the workhouse on the grounds of 'public security'. This combination of controlling movement and concentrating Gypsies in designated sites laid the foundations for early Nazi legislation. Bavaria was aided in its work by the ongoing existence of its police Gypsy department, which by this stage held the biographical information, fingerprints and photographs of 26,000 individuals.[57]

Yet even here, with this obsessive cataloguing and constructing of family trees, the Bavarian police and legislators were not able to define in any satisfactory way who constituted a 'Gypsy'. As much as in the nineteenth century, overlaying racial considerations were those of behaviour. Consequently the 'workshy' and those 'living like a Gypsy'– increasingly labelled *Landfahrer* – were included in the new measures. The only clear guidance over how the distinction between these different labels might be made was through assessing their conduct: 'The decisive factor was way of life. Everyone with a fixed abode was exempted . . . it was assumed that Gypsies could never meet these criteria.'[58] In fact, a significant number of travelling showpeople and pedlars claiming no Gypsy ancestry but with no fixed address were included within its powers, while the increasing number of Gypsies who had settled owing to the difficulties of gaining the *Wandergewerbeschein* were technically excluded.[59]

In 1927 Prussia made the decision to fingerprint and photograph all adult Gypsies and those travelling *nach Zigeunerart* ('in a Gypsy manner'). All those recorded were then to be issued with identity papers, which they needed to carry with them at all times, and in addition one copy was retained by the state and a second sent to Munich.[60] And indeed, from 1929 Munich was to become central to the system, as it began to coordinate the control of Gypsies at the national level, reducing from this point onwards the differences between states across Germany. These years provide evidence that while the state's reach was increasing, it was by no means insurmountable. Records show that family registration documents might still be falsified, or obtained in Alsace, which had been returned to France in 1918 but still saw many German Gypsy families travelling through its territories.[61] And still Gypsies might find a measure of protection from the law: in 1930, when 500 Frankfurt residents petitioned the city authorities over the 'Gypsy Plague' living in their midst, the magistrate replied that there was no legislation which allowed him to remove them. All the city's existing measures were based on the assumption that they were nomadic and under the Weimar constitution freedom of residence for all citizens was enshrined in law.[62]

What was the effect of these increasing pressures on the every-day lives of German Gypsies? The fact that freedom of residence remained a right in the republic meant that where circumstances permitted Gypsies bought or rented plots of land or houses and carried out their trades from these bases. If private plots offered some measure of independence from state interference, in Bavaria the designated sites formed under the 1926 legislation rapidly became places of rigid supervision and social marginalization. High rents, frequent police raids and a virtual absence of sanitary facilities ensured that many Gypsies, if they could, moved out of the area rather than being subject to the controls they faced.[63]

Over a few short years the local authority sites of the 1920s acquired permanent guards and fences, residents moved from being able to choose their employment to being forced into labour units, and gradually their ability to move outside the camps and to buy food and other items was restricted. By the late 1930s the sites had become internment camps acting as a pool of forced labour, and were the stepping stone to the deportation of Gypsies to the Polish ghettos and concentration camps. It is helpful here to separate out the two distinct but complementary processes at work: the ideological justification for the policies, and the bureaucratic measures that gave the ideology its material expression. Together these ensured that Gypsies were sufficiently physically and socially marginalized so that when the order came in December 1942 to intern all Gypsies in a specially created 'family camp' at Auschwitz–Birkenau, by the end of February 1943 the vast majority had been deported without resistance or objections from the wider community.

The Nazi era saw Gypsies positioned between deterministic ideas of antisocial behaviour and racist doctrine: this period is characterized by intense debates over whether 'Gypsies were predominantly antisocials who had to be sterilized, or member of a separate race who ultimately had to be exterminated'.[64] Even after over 30 years of data collection the Munich police bureau exhibited a degree of confusion over this issue. Arguably, however, this is unsurprising, as ever since the sixteenth century Gypsies had been treated as suspect, sometimes because they were 'foreign', sometimes because they were vagrants, and sometimes because they were both. While dressed up in the language of pseudo-science, in which reactionary attitudes were lent the cloak of modernism, the

Nazis did not fundamentally change the ground on which the arguments were made. If the Jewish experience in the Third Reich can
be argued as exceptional for their being the only group targeted
solely on the grounds of race, then the Gypsy experience might
similarly be positioned as exceptional on the grounds that they
were persecuted on both racial *and* asocial grounds.[65]

Essentially Nazi racial ideology towards Gypsies was always
bound up within its own internal contradictions. Nazism was clear
in seeing Gypsies as a separate racial group, and it devoted effort
and resources towards establishing a scientific rationale for this
belief. And yet, by its own admission, the acknowledged Indian
heritage of the Gypsies meant that they too were 'Aryan', which
theoretically meant that they could not be discriminated against
on racial grounds. Consequently the designation of Gypsies as a
group as *Asoziale* (antisocial) was an ideological sleight of hand:
while apparently condemning Gypsies for their way of life –
assumed to be both nomadic and criminal – in fact the designation
of an entire people as antisocial on the grounds of assumed biological characteristics made it clear that this was underpinned by racial
thinking. Fundamentally doctrines of race meant that there was no
ameliorative hope for these asocials: at this point the way was paved
to sterilization and murder.

We should, however, be wary of granting the Nazi regime the
dignity of a fully thought-out and coherent programme of action.
The political style of Hitler and other Nazi leaders was to issue general guidelines, based on broad ideological or strategic precepts,
and to expect subordinates to find the ways to realize them. This
meant that participants in Nazi crimes, both before and during the
war, acted as 'creative conformists', navigating the different policies
of persecution and destruction as the evolving conditions of the
war allowed, in order to implement what they believed to be their
superiors' wishes.[66] Consequently just as we should not be surprised
that there were often contradictions between actions at the local
level in different places, we should know that there were many
paths to the death camps.

Directly after the Nazis came to power, in March 1933 the
Agreement by the States to fight the Gypsy Plague was passed which
harmonized anti-Gypsy legislation across Germany, bringing all
states in line with Bavarian regulations. Two months later laws were

passed authorizing sterilization on eugenic grounds, which were further reinforced with the outlawing of the propagation of *Lebensuntwertes Leben* ('lives not worthy of life'). Between them these framed the twin approach taken by the Nazi towards Gypsies over the next decade: as laws governing their 'antisocial' habits tightened, so too did the racial justification for their oppression.

Central to the Nazi regime's racial project against Gypsies was their inclusion in the supplementary decree to the Nuremburg Law for the Protection of German Blood and German Honour issued in November 1935. This made it clear that those of 'racially alien blood' included 'members of other races whose blood is not related to German blood, as, for example, Gypsies and Negroes'. In order to be able to close the gap between existing racial legislation and the knowledge the regime held about its population, the Race Hygiene and Population Biology Research Centre was founded in 1936, under Dr Robert Ritter and with Himmler's direct support. Its aim was 'to reveal with exact methods the root cause of social developments in the biological', in order to begin the eradication of the 'unintegrated and the unproductive'. Seen as being 'the first and most easily resolvable part of the problem, the Gypsy Question was taken up' by Ritter.[67]

The first step was to resolve who might constitute Gypsy or 'part-Gypsy' through deploying a combination of genealogical, 'biological' and anthropometric methods, 'as well as threats and coercion'. Building on the work of the Munich police it began meticulously categorizing people as 'pure' Gypsies, various grades of 'mixed' Gypsy and sometimes 'non-Gypsy nomads'.[68] In this way, by 1940 Ritter had determined that there were around 30,000 Gypsies in Germany, of whom 90 per cent were deemed to be *Zigeunermischling* (Gypsy of mixed blood). In Ritter's view, the Sinti and Roma were 'primitive Aryans', but the majority were no longer 'racially pure' as their ancestors had mixed with 'criminal and asocial elements'. Contemporary criminal biology insisted that behaviour and criminality were inherited traits and so mixed-race Gypsies were 'born criminals and Gypsies at the same time, their blood doubly tainted . . . [and] doubly inferior'.[69] Consequently it was mixed-race Gypsies who were the main target of race scientists' recommendations for forced labour camps and sterilization, with a view to annihilating them over a generation if not quicker:

Our investigations have allowed us to characterize the
Gypsies as being a people of entirely primitive ethnological
origins, whose mental backwardness makes them incapable of real social adaptation . . . The Gypsy Question can
only be solved when the main body of asocial and good-for-
nothing Gypsy individuals of mixed blood is collected
together in large labour camps and kept working there, and
when the further breeding of this population of mixed
blood is stopped once and for all.[70]

Ritter's Centre was not the only organization interested in this
question. Also based in Berlin, the Kaiser Wilhelm Institute for
Anthropology, Hereditary and Eugenics, established in 1928 was
another key breeding ground for race scientists focusing on links
between heredity and criminality. Most notable for our purposes
was the assistant of one of its directors, Josef Mengele, Auschwitz's
notorious camp physician. As part of his work he sent the eyes of
murdered Gypsies, the internal organs of murdered children and
the sera of those deliberately infected with typhoid back to the
Institute for analysis.[71]

Systematic pseudo-scientific research justifying racial exclusion
both fed into and took place against a backdrop of ever-more
extreme government intervention. In 1938 the 'Decree for the Fight
against the Gypsy Plague' declared that 'based on knowledge
gained from race biological research' it was clear that 'the solution
of the Gypsy Question should be based upon the nature of race'.
By this point it had been determined that, unlike Jewishness which
was defined as an individual having at least one Jewish grand-
parent, an individual only needed two great-grandparents to have
been part-Gypsy in order to be designated *Zigeunermischling*. And
yet, despite this emphasis on race, its definitions in fact revealed
how there was still no clarity over definition, as its terms covered
all 'sedentary and non-sedentary Gypsies and persons travelling as
Gypsies'. The decree ordered for the Munich Gypsy department to
move to Berlin, so it was better placed to complete its task of
registering the details of all Gypsies living in the Reich, and where
it was renamed the National Centre for the Fight against the
Gypsy Menace.[72] From this point everyone covered by the decree
was required to be registered both through the local police and

with the national centre, while the authorities were ordered 'to put all sedentary and non-sedentary Gypsies under constant surveillance'.[73]

If then the ideological underpinning of Nazi actions continued to confuse racial and behavioural stereotypes, and hence exhibit a surprisingly old-fashioned anti-Gypsyism, what had undoubtedly changed was the means of the state to carry out its intentions. Throughout history, states repeatedly expressed the desire for Gypsies to be removed from their borders or societies, but far more rarely did governments have the capacity to implement these intentions. Nazism combined both the desire and a determination to back up ideology with action. A number of historians of the Nazi period have emphasized the bureaucratic, almost mundane nature of the Holocaust, in which *Kristallnacht* was the exception rather than the rule. It was not mob chaos in the throes of violent emotion that killed the majority of those who died as a result of Nazi policies, but rather obedience and a highly focused bureaucratic system.[74] And indeed, when we look at the detail of police inter-actions with Gypsies in the first years of the Nazi regime what comes across most strongly is the ever tighter control by the state over their lives.

The years between 1933 and the passing of the decree of 1938 saw a proliferation of regulations governing the minutiae of Gypsies' lives, including banning public displays of dancing bears and monkeys, as well as the decision that Gypsies could not have visits from kinsmen after arrest, and women in particular should have no opportunity to make eye contact with kinsmen 'to avoid consultations' of a supernatural nature.[75] This period also saw the first Gypsies being sentenced to concentration camps, typically on the grounds of their 'criminality': as early as September 1933 a group were arrested for begging and sent to Buchenwald, Dachau and Sachsenhausen. One of the most high-profile actions against Gypsies in the first period of the Nazi regime came as a result of the Berlin Olympics of 1936. All nomadic Gypsies in the city were relocated by the police to a camp in the Marzahn suburb in order to remove them from public sight, where they remained after the close of the Games, acting as a pool of forced labour.[76]

And yet archival material from this period also sheds light on the multitude of bureaucratic difficulties the regime created for itself in the course of trying to enact its policies. The police in the small town of Gross-Umstadt in 1934 recorded the problems of Gypsies begging, complaining how, as they often arrived in town late at night, it was impossible to deport them. More vexing however was the fact that many of them were in possession of the *Wandergewerbescheine*, which stated that '*fällt nicht unter das Zigeunergesetz*' ('Gypsy Law does not apply') because they were defined as *Halbzigeuner* (half-Gypsy).[77] Three years later the police were becoming preoccupied by the issue of the high costs of deporting Gypsies and the lack of available public funds. Policemen were urged to check that any damages to Gypsy families' modes of transport were not caused deliberately, and were advised that 'if there is no other option it is better to pay five Reichsmark for fixing a broken wheel than to spend twenty Reichsmark organizing deportation by the police'.[78] This gives us a valuable glimpse into the bureaucratic challenges of implementing higher-level decrees and also, crucially, of everyday strategies of resistance that Gypsies deployed in the face of repression. The holders of the *Wandergewerbescheine* had obviously managed to comply with the regulations, despite apparently also appearing as Gypsies to the local police (and here we also get a sense of ongoing official confusion over who was or was not a Gypsy); late arrival in town in order to go begging was perhaps a strategy developed to try and maintain a livelihood; while deliberate breaking of caravan wheels to prevent deportation was a time-honoured tactic for slowing down evictions. Personal testimonies from this time also show how many Sinti and Roma responded to the worsening climate by trying to be as unobtrusive as possible:

> After 1933 we behaved as my father told us to: 'Don't attract attention, behave correctly, do not provoke anyone! You see how it is.' We heeded our parents. We kept a low profile . . . We were dressed no differently from others, but we were dark skinned. You could really sense the looks boring into our backs.[79]

After the decree of 1938 the option of being unobtrusive became far more difficult. One common local-authority response to the new regulations was to interpret 'constant surveillance' as requiring the creation of a specific Gypsy camp, if they had not already established one. So, in Gelsenkirchen, for example, Sinti and Roma from private caravan plots and rented lodgings were interred in a single Gypsy camp initially located in Crangerstrasse. Here, 42 families comprising 220 people were accommodated in 50 caravans and huts. The following year they were moved to a new camp:

> Reginenstrasse had to be closed to traffic and is barred with barbed wire barricades. The caravans are set in a row and consecutively numbered and in front of every window there is a list of the residents of the caravan divided into adults and children. Up to September 1st [1939] the camp was continually checked by SA brigades [during the day] and at night.[80]

Where camps were already in existence their regulations became more stringent, so those running the Berlin Marzahn camp, for example, decided to introduce 'severe camp regulations on the [harsher] model of a concentration camp'.

Further developments along these lines were slowed down owing to the changing situation brought about by the invasion of Poland. Initially it was planned to deport all 30,000 Austrian and German Gypsies to occupied territory as part of the wider resettlement of 160,000 Poles and Jews. In preparation for this removal all Gypsies were forbidden to move from their current residence, but organizational difficulties intervened. In the spring of 1940 only 2,500 were moved into Poland, mainly to pre-existing Jewish ghettos such as Łódź, as well as to forced labour and concentration camps. That the majority of Gypsies and Sinti were not deported meant the movement ban remained in force for several years, leading to all temporary, private and official sites used by Gypsies turning overnight into long-term stopping places. This inevitably resulted in highly unsatisfactory and rapidly declining conditions, where overcrowding, water shortages and inadequate sanitation were the norm.[81] Camp inmates were assigned work in forced labour brigades, carrying out often gruelling and dangerous work, sustained by inadequate and increasingly limited rations. These conditions then fed into a self-fulfilling prophecy: Gypsies were seen as dirty and criminal, and conditions in which they were forced to exist ensured diseases spread rapidly amongst the under-nourished population, confirming to the wider population the justice of treating them in this manner.

Preparations for and subsequent invasion of the Soviet Union in June 1941 gave some pause to the advance of anti-Gypsy regulations in Germany at least. In contrast, Austria, in the months following the *Anschluss*, moved rapidly against its Gypsy population, most of whom were concentrated in the Burgenland. This was the area that up until 1919 had been part of Hungary, and where Gypsies had been settled under the imperial assimilation schemes. As early as June 1939 the region's 8,000 Gypsies were taken into 'preventive custody', with some sent directly to Dachau and Buchenwald concentration camps, or the newly created Ravensbrück women's camp. Others were sent to the Mauthausen Gypsy camp, which opened in November 1940, and where conditions were described as being comparable to those in concentration camps.[82]

The combination Ritter's work, that of the central police department and the experiences in Austria and Poland fed into a decisive change in policy within Germany in December 1942. A decree issued by Himmler on 16 December ordered the internment of all Roma and Sinti in the newly created Gypsy Family Section (B-IIe) in Auschwitz–Birkenau. Deportations began at the end of February 1943 and were virtually completed by the end of the month. Not exterminated immediately on arrival, the inhabitants of the Gypsy camp who did not die through malnourishment, summary execution or medical experiments became forced labourers for the next seventeen months. During its existence the camp housed around 23,000 people and of these 20,078 died. Numbers were reduced from May 1944 and on 3 August 1944 the camp was cleared overnight. The remaining 2,897 men, women and children were gassed in order to make room for a new consignment of Hungarian Jews.

The extension of Nazi control and ideology across the Continent from 1938 was by no means total, as although German invasion meant some parts were under its direct control, other parts of Europe were ruled indirectly through collaborator or puppet governments, and the ever-shifting and increasingly troublesome Eastern Front created a huge and shifting zone of military and political flux. This meant that the politics of place and time were vital aspects of the lives and chances of survival of Roma, Sinti and other Gypsy groups across Europe during the war years. Across Europe as a whole there are 219,700 documented Roma and Sinti deaths, although the actual number is thought to be around 500,000.[83] These deaths were concentrated in Germany, Austria, Serbia, Romania and Hungary, and although their total populations were smaller, almost the entire Croatian, Latvian and Estonian Gypsy populations were exterminated.

As German control over Poland became consolidated, the Nazis began tackling the issue of the presence of Gypsies within its borders. Chełmno extermination camp became the base for death trucks using carbon monoxide to kill Gypsies who had been rounded up from a range of places – some were Germans who had been part of the original deportations from Germany, and included some who had survived the typhus epidemic in Łódź ghetto, while others were recently interred Polish Gypsies.[84] As the *Wehrmacht* advanced across the Ukraine and into Russia Gypsy populations were caught up in fighting and also became targets for mass executions: 176 Roma from three Romani showcase *kolkhozes* around Smolensk were shot or buried alive in a mass killing in 1942, with emerging evidence convincingly demonstrating that this was the typical reaction of ss units whenever they came across Roma communities as they advanced.[85]

On the Western Front, in France, the growth of concerted state control of nomads, use of the anthropometric identity cards and the increasing restrictions on foreign Gypsies would all seem to point towards providing a basis from which the racist policies of the Third Reich could take hold. Indeed the Germans profited from both the anthropometric identity cards and recent legislation: two and a half months before the French surrender the government banned movement by *nomades* for the duration of the war, requiring them to remain in an assigned area under police surveillance on the grounds of their supposed security risk.[86] In Limousin the initial response of the authorities when receiving the April decree was to increase policing at its borders to prevent any new groups of Gypsies entering its jurisdiction, so that it would not have to expend extra resources on them. As food shortages intensified and evacuees and refugees came into the region, thefts of wood, food and fuel increasingly came to be blamed on *nomades*. Though evidence shows all sectors of the population regularly engaged in such thefts, long-standing stereotypes of 'thieving Gypsies' were deployed in order to concentrate blame on people already deemed antisocial outsiders.[87]

So while the German ordinance of 4 October 1940, which described Gypsies as 'of an ethnic character which is particular to the romanichels', was racially defined, it also included those who 'pretended' to have an occupation and built on pre-existing French legislation. Those classified as such were sent to internment camps and forbidden from crossing between the occupied and unoccupied zones: overall 6,500 were interned, 4,650 of these in the occupied zone and 1,400 in Vichy France.[88] Originally internees were dispersed between a number of smaller camps, but over the course of 1941–2 these were rationalized so that Montreuil-Bellay, which was the largest in the occupied zone, held around 1,000 internees at any one time, while by March 1942 in the Vichy zone inmates were concentrated in Saliers in Bouches-du-Rhône.[89]

The fact that *nomades* conformed neither to generally accepted standards of behaviour nor ideals of 'work, family, fatherland' promoted by the Vichy regime's National Revolution meant that there was widespread public support for the internment of Gypsies. Significantly, within both the justification for internment camps and daily life in them, French state insistence on 'reform' through changing behaviour and encouraging sedentarization remained more important than racial categorizations. French bureaucrats saw the camps as an opportunity to teach *nomades* trades that would help them to settle and to provide schooling for the children.[90] In camps, theoretically at least, if they changed their work habits and acquired the ideals of family and society as pushed by the National Revolution, they could re-enter the French national community.[91] In fact, despite the plans of architects to turn Saliers into a 'concentration camp [with] the look and feel of a village and of allowing family life there', deplorable living conditions led to persistent escape attempts.[92] Indeed, all surviving accounts of the French camps indicate unforgiving living conditions: inmates burnt furniture to keep warm; while the population of Montreuil walked out to the camp on Sundays to throw bread to inmates for the entertainment of watching starving people throw themselves on the bread and fight for it.[93] A Swiss nurse, Friedel Bohny-Reiter, describes roasting summers and freezing winters with a ceaseless wind at the camp at Rivesaltes; overall, camps lacked food, hygiene, bedding and clothing, and residents suffered persistent infestations of vermin.[94]

While much of the story of the war in France centres around the creation of internment camps, it is important to stress how significant numbers of Gypsies were involved in the resistance. This included such prominent people as Jean Beaumarie, who worked with the *Maquis*, as did his brother who was caught and hanged. Armand Stenegry, later president of the Manouche Gypsy Association, and well known musician, became a guerrilla officer. With his unit, which included other Gypsies, he participated in partisan attacks carried out in coordination with the Normandy landings in 1944.[95] There is also evidence of more general involvement in the resistance, as some groups of Gypsies joined partisan groups living in forested and mountain areas. Exchanging live-in caravans for farm wagons and adopting local peasant dress they ran explosives, transported fugitives and British agents, as well as participating in raids, arson attacks and combat situations.[96]

Despite the apparent malleability of French attitudes towards Gypsies to Nazi ends, in fact the position was not so clear cut. As we have already seen, the law of 1912 applied to *nomades* rather than 'Gypsies', and so settled Gypsies did not require them while non-Gypsy nomads did. The French state's concentration on settlement and regular employment as the means by which Gypsies might be 'turned into Frenchmen' stymied an easy 'racial' separation of Gypsies and non-Gypsies. Although offering no protection to its Jewish population, in this case the French republican tradition of resistance to ethnic differentiation played a crucial part in ensuring that Himmler's December 1942 order that all Gypsies to be sent to Auschwitz–Birkenau was not enforced in France.[97] French Gypsies may have been interned for the duration of the war, where they faced privation and social isolation, but this was in contrast to the experiences of those living in the Nazi-controlled Nord *département*. Interned in far higher numbers than in Vichy France on 15 January 1944, 351 interned Belgian and French Gypsies made up Convoy z, which went straight to the Gypsy camp at Auschwitz–Birkenau.

We see some similarities in the position of Roma in Bulgaria, where they became entangled within wider notions of national identity and independence. Although Bulgaria entered the war on the side of the Axis powers in early 1940, and despite King Boris's personal ease with many fascist policies, what was most notable about Bulgaria's relationship with the Third Reich was the reluctance with which it engaged both with the war generally, and the racial policies of Nazism specifically.[98] Boris consistently resisted Nazi attempts to engage Bulgaria in the Eastern Front and Macedonia, and when from late 1941 the Germans began pressing for more restrictions on Bulgarian Jews, Bulgaria rejected the increasing stigmatization and deportation of its well-integrated Jewish population. Bulgaria's ability to protect the Jewish population was undoubtedly limited: those in Bulgarian-held Macedonia and Thrace were not shielded from the round of deportations that began in March 1943. However, deportations in Bulgaria itself were staunchly resisted: 40 deputies from the government party signed a petition and condemnation and resistance came from all strata of society, including the Orthodox Church, pro-fascist MPs, trade unions and the (illegal) Communist Party. Backed so strongly by the nation Boris stood firm against the Nazi demands, and the country's 50,000 Jews survived the war.[99]

It is in this context that we can place the treatment of Bulgaria's Roma population, and the implementation of the decrees directed against them. Ordinance 129 included Gypsies along with Jews in prohibiting marrying Bulgarians; while in May 1942 a decree ordered 'Gypsies to be directed to compulsory employment'; and another allocated them lower ration entitlements than the wider population. This period also saw some hardening of attitudes towards Gypsies, and the summer of 1942 brought an increase in attacks on them encouraged by the discriminatory decrees. The following year, in part because the compulsory labour order had been inconsistently applied, all Gypsies aged between seventeen and 50 'found idle' were mobilized for the harvest, and other public works, prompting raids across Sofia on 'restaurants, coffee-houses, sweetshops and taverns'. Although this was combined with orders from the Ministry of the Interior to restrict their movements, 'under the pretext that Gypsies were spreading infectious diseases, especially spotted typhus', this translated into neither rounding them up into internment camps, as in France, nor deportation to extermination camps.[100] Overall, most agree that these decrees were largely ineffective and that many Gypsies found ways to avoid labour mobilizations. Given that the decrees were policed by the Bulgarians themselves, and that the measures had only been passed to placate Germany, turning a blind eye to anti-Gypsy measures was one way for officials to undermine Nazi domination of daily life.[101] In their position of relative safety, the Roma of Bulgaria were like those of Albania, an Italian protectorate; Montenegro (divided between Italy and Albania); and Macedonia (divided between Albania and Bulgaria). As in Italy, the Roma living in Italian areas faced relatively few extra restrictions – although there is some evidence of local internment and imprisonment – until the German occupation in August 1943.[102]

Roma experiences in Serbia were rather different, as the territory became a zone of German military occupation under the collaborationist regime of Milan Nedić from April 1941. Nazi racial policies were swiftly implemented, although the standard definition of who constituted a Roma was changed slightly: Serbian Gypsies able to claim that their families had been sedentary since 1850 and integrated into mainstream life were free from the restrictions applied to those with three or more Romani grandparents. Those unable to prove their exemption, in common with Gypsies across German-occupied territories, lost professional positions, were subject to property confiscations, forced labour and curfews and were barred from most public places. They were also some of the first to be taken and executed as hostages at ratios of 10- or 100-to-1 for reprisal for casualties caused by partisan attacks on German forces. As slave labourers they were forced to construct concentration camps in both Serbia and Croatia, including the notorious Semlin camp, where later as inmates they starved, died of exposure or committed suicide. And yet, despite the restrictions they faced, owing to the high level of integration into the wider community – speaking and looking Serbian, and being primarily settled – it is estimated that only one-third of Serbia's Roma population were affected by the racial laws. Many 'fled, evaded, hid and were hidden' or joined the resistance, either separate Roma groups or Tito's partisans.[103]

Across the border in the Independent State of Croatia, led by the fascist *Ustaša* under Ante Pavelić (the 'butcher of the Balkans'), Roma faced one of the most savage regimes of the period. Pavelić's project of radical ethnic homogenization meant that the genocides committed against Serbs, Jews and Roma were very much inter-twined, and overall it is estimated that 10 per cent of Croatia's total population were killed as a result of racial policies.[104] As part of this Croatia constructed some of the strictest racial categorizations – here a Gypsy was anyone with two Romani grandparents – as well as some of the most ruthless concentration camps. Indeed, Gestapo reports to Berlin of its camps commented on their brutality, ex-pressing concern that the 'excessive viciousness lessened efficiency'. While the largest number killed were Serbs, the annihilation of the Croatian Gypsy population was almost total: up to 30,000 Roma from all over Yugoslavia were killed in Jasenovac extermination camp, and by October 1943 only 1 per cent (200–300 people) of Croatia's pre-war Roma and Sinti population remained. There are accounts of Roma who, against the odds, escaped Jasenovac under fire by swimming the river, and who subsequently joined the partisans for the rest of the war. However, overall, it is estimated that of the approximately 200,000 Roma killed across what became Yugoslavia the majority were from Croatia.[105]

Romania's fascist Iron Guard came up with a different solution to its 'Gypsy problem'. Dressed up as a preventative public health and anti-crime measure, it saw the deportation of the bulk of its Roma population, alongside its Jews, to Transnistria. In a six-month period in 1942 over 11,000 nomadic Roma were expelled and forced to make their way on foot and with carts to this region of south-western Ukraine across the river Dniester, where they were to live in 'colonies'. This was part of an explicit and coordinated racially motivated attempt to annihilate Romania's Roma population, which built on pre-existing eugenicist preoccupations:

> Nomadic and semi-nomadic Gypsies shall be interned into forced labour camps. There, their clothes shall be changed, their beards and hair cut, their bodies sterilised [. . .] Their living expenses shall be covered from their own labour. After one generation, we can get rid of them. In their place, we can put ethnic Romanians from Romania or from abroad, able to do ordered and creative work. The sedentary Gypsy shall be sterilised at home [. . .] In this way, the peri-pheries of our villages and towns shall no longer be disease-ridden sites, but an ethnic wall useful for our nation.

Overall, it is estimated that 26,000 Roma were deported to the region, with over half dying of starvation, exposure or in the typhus epidemic of the winter of 1942–3.[106]

The evidence from Hungary similarly confirms the importance not only of Nazi occupation or alliance, but of internal national preoccupations, in whether or not the Roma population were savagely persecuted. As a German ally, Hungary took an active role in the war, with regiments of Hungarian soldiers (including Roma) fighting alongside the Germans on the Eastern Front. Yet it was not until the 1944 coup by Ferenc Szálasi's fascist Arrow Cross that the way was opened for an active, nationally led racist terror campaign against Roma. The collective persecution they had experienced up until the coup – a mix of racially applied laws, mass arrests, forced labour brigades and continual police harassment – suddenly intensified. Although lasting only a few months – until April 1945 – the closeness of the new regime to the Reich's ideology and the sophisticated extent of the machinery of annihilation by this point in the war meant that most of the estimated 50,000 Hungarian Roma killed during the war died in these months. In October 1944 orders were given to intern all Gypsies in local camps and other places of confinement; from there they were sent to transit camps such as Komárom castle on the Slovakian border. Here they were held in underground bunkers, experienced torture, starvation, extreme cold and death camp selections. Some, mainly women and young children, were released, but the majority were sent on to concentration and death camps, primarily Ravensbrück and Auschwitz:

> We were nomadic at that time, from one village to the next. I was twelve . . . the fascist Nyilas [national socialists] came and took us, we were transported in trains . . . it took some two weeks before we reached Komáron. I can remember Komárom as if it were yesterday. Anyone who collapsed was immediately thrown into the Danube. They squashed us in . . . Those who couldn't move were put on top of the bodies of those who had died . . . There was one Romani woman, she was so beautiful . . . They abused her so much she could no longer stand. Then they tied a rope between two trees and took a tin of petrol and hanged her by her hair on the

rope and put the tin under her. It was petrol or oil or something. They burnt her alive. She couldn't even scream.[107]

Across Europe, then, Gypsies were harassed and persecuted, their
lives increasingly restricted. They were often interned, imprisoned
or forced into slave labour brigades. And yet this was not the worst.
Despite the vast and painful literature devoted to the subject it
remains impossible to do justice to the experiences of those who
faced deportation and internment in death camps or those whose
lives ended in the gas chambers. As survivor Bernhard Steinbach
from Worms put it, 'What I describe is only scraping the surface.'[108]
Part of that scraping the surface involves briefly looking at first-
hand accounts of two Auschwitz survivors. In doing this we are able
to construct some understanding of how personal histories and
circumstances produced different routes to the camps, allowing us
a small insight into what they experienced and witnessed.[109]

Walter Winter was a German Sinto whose family had travelled
widely around northern Germany but by the inter-war period had
made its base in Cloppenburg in Lower Saxony.[110] His memories of
these years demonstrate the extent to which the state and wider
socio-economic changes had shaped his family's decisions: the requirement to have a permanent address in order to qualify for a
Wandergewerbescheine meant they bought some land. Here they
settled each winter, while using it also to raise fowl which they
bartered for provisions. He and his siblings attended school either
in their home village or when they were travelling, and so all of
them were literate. Although his memories of the years up to 1933
show they encountered prejudice, 'generally, the people in the
country were not so unfriendly', and they were able to make a comfortable living. After 1933 they started to run a travelling shooting
gallery and so 'became' showpeople, able to carry a legitimate *Wandergewerbescheine* and continue moving around. In fact, during
these years they did well economically, although they faced growing
official pressure, including in 1936 being barred from the meetings
of the Association of Fairground Workers. On the outbreak of
war their preoccupation was with being called up rather than being
singled out. Barred from promotion, Walter and his brothers
nevertheless served in the *Wehrmacht* until the autumn of 1942
when all Sinti and Roma were deemed 'unsuitable material' and

discharged. For the next six months, aided by the fact that his family owned two vehicles, his forced labour involved driving for the local council. But this did not prevent him and his siblings (although not his parents) from being deported to Auschwitz in March 1943. They arrived at the camp as the work details were returning from their day's labour:

> I thought, 'You aren't seeing right'. They were carrying two corpses covered in blood. The corpses were slung from poles, tied by the hands and feet, like deer. Two men carried each corpse, streaming with blood. Our column became as quiet as a mouse despite there being children among us. You could have heard a pin drop . . . we were unable to utter a word. We thought, 'Is this going to happen to us? Oh God, oh God, oh God!'

His testimony, as with that of all survivors, shows the importance of a combination of luck, contacts and determination in contributing to his survival. Being literate and an ex-serviceman led him to being appointed roll call clerk and his brother block senior. Together they were able to run their block with as much humanity as conditions allowed. A friendship with someone working in the kitchens ensured access to vital extra food, and while he, his brother and sister all at various times stood up to and were punished by camp guards, this did not result in summary execution. Most crucial to his survival was the fact that on the eve of the closure of the camp, all those who had served in the *Wehrmacht* and their families were moved to Ravensbrück and so escaped the gas chambers. During the final period of the war he was conscripted back into the army, where he remained until able to surrender to the Russians.

Roman Mirga, in contrast, was a Polish *bareforytka Roma* ('big-town Gypsy') who spent the years up to 1942 playing accordion in his family's band in the prestigious nightclubs of Warsaw.[111] There they played for a clientele of Polish elite and occupying German officers, including Josef Mengele. Alerted by a cousin who had been interned in the Łódź ghetto, the family rejoined their *kumpania* (extended kin group with whom they would normally have travelled) with the aim of persuading them to move to Hungary, where conditions at that point were better. Over the late spring of 1943 the *kumpania*, which had only then been finally convinced to move after the overnight deportation of a neighbouring Kalderashi group, made the journey south, attempting to evade the ss as they did so. While hiding in the forests Roman witnessed the execution of some Lovari Gypsies. After the men were forced to dig their own mass grave before being shot, the women and children were then made to get out of the trucks:

> They were hit by rifle butts or booted down, and then shoved ahead until they, too, slid into the ditch. Those who, in their rage, spat at the Nazis and their Ukrainian helpers, had their babies wrested from them and, in front of their mothers' eyes, the babies heads were smashed against the tree trunks . . . As the lamentation and cries for mercy got louder, the ss officer impatiently gestured to the machine-gunner who lowered his fire directly into the ditch. The screaming ceased almost immediately.[112]

Nearly half of their *kumpania* were caught and shot on the way or when crossing the Hungarian border. The survivors were able to live relatively easily until March 1944 when an invading German convoy caught them on the road and sent them straight to Auschwitz. In a vivid passage, Roman remembered the shaving of his wife's head and body hair. This act features in many survivor testimonies as epitomizing the 'worst possible humiliation' and sense of shame felt by people whose cultural values centred on the strong separation of male and female spheres, and of numerous taboos around nakedness, cleanliness and the dignity of elders.[113]

On arrival Roman's family were recognized by Josef Mengele, who assigned his father to play in the Gypsy orchestra, while the women were detailed to the kitchens. Roman, as he could speak Polish, German and Romani, worked under Mengele himself as a clerk and translator. In this capacity he witnessed the experiments carried out on Gypsy inmates: 'a world of spot fever and scarlet fever, typhoid and dysentery, tuberculosis and noma, and smallpox or varieties of scurvy which inevitably led to gangrene and death', as well as Mengele's notorious experiments on twins.[114] Roman also witnessed the final clearance of the camp:

There was furious resistance. I heard sounds of terror, the screams of sobbing children trying to reach their fathers for protection, the women's shrieks of 'Mörder!', but also the cries of men, even the old ones, fighting back. From the dark camp came the vicious howling of dogs, gunshots and bursts of machine gun fire, as those who threw themselves on the Nazis with knives, razors, sticks or their own bare hands, willingly selling their lives dear . . . The operation lasted for several hours, because the Germans were short of transport . . . I saw the ss men and their dogs turning on their assistants, the Gypsy *kapos* who had been helping them to round up their own people . . . finally only Barrack No. 1 was left. Just one squad of young workers who were still needed to speed up the process of dispatching to their death the incoming mass of Jews . . . Mengele pointed with his riding crop at the empty barracks, 'Schade um die Romatik des Zigeunerlage' ['What a pity we have lost the romance of the Gypsy camp'].

Roman was able to escape with the one surviving member of his *kumpania*, and was hidden by a local Polish woman until the Russian arrival in January 1945. That only two from the original *kumpania* of 84 survived gives some sense of the devastating impact of the Nazi period not just on individuals but on the wider kin and social networks which were absolutely central to Gypsy society and identity. Like all concentration-camp survivors, ex-prisoners were marked for life by the physical and emotional scars of their experiences. Added to this the Nazi policy of sterilization ensured that the ramifications of its racial doctrine extended far beyond the liberation of the camps, as the oral testimony of camp survivor Anna W makes clear:

I was sterilized myself, but in Ravensbrück.
Q: In Ravensbrück. How old were you back then?
Sixteen.
Q: And did you know what . . .
Not quite sixteen.
Q: Did you know what kind of . . .
No, I did not know that. They said they were just examining,

but the pain afterwards, so then you realized.

Q: That was of course very, very . . .

There were several young girls, of, how old were they, twelve years, twelve, fifteen-, sixteen-year-olds.

Q: And Friedel [her husband], too?

No.

Q: No, not him. Because I know that they also did this to the boys . . .

Yes, I even know some where they did it.

Q: Yes, I think Ranko B., no?

Yes.

Q: He spoke about it. This is something very terrible, for a woman, no?

Very much, yes. For now I have to suffer from it. Since I could have had a family, could have, I could have had grandchildren who would be twenty years by now, my grandchildren . . .[115]

Consequently it was not only through the devastation of entire communities that the legacy of the war and Nazi policies were felt: forced sterilization ensured that racist ideology was to be carried in the bodies of Roma and Sinti women, ensuring that their loss was felt in the absence of future generations. And it is no accident that Anna W's testimony above, as well as the writings of both Walter and Roman, appeared decades after the end of the war. Now often regarded as the 'forgotten Holocaust', as we shall see, one of the central experiences of Gypsies and Roma trying to go forward into the post-war world was repeated denial and silence over their experiences.[116] In part this came from individuals and Gypsy communities themselves, as a combination of shame, deep trauma and a desire to 'get on with life' served to bury their memories of the war years. And yet this was overlaid by the active suppression of the facts over the fate of thousands of Roma and Sinti on the part of governments and majority societies which went hand in hand with ongoing harassment and persecution.

IN REFLECTING ON THE DEEP SIGNIFICANCE of the Roma Holocaust to both Roma and Gypsy communities and to wider European history, we have seen the importance of paying attention to time and place. Roman's account, taken alongside Walter's, demonstrates something of the complexity of experiences of Gypsies under Nazism. Whether settled in a town, or still travelling, serving in the German army, or as a civilian carrying out a 'typical' Gypsy occupation, the racial policies and regulations governing everyday life affected Gypsies, but often in different timescales and in different ways. Some Gypsies lived in camps from the early 1930s, others were able to sustain something like a 'normal life' until the decree of 1938, or sometimes until as late as 1942 or even 1944. The wartime experiences of a Gypsy in France was likely to be different to that of one in Croatia, Germany or Romania: while all experienced degrees of marginalization and repressive legislation, those in France experienced internment, but were unlikely to have been deported to Auschwitz; Romanian Roma experienced racially motivated policies which were translated into the trauma of harsh deportation policies; while Croatian and German Gypsies were most likely to feel the full force of Nazi genocidal intentions. All this shows, that despite near universal negative stereotypes of Gypsies, the actions of different regimes at different times were crucial to the treatment and survival of their Gypsy populations. And as we move on to the second half of the twentieth century it is the actions and ideologies of states which were to remain so telling.

SIX

A New Dawn?

IT IS HARD TO OVEREMPHASIZE the extent to which Europe
lay in ruins in 1945: it was not only physically devastated, but
socially, politically and culturally battered. The protracted fighting
in 1944 and 1945 produced millions of refugees fleeing mass bomb-
ings, the terror of the advancing Soviet forces, the shifting Western
Front, as well as the increasingly savage actions of the Nazi regime
as it tried to maintain a grip on its domestic population. While
impossible to count, estimates put the number of refugees in 1945
at around 30 million.[1] Ruined harvests and broken supply lines
meant they faced starvation on top of homelessness and violence.
The closing months of the war saw the biggest mass migration in
German history, involving 20 million people – Jews, forced labourers
and ethnic Germans from the east, as well as those fleeing bombing
and military advancements – moving in all directions, as they tried
to return home, escape further persecution, or formed part of one
of the mass population transfers.[2] As much as others, Gypsies formed
part of this churning population, as refugees, camp survivors and
as part of population transfers.

Politically, of course, alongside material problems and infra-
structure collapse, the complete disintegration of both the Nazi
state and its ideological basis affected not only Germany, but the
fascist regimes of Hungary, Croatia and Italy. This was further
compounded by the major redrawing of international boundaries –
notably the massive German loss of territory east of the Oder-
Neisse line and the imposition of direct rule by the Americans,
French, British and Soviets. And on top of this within a very
short time Communism was able to assert itself as the dominant
ideological force of eastern and south-eastern Europe. Having

learnt something from the aftermath of the First World War, the American-funded Allies rejected a humiliating package of reparations in favour of a more generous notion of reconstruction. This was given material expression in the Marshall Plan of 1947, whose aid and trade packages aimed to ensure that the German territories under western control were increasingly dissociated from the Soviet zone, and were firmly incorporated in the wider network of economic and political organizations emerging to counter Russian influence in the east.

Hindsight allows us to see how the Cold War, in exporting active conflict beyond Europe's borders, gave four decades of peace to the Continent. For those living through these years, however, this was by no means given: one of the reasons that Hungarian refugees to Britain in 1956–7 were so desperate to emigrate immediately to the US, for example, was because they feared immediate nuclear reprisals from the Soviet Union. And yet despite such fears, these years undoubtedly gave Europe the breathing space it needed to engage in reconstruction. The post-war period saw not only new visions of the built environment realized, but the emergence of new socio-economic conditions and political entities aimed at protecting populations and removing the future possibility of total war.

Reconstruction was therefore one front on which the Cold War was fought, yet what is perhaps most remarkable is not the differences between these two political systems, but rather their similarities. Both socialist and capitalist nations sought to create welfare systems, provide employment and a new vision of the world for their citizens. At their core both were wedded to modernist ideas of progress, built around industrialization, technology, urbanization, control of physical space and expanded state support, including free education and a package of welfare benefits. Bureaucrats and regulations, instructed either by Party committees or parliamentary bodies, took centre stage in the creation and enactment of policy. What is noticeable for Roma and Gypsy populations is that, despite apparent ideological differences, intentions towards them on both sides of the Iron Curtain were remarkably similar. After an initial post-war divergence in attitudes, all states moved very rapidly towards policies pushing settlement and assimilation, differing only in their methods and the extent to which they realized their intentions. By the end of the century what was obvious was how partial their successes in this area actually were.

We must not mistake the stability provided by the Cold War for stasis. It was with remarkable rapidity that Europe moved into a period of something like full employment, mass education and unprecedented affluence, although this was more pronounced in western than eastern Europe. In the West the space created by being able to focus on matters beyond immediate material concerns allowed the emergence of new forms of political expression in which issues of identity and self-determination came to the fore. Socialist states could not remain insulated from these changes, and although regimes attempted to adapt, economic crises and nascent protest movements ensured, by the end of the 1980s, the collapse of state socialism. The closing years of the century saw ex-communist states struggling with the impact of uncontrolled capitalism as well as the revitalization of the paused politics of nationalism. In this new climate, alongside new political freedoms and possibilities for self-organization, Roma communities felt the brunt of economic uncertainty, resurgent racism and the collapse of state support. On the accession of many of the eastern European states to the European Union in 2004 it was by no means clear that their social or economic position was any better than it had been 100 years previously.

And yet, despite all the disjuncture and change, there were strong continuities too. For Gypsies, foremost in these continuities was their marginalization and absence from the official record. Within Germany this was translated into a lack of recognition for the persecution they had experienced during the Nazi period. Given that the Nazis themselves had built on pre-existing attitudes towards, and legislation targeted at, Gypsies from the Weimar and indeed imperial periods, this is hardly surprising. Although such silence, particularly around the complicity of the wider population, extended to include the treatment of the Jews at the hands of the mass of the German population, at an institutional level there was a big difference. The Allies had made it clear that German attitudes towards its remaining Jewish population would be taken as a measurement of German desire to be included in the democratic world. Consequently the Federal Republic developed a proactive attitude towards both individual Jews and Israel. Laws of restitution from the early 1950s ensured that Germany paid financial compensation, firstly to Israel, and later to Holocaust survivors, so from the mid-1950s returning German Jews received 6,000DM.[3] In contrast, the Nuremberg trials, as well as subsequent military tribunals prosecuting SS personnel and other individuals for their actions in the camps, barely mentioned Roma and Sinti in their considerations: SS officer Richard Bugdalle was sentenced to life imprisonment in 1960 for the personal murder of a number of inmates of Sachsenhausen camp. Along with the evidence used in the prosecutions over Chelmno extermination camp, this was a rare case of evidence of a Sinti or Roma death being explicitly used to build the case for the prosecution. In the major Auschwitz trial, held in Frankfurt am Main in 1963–4 the persecution of Roma and Sinti as well as the liquidation of the Gypsy camp in August 1944 had no influence on the eventual verdicts.[4]

Denied recognition and initially disqualified from compensation as racial victims, the treatment of Roma and Sinti survivors showed how the Federal Republic was content to carry forward Nazi stereotypes of asociality. The decree of 1950 of the Baden-Württemberg interior minister was typical: 'Gypsies and Gypsies of mixed race . . . [have] not been persecuted and imprisoned for racist reasons, but rather *because of their asocial and criminal attitude* [emphasis added].' Similarly the Federal High Court in 1956 found that Himmler's measures of 1938 were 'not by their nature, specifically geared to racial persecution, but within the scope of standard police and security measures'. It was not until 1963 that the idea of Gypsies' inherent criminality and asociality was challenged, when the courts accepted that racial motives 'may have been a contributing factor' in the treatment of Roma and Sinti. Resulting compensation claims were, however, restricted to incidents occurring after 8 December 1938, thereby excluding restitution for incarceration in early internment camps, such as Berlin's Marzahn. Claims could not be made for deportations to ghettos after May 1940 (primarily Radom and Białystok) and were highly restricted in relation to health disabilities caused by sterilization and medical experiments. Regulations also required individuals seeking compensation to have endured minimum periods of detention in certain officially recognized camps.[5]

Added to these difficulties was the fact that any claims made were to be assessed by the police department, often largely staffed by the same personnel as during the Nazi period. Walter Winter tells how, once back in his home town, he went to register with the local authorities and only avoided being registered as 'stateless' because not only had he been at school with the clerk registering him, but because he protested vigorously and stood his ground. He also had to fight to have his family land and home returned, and also faced the fact that while he had to be denazified (as he had served in the *Wehrmacht*), 'the old mayor, the Nazi, was still in office'.[6] Indeed, his experiences were indicative of a wider phenomenon: although the Allies issued identity papers to returning Roma and Sinti survivors, German authorities commonly confiscated them on the grounds that the holders lacked proof of German nationality and were consequently stateless. Such denial of citizenship to Sinti survivors had wider repercussions, as it meant the loss of civil rights, including the right to vote, as well as being required to renew their passports every two years at a cost of 40DM.[7]

In-depth interviews with survivors reveal how well-placed fear of authorities and feelings of shame fed into a deep reluctance to submit to the examinations and bureaucratic procedures necessary to receive compensation. Ottilie Reinhardt's mother

> was declared 100% disabled, but one of the doctors contested the finding, so my mother had to go through yet another medical examination. After that, my mother simply refused to let the doctors examine her anymore. She didn't want to be tortured again. My mother was always afraid, she said she didn't want to repeat her experience of the war. And she had the same kind of fear of doctors. My mother did not receive any compensation.

On top of these humiliations, interviewees, although acknowledging the pain and fear associated with the initial sterilization, stressed it was in fact the far-reaching repercussions which damaged them more. Their inability to find a place within their community, and to play a role in the passing on of culture, mattered far more than any physical pain caused by sterilization. With almost an entire generation wiped out and a second generation irrevocably damaged, German Roma and Sinti communities struggled to re-form. Nazi persecution had ensured that it was almost impossible for Roma and Sinti customs and culture to be maintained: the humiliations and treatment faced by individuals within the camps had destroyed the fundamental structures of authority and respect, which formed the basis of traditional culture; and the deaths of most elders in the camps ensured there were fewer people to pass on traditions. Something of the impact on the community's population structure is revealed in a 1960s study of the Roma community of Hildesheim. Of the 183 individuals, over half were under fourteen and only five over 60. When we consider these factors in combination with the sterilization programme, as well as ongoing levels of illiteracy and social marginalization, we begin to get something of the sense of the internal challenges faced by the surviving German Roma and Sinti.[8]

Layered on to the devastation of Roma and Sinti communities was the added fact that although the German population was aware of how Gypsies had been persecuted during the war, this did not translate into sympathy in the post-war period. As one commentator observed, 'Hitler has sunk, but the racial hatred has remained unchanged; to those who do not believe this, I recommend a walk, accompanied by a Gypsy, in the streets of a city.' Even in the chaotic months following the collapse of Hitler's regime, the population of Marburg found the time and institutional energy necessary to approve the deportation of Gypsies from the town.[9] Hesse in autumn 1947 saw administrators complaining how Gypsies were travelling in *Rudeln* (packs) again, and were again constituting a *Landplage* (menace).[10] Similarly Bremen issued a measure for 'the protection of the population from molestation by Travellers' based on the Bavarian legislation of 1926, which was simply one of number passed across Germany in the late 1940s. Both Cologne and Düsseldorf from 1949 actively registered all Gypsies in their area through the local police stations, as part of a stated policy on 'Combating the Gypsy Menace'. Registration also included continuing Nazi restrictions over the issuing of *Wandergewerbescheine*, as well as regulations over the registration and surveillance of all local Gypsy employment.[11]

Lest we think that such attitudes were solely the feature of post-war Germany, a look at France and Britain in these years shows similar preoccupations around ideas of asociality and the need for assimilation. France's wartime internment policies were followed seamlessly by assimilatory measures and harassment via the anthropometric notebook. Although internment technically ended on 30 August 1945, the last inmates were not released until May 1946 with the minister of the interior declaring 'we liberate [the Gypsies] with the greatest of regret, and recommended the severest possible application of the law of 16 July 1912', making plain the fact that internment was as much a French solution as it was Nazi policy.[12] The refusal of the French state to extend compensation to Gypsies who had suffered internment, with the attendant disruption of familial and economic routines and networks, trauma, starvation and loss of property, can also be understood in this light. Compensation would have been an acknowledgement that French preoccupations with assimilation were flawed or morally wrong.[13] Right up to 1969 *nomades* were prosecuted and imprisoned for offences relating to the law of 1912, and the emphasis at both national and *département* level remained on using legislation to heavily encourage settlement.[14]

In Britain, Gypsy Travellers' invisibility in relation to the war effort spilled over into a denial of their rights to the benefits of the welfare state as well as their absence from new planning considerations embodied in the Town and Country Planning Act of 1947 governing the use of space. In popular imagination the new welfare state (1944–8) had been 'won' through people's individual and collective engagement in the war effort, and consequently was seen as a 'right'. The reverse side of this was that those who were not perceived as having pulled their weight were vilified and marginalized. Lack of understanding of Gypsy Travellers' roles in the war, added to traditional stereotypes of Travellers as antisocial, gave rise to a new sense that they had undermined Britain in its time of need.[15] So while universal provision of services and benefits theoretically removed both the stigma and the overt social control elements from post-war welfare provision, for Gypsy Travellers things were far more problematic. Gypsy Travellers were seen as undeserving, yet it was accepted that it was both difficult and counterproductive to withhold benefits from these less-than-perfect citizens. While rarely made explicit, officials ensured that services were bestowed with discretion, based on understandings of social improvement and with a view to promoting assimilation. We can see this in punitive calculations of National Assistance payments made by local officers, who questioned the right of Travellers to receive public money, and made arbitrary deductions. Often they assumed claimants were not declaring their full income or that they did not need to maintain the same standard of living as settled people:[16]

> There can be no doubt that there are undisclosed resources in most cases. A number of them have ancient cars in which they move around while our allowances are largely disposed of in the nearest bar that sells 'wine' . . . no injustice would be done if allowances were withheld from all but the oldest and, exceptionally, those with large families of young children.[17]

Gypsies and Travellers also experienced problems when they sought spaces for caravans or housing. For them the general problems presented by the post-war housing shortage was compounded by local authorities' reluctance to put them on council-housing lists as they were not considered 'local', and by the absence of designated space for caravans as part of new planning controls. Where councils did develop particular housing schemes directed at Gypsies and Travellers, such as in the New Forest, authorities generally provided inferior accommodation, on the grounds that the inhabitants were not ready to meet the standards of settled society but that these dwellings could act as a stepping stone towards full assimilation.[18] For the most part, they were affected by the post-war housing programme only in that it created pressure on the marginal spaces traditionally used by Gypsies. In more than one case families arrived at an old camping ground only to discover that a council estate had sprung up since their last visit. By the early 1950s it appeared that just as the physical space open to Gypsy Travellers was drastically reducing, so too shrank their – always tenuous and partial – social legitimacy.

If western Europe was characterized by denial of both the specificity of Roma and Gypsy experiences of the war and of their distinctive culture, was this the same on the other side of the Iron Curtain? As ever, we need to be wary of generalizations: although the West depicted the 'Eastern Bloc' as a monolithic totalitarian system directly under the sway of Moscow, in fact while all the governments were based on versions of Marxism–Leninism, these played out differently across the region. Countries differed both in their relationship with Moscow – Tito's Yugoslavia and neighbouring Albania maintained their independence from the Soviet Union – and in how they dealt with their different ethnic groups. Some, such as Poland, Hungary and Bulgaria, understood national identity as being fundamentally ethnically homogeneous, containing only small 'minority' populations. Others, most typically the Soviet Union and Yugoslavia, officially had no dominant nation, but instead a complex hierarchical structure of national/ethnic communities now unified in new, 'higher' socialist formations such as 'the Soviet people' or 'Yugoslavs'. However, within this, and as in the West, Roma were denied recognition of a separate identity, for by Stalin's criteria, they fell short of the definition of a national minority: they had no territorial base or 'history', and were seen as having no unifying language or culture. As a result there was no apparent justification for extending to them any of the special measures granted to designated 'national minorities'.[19] And yet, it would be too simplistic to say that Roma experiences under state socialism were either uniform or wholly negative.

Initially, as with the *korenizatsiia* policy of the Bolsheviks, many new regimes courted this most marginalized section of their populations in the hope of sowing the seeds of socialism amongst them. A year after the communist takeover of Czechoslovakia, the government commissioned a study of the country's Roma population, which firmly placed responsibility for their poor socioeconomic position on the attitudes of previous bourgeois governments. In contrast, the new People's Democratic State would 'successfully solve the Gypsy Question'.[20] Similarly, criticizing their fascist predecessors for having neglected Gypsies, Bulgaria's government's aim was to 'make every effort to change the life of the Gypsies for the better, and to weld them into the political and social and economic life of the Bulgarian People's Republic'.[21] So, the first issue of the state-sponsored Roma newspaper *Romano esi* in 1949 carried an appeal from the Communist Party to those who called themselves 'Turks' or 'Christians' rather than identifying themselves as 'Roma' to 'tear off the mask from their faces, stop being ashamed and say that they are Gypsies'.[22] Official support for Roma was also signalled through state sponsorship of the Gypsy Organization to Fight against Fascism and Racism, and for the Cultural Development of the Roma Minority in Bulgaria. At first, under the

Dimitrov Constitution of 1947, Gypsies were defined as a specific nationality with their own rights. The Bulgarian Communist Party and the Fatherland Front committees actively courted the Gypsy intelligentsia, resulting in Roma – most notably the inter-war activist Shakir Pashov – acquiring seats in the national legislature and being integrated into the Communist Party hierarchy. At the same time they began actively participating in the national Gypsy cultural organization, forming more than 200 local clubs, and which boasted its own theatre in Sofia.[23]

Acknowledging the cultural life of Roma was not the same as leaving them to live life as they might wish. New socialist regimes across the region moved rapidly towards implementing policies aimed at reshaping society. Dominated by Soviet party agents, emerging governments set about programmes of land reallocation, industrial restructuring and rapid urbanization. So, within Czecho-slovakia, for example, thousands of Gypsies from rural Slovakia made up some of the 1.5 million people who were relocated into areas stripped of their German populations, where they formed part of the new urban proletariat in the expanding industrial conurbations.[24] Other Slovakian Roma were deployed to labour camps in Moravia and Bohemia, as part of the regime's attempt to deal with the severe labour shortage, and as a means of 'extracting social and labour conformity from Gypsies'.[25]

As in other parts of the Soviet bloc, the post-war years in Bulgaria saw rapid land collectivization and the large-scale migration of young rural Bulgarians to the towns, altering profoundly relations in rural areas. Previously, a small proportion of Gypsies had been engaged permanently in agriculture, and then mainly as labourers on farms belonging to rich Bulgarians and Turks in northern Bulgaria, or as hired shepherds and cattlemen across the country. However collectivization opened the way for Gypsies to find a permanent role on the new cooperatives and state farms. Still others left their villages, and moved to what rapidly became illegal settlements on the edges of the expanding cities.[26] Rural Gypsies, then, although often largely untouched by the 'Roma renaissance', had good reason to support the new regime.

The policy of land allocation in Bulgaria of course can also be seen as one way in which the wider policies of the state promoted sedentarization. Often this was part of broader regulations that typically included a requirement for a fixed place of residence and employment. In Hungary this process took place during the second half of the 1950s, and in Albania and Yugoslavia in the 1960s and '70s. On top of such measures some countries also passed special legislation banning an itinerant way of life with the Soviet Union taking the lead through its decree of 1956 on 'the inclusion of itinerant Gypsies in labour activities'. Bulgaria's 'resolution of the issues of the Gypsy minority in Bulgaria', and Czechoslovakia's 'settlement of itinerant persons' followed a similar model and were both passed in 1958. In Poland, after the unsuccessful attempt of the government to persuade itinerant Roma to settle voluntarily in the free western territories following the deportation of the German population in 1952, the Ministry of the Interior issued a resolution on the obligatory sedentarization of itinerant Gypsies in 1964.[27]

As other intellectuals and artists found, where possible socialist regimes attempted to co-opt the emerging Roma artistic elite for their own ends. Probably the most prominent case of this was that of the Polish Roma poet Bronisława Wajs, commonly known by her Romani name Papusza. She was 'discovered' by the Polish poet Jerzy Ficowski, who published her work in *Problemy* magazine. In the tradition of much Romani poetry, her writing expressed yearning for life on the road, but in the new socialist context this yearning was interpreted as a yearning to be settled. Her work appeared in the magazine alongside a pro-settlement piece and Ficowski soon became an adviser for the state's sedentarization programme 'Action C' (also known as the 'great halt'), often using Papusza's poems to back him up. Although Papusza maintained to the last that her work was misused, she was regarded by Polish Roma as a traitor, was ritually banished and forced to live the rest of her life apart from her community.[28]

Here it is worth reflecting on the need to understand the changes experienced by Roma across the Eastern Bloc in the context of broader shifts in society that were affecting the whole population. Moves towards urbanization and industrialization and opportunities for education and training profoundly affected what had still been primarily rural populations across the whole region. And although socialist regimes generally existed within an economy of shortages, it is undoubtedly the case that for the majority of their populations material prosperity and opportunities for social advancement through free education and the party system were greater than in the pre-war period. Sedentarization might have been experienced as a repressive policy by Roma – notably in Poland and Czechoslovakia where it was backed up by the confiscation of horses, wagons and other property – but might also have been seen as an opportunity. The changing socio-economic climate was making nomadic lifestyles more difficult, and many Roma, particularly in the Soviet Union and Bulgaria, had been moving towards a position of (semi-) settlement. In such cases loans and subsidies for housing and land supported moves that Roma communities were already making. And settlement did not necessarily mean assimilation – indeed, across the Balkans and Hungary in particular, there had been a long tradition of identifiably settled Roma communities – and nor did engagement in new forms of economic organization:

> In Hungary, there is a small number of blacksmith cooperatives which are run by Roma on their own behalf. The blacksmith cooperative of Nogradmegyer . . . has existed since 1951. The village had been inhabited by Gypsy nailsmiths and musicians, both groups through a long process established the cooperative, which today produces a multiplicity of products.[29]

And yet not all regimes were so open to the idea of difference: the insistence in Poland on sedentarization, for example, was simply one manifestation of a broader policy of cultural homogenization. In Bulgaria, state emphasis on cultural and ethnic homogeneity was pursued through active 'Bulgarization', which, while primarily focusing on the country's Muslim population, was to hit Muslim Gypsies doubly hard. We must not see this, however, as a particularly 'communist' measure, but rather something that had been a feature of Bulgarian life since independence. Although now backed up by the bureaucratic weight of a totalitarian regime, the removal of Turkish influence had been a persistent theme in national life, and the state's initial encouragement of a positive Roma identity had been one way to halt the perceived integration of Roma into the general Turkish minority. As well as heavily pushing Muslim

Roma to Christianize their names, Bulgarization was behind the granting to all Jews of exit visas in 1948 and the official encouragement of a quarter of a million 'Turks' (Muslim Bulgarians) to 'return' to Turkey in 1950.[30] Revealingly, not only did Muslim Gypsies form an important part of the exodus but their presence caused considerable diplomatic difficulties. The Turkish authorities swiftly warned the Bulgarians against including Gypsies among the 'Turks', and after a trainload of deportees containing 97 Roma tried to enter Turkey, the Turks closed the border. Istanbul argued that the Roma had no claim to Turkish origins and therefore could not be granted entry. Although official Communist Party records indicate that only fifteen Roma emigrated in 1950s, in reality the Bulgarians continued to force both Turks and Roma across the border in isolated areas, with up to 5,000 Bulgarian Gypsies entering Turkey in this way.[31] Such actions proved that despite the rhetoric of equality, Gypsies were still somehow less Bulgarian than their Bulgarian comrades.

If socialist regimes teetered between trying to treat Roma in the same way as their majority populations, and implementing special measures aimed at specifically changing their way of life and relationship with society, then they were not alone. On the other side of the Iron Curtain exactly the same dilemmas were being acted out. By the 1960s the West had moved on from its initial post-war preoccupation with reconstruction. The unexpected prosperity which started to blossom from the mid-1950s brought on a wave of full employment, urbanization, expanded university education, rising consumerism and higher expectation, heralding what the French called the *Trente Glorieuses* (the years 1945–75, which followed the end of the Second World War), which across the Channel was encapsulated in the observation that Britain had 'never had it so good'. For Gypsy populations we see two contradictory trends – one reinforcing marginalization, the other promoting inclusion.

On the one hand, Gypsies were pushed increasingly towards city edges, partly following general patterns of urbanization, but also resulting from the growing scarcity of stopping places caused by the physical expansion of towns and urban zoning limiting use of open spaces. Such physical marginalization reinforced increasing disparities between *nomades* and Gypsy Travellers' standards of living and those of wider society. In the late nineteenth century, and even in the inter-war period, there might not have been much difference between the standard of living of Gypsies and the urban and rural poor: lack of electricity, running water or washing facilities was common, and for both groups standards of schooling might be low or non-existent. More than this, evidence shows that they lived side by side in areas of cheap urban housing, worked alongside each other in the fields for fruit, vegetable and hop harvests, and met face to face through door-to-door selling and other interactions. Indeed, the high level of cross-over in folk songs sung by British Gypsy Travellers and the wider working-class population suggests that there was meaningful social interaction too. However, this did not mean that they were fully accepted by their neighbours and fellow workers. The Stewarts had lived in the Scottish town of Blairgowrie for at least three generations by the 1960s, and as one of them put it, 'I've worked in this toon, Blairgowrie, as a labourer, as a bricklayer, as an electrical engineer, and they liked me as far as my work was concerned, but at the end of the day, ye're still a Tink.'[32]

Such discrimination and social distancing was reinforced by two key factors. The first was the arrival of new, more visible Roma or Traveller groups, which increased pressure on the already over-stretched network of stopping places, and made travelling populations generally more visible. In France it was the significant migration of Yugoslavian Roma, such as the Kosovan Xoraxané Roma, who arrived along with large numbers of other Yugoslavs seeking prosperity when border controls were lightened by the Titoist regime. In Britain, it was the migration of large numbers of Irish Travellers, who crossed the Irish Sea following concerted state action against 'Itinerants' from 1963. While in France some Roma managed to secure space in sites allocated to Gypsies, most ended up in shanty towns on the edge of the cities; in Britain Irish Travellers joined British Gypsies in living on a succession of insecure roadside stopping places.[33]

The second factor was the changing economy: many of the visible 'Gypsy' occupations – horse dealing, peg making, hawking, field labour – were becoming more marginal or even obsolete. And while Gypsy Travellers diversified their work into almost anything where mobility, versatility, negotiation and self-employment were central features – the Stewarts worked as builders, for example, on the new towns, and erected pylon lines across Britain; others worked on the nuclear power plant at Dounreay, or moved into car and furniture dealing, scrap metalwork, tarmacking, 'lopping and topping' – these were not acknowledged by the majority population as 'legitimate' trades for Gypsies. The shortage of stopping places, in combination with increased motorization, meant that people stayed in one place for longer, and in often larger numbers than in the past. To this was added the modernization of nomadic lifestyles – new motor-drawn caravans, generators providing much-valued electricity – reinforcing the lack of visible 'Gypsy' markers such as bow-topped caravans, horses, peg-making around an open fire.

These factors were to coalesce in a peculiarly toxic mix of stereotypes over race, lifestyle and perceptions of unfitness for the modern world. In both France and Britain, as we have seen, there was a long-established tradition of the state denial of difference, meaning that all citizens in theory were to be treated the same. West Germany, in an attempt to distance itself from its Nazi past, similarly moved towards explicitly non-racial legislation. In the context of the post-war world this combined with the seemingly relentless expansion of state control over people's lives, and a changing socio-economic context in which Gypsies no longer seemed to fulfil an obvious function. Put simply, a rejection of ethnic difference in combination with the denial that 'real Gypsies' still existed in the modern world resulted in civil servants insisting that while 'true' Gypsies might be free to live how they pleased, compulsory housing, regular employment and education were the best means of solving any lingering 'nomad problem'.

This position involved deploying racialized and spurious definitions of 'Gypsies': 'true' Gypsies, who carried an inescapable wanderlust, did not want or need official intervention, while racially impure 'didikais' (Travellers of mixed Romani heritage) and other Travellers – ancestors of the Tudor 'counterfeit Egyptian' – could be subsumed under the wider 'caravan' problem and the housing programme. Rather than examining the structural reasons behind repeated evictions, officials dismissed their importance by denying they involved true Gypsies:

> From time to time there are articles in the Press and ques-
> tions in the house about Gypsies being evicted from their
> customary camping sites . . . In all these cases the people
> are referred to as 'Gypsies', though the Romany element

seems to have been diluted, with *Irish tinkers* in Cardiff, and with *scrap metal dealers* in Iver and Brierley Hill [my emphasis].[34]

Concentrating on living style and economic occupation allowed British civil servants to suggest that all those affected by the Act of 1947 were 'not Gypsies at all', but rather 'people who without any special claim, choose to live in a way which does not harmonize to the local pattern'.[35] We see a similar process at work in Germany as bureaucrats were aided by the official adoption of the label *Landfahrer* [Traveller]:

> many people that are travelling around today are not real Gypsies anymore but *Wandergewerbetreibende* [people whose profession is itinerant trade], or fairground and showpeople, who differ in their outer appearance and their demeanour from Gypsies; they don't have a deep-rooted affinity with travelling and therefore it is possible to make them settle down permanently again, perhaps through a permanent obligation to report to the authorities . . . One problem is that many *Landfahrer* have vehicles and can escape quickly in them.[36]

And yet, while apparently shorn of racial associations, as these people were not 'real Gypsies', the official definition also made it clear that a *Landfahrer* was someone with 'a deep-rooted affinity with travelling around, or has a strong aversion against settling down and who travels around especially with caravans, horse-drawn carts and different mobile possessions'. And now, perhaps learning from the Weimar period, having 'an official permanent place of residency' was not enough to be excluded from the definition.[37] Simultaneously deploying and denying race, while also implying endemic criminality and the ability to 'escape quickly', official attitudes towards *Landfahrer* justified assimilationist policies alongside policies of surveillance and control. In Cologne and Düsseldorf, *Landfahrer*, many of them in fact concentration-camp survivors, were resettled in the old municipal internment camps, while people parked in unapproved places were evicted and prosecuted. Once again survivors were 'in barracks surrounded by barbed wire . . .

[where] they still live with the filth and most primitive conditions'. There was continuity in other ways too: the Bavarian police managed to retain the records of the Central Office to Combat the Gypsy Menace. Its renamed *Landfahrerzentrale* [Vagrant Department] continued to use the records to assess restitution and citizenship claims up until it was disbanded in 1970 and its files 'lost'.[38]

By the mid-1960s it was becoming clear that post-war policies towards Gypsies across Europe were failing. Britain was experiencing an increasing number of high-profile and violent evictions as many West Midlands local authorities in particular adopted 'zero-tolerance' policies towards Gypsy Travellers. Jimmy Connors, an Irish Traveller, recounted the persecution they faced in Walsall:

> Twenty-eight times that day I produced my driving licence and insurance. The first day's summonses totalled sixty-two and the full total was three hundred. Every two minutes of the day we were summonsed for an offence. The persecution went on and on, night, noon and day. The police thought we would move away from the Midlands . . . But the question was where could we move to? All camping sites were banked up with piles of earth, and trenches dug across all open land to prevent us from camping on them . . . A harmless child is blown to bits at the hands of the local authorities; Ann Hanrahan, two and a half years old, crushed to death during an eviction near Dudley, two miles from Walsall. My own little son very badly injured and my caravan smashed to pieces . . . Walsall – during an eviction, three little girls burned to death. Walsall – my wife kicked black and blue by the police in her own caravan three days before her baby was born. Walsall – I was kicked unconscious. Walsall – a sister at Walsall Hospital refused to treat us.[39]

In the Eastern Bloc it was equally clear that the optimism of the early post-war years was being replaced by the reality of ongoing marginality, socio-economic problems and prejudice. These years saw disillusionment on the part of the regime as they realized that while some Gypsies, primarily those already settled, engaged with Communism, there were still large numbers who did their best to ignore it and tried to maintain more traditional ways of life. An internal document of 1959 tried to give a positive gloss to the progress made by the Bulgarian Roma:

> Among the Gypsies there are now doctors, officers in the army, mechanics, etc. There are 3,500 Gypsy members of the organizations of the Bulgarian Communist Party, and tens of thousands of Gypsy members of the Fatherland Front, the Komsomol, and other organizations.[40]

However, it was admitted that this was not necessarily typical of broader experiences, and that for most Bulgarian Roma the reality was one of leaving school early and often illiterate, and moving between a number of low grade jobs or semi-unemployment:

> Certain industrial managers support the theory that the Gypsies are lazy and cannot learn to work and be disciplined, so they are reluctant to give them work in their factories and are ready to fire them at the smallest occasion.[41]

Laziness and other 'innate' characteristics were also the normal explanations given for their poor performance in school and tendency to leave formal education as early as possible. Overall, it was made explicit that the behaviour of Gypsies themselves was central to their failure to progress satisfactorily under socialism. There were still 14,000 nomadic Gypsies across the country who 'wander from town to town' and 'practise begging, fortune telling, stealing', which may have been understandable under bourgeois and fascist regimes but, 'today in the conditions of socialism this way of life is harmful and disgraceful'. In Romania, as late as 1977 the official census recorded that there were still 66,500 nomadic Roma, suggesting that despite regulations to the contrary they were able to circumvent restrictions.

In rare cases, regimes accepted that positive measures needed to be taken, and that rather than the problem sitting with the Roma community, majority society bore some responsibility. In Hungary this was partly a result of a gradual evolution of a more proactive policy towards minorities following the 1956 revolution. By 1961 the Central Committee had declared that although its Gypsies did 'not constitute a national minority' they should be accorded the same privileges as other groups. This resolution admitted that the major barrier to their progress, particularly in rural areas, was a 'phalanx of prejudice', which prevented them from being allocated adequate housing or being hired for work. Research into their conditions over the next decade found that there were 2,100 Roma settlements throughout the country, with 126,000 living in what were described as 'shanty towns', over a half of which had no water, and two-thirds had no electricity.[42]

Often portrayed, particularly in the West, as an example of the repressive policies of communist regimes towards Roma, in fact the effects of targeted housing schemes were rather more complex. Across Hungary, government mortgages were made available to Roma families whose head of household had 'worked steadily for two years', and under this scheme in the five years from 1965 2,500 new houses were built. As the shanty areas around the major cities, which housed an estimated 65,000 Roma, were cleared, 3,000 apartments were made available to them. In tandem with the schemes, there were labour-development programmes aimed at semi-skilled Roma: in the Baranja mining area of the south-west officials proactively recruited Roma men at all levels of production, as well as encouraging them to become active in local government bodies. And yet, the impact of such schemes was partial. New housing was insufficient to adequately house displaced Roma, so not only did large numbers remain in shanty accommodation, but they were blamed for failing to take advantage of the benefits of socialism. Similarly, although in some areas Roma were successfully included in the workforce, by the late 1970s only 1.5 per cent were classed as skilled workers, and illiteracy levels among the Roma population remained high. Still largely speaking Romani as their first language, they entered school with limited Hungarian, where they were often treated as 'retarded', leading to drop-out rates of 50–60 per cent in the early 1970s.[43]

We see similar efforts in Bulgaria during this period, although here the policies were part of a specific package of measures aimed at eradicating Roma lifestyles and the anti-socialist individualism it was seen to foster. The decree of November 1958, directed solely at the Roma population, stated that 'the vagrant way of life is forbidden in every form', outlawed begging, and made illegal the unauthorized settlements that had grown up on the outskirts of all the major cities. Residents of these shanty areas were consequently ordered to return to 'their place of permanent residence'.[44] In the same month a decree set out a concerted programme of enforced settlement and assimilation. Mobilizing long-standing stereotypes but couched in the new language of bureaucratic socialism, this decree made no bones about the problems the Gypsy population caused to the wider population:

> they do not work, do not settle, beg, tell fortunes, steal and commit other violations of public order. In many cases the Gypsy population spread illnesses and are the bearers of huge underdevelopment . . . The cure is to settle the Gypsy population, to make them work, and to make their culture and everyday life higher.[45]

Those drafting the decree had also made sure that it specified exactly who was to do what: the Ministry of Agriculture and Forestry was obliged to 'find not less than 1,000 jobs and to build homes for the workers'; the Central Union of Labour Producer Cooperatives was expected to create cooperatives and to include in them 'Gypsy people who do hand-craft work such as basketry, iron-smithery and others'; while the Executive Committees of People's Councils were tasked with tackling the 'regulation, development and sanitation of the Gypsy quarters'.[46] The 'most stringent measures' (essentially internment in a 'correction' camp) were to be applied to officials who 'fail to act' and Gypsies who refused to comply.

Central to the programme was the principle that any new homes for Roma were to be 'dispersed in different parts of cities or regions in order to prevent their concentration in compact groups'. As in the past, allowing them to live and socialize together was seen as potentially undermining the good work promised by settlement. So Gypsies were to be offered new apartments in Bulgarian neighbourhoods, with only one or two families housed in each development.[47] Often apartments were made available to Party members as a perk, and were 'showpieces' for state policy, meaning that Gypsies often accepted the new apartments willingly, even though they knew it was tied to a policy of dispersal. As the Gypsy activist Manush Romanov observed, 'when you live in bad conditions, you want to move'.[48] Overall the policy of supported 'resettlement' had a significant impact, in good part due to the fact that money was made available via loans and from central funds. In total around '20,000 families . . . received plots of land and low-interest loans to build their own houses and numerous settlements [were] created on collective farms'.[49]

Unlike the housing schemes, which were based on a premise of dispersal, from 1964 the state aimed to tackle the low standards of formal education and literacy amongst Gypsies through the creation of a network of designated Roma schools. These special, often boarding, schools – of which there were 145 at their height – targeted pupils from 'the poorest families' or areas in which there was deemed to be a 'bad social atmosphere'. By the early 1970s there were approximately 10,000 Gypsy children in these schools, with a majority in mainstream Bulgarian institutions. And yet, by 1978 an investigation concluded that 'only 30% of Gypsy children completed primary school, while the number who finished secondary school was negligible', contributing to more than half of Roma aged over 30 being illiterate.[50]

Other socialist nations were even most explicit in their intentions to deconstruct Roma culture. Along with Poland, Czechoslovakia had a rigorous policy of dispersal and settlement. In 1965 a decree was issued aimed at the destruction of Roma quarters, mainly those of eastern Slovakia where the majority of Roma still lived. Gypsy villages were emptied and their populations dispersed to Slovak villages and towns, as well as to the industrial Czech regions. Soon after this a sterilization decree was passed in 1972, authorizing the 'voluntary' sterilization of women who had given birth to more than four 'mentally retarded' children. While neither technically coercive nor directed specifically at the Roma population – and therefore distinct from Nazi sterilization policies – it was backed up by heavy persuasion from officials, as well as a significant financial incentive, and more than half of those sterilized in the 1970s were Roma women. Rather than this being a particular feature of totalitarianism, however, we need to remember that it was very similar to contemporary practices across Scandinavian countries and Switzerland. Consequently we can see it as more in line with eugenicist and 'national efficiency' ideas of social engineering that had a pedigree stretching back to the late nineteenth century. And yet, as with many theoretically mainstream policies, its impact on Roma was disproportionate and discriminatory in practice. Roma remained some of the poorest in society, and therefore most likely to be affected by the financial benefits, while ongoing poor educational attainment of Roma children rendered them disproportionately liable to be labelled as 'retarded'. Romania took a less draconian route to trying to reduce the number of children in Roma families, only giving allowances to families with fewer than five children.[51]

While superficially the measures taken by socialist governments were far more coercive than those in the West, in fact the late 1960s and early '70s also saw the emergence of particular policies directed at Gypsies in western Europe, as governments accepted that straightforward assimilation or strategies based around ignoring the mounting problems faced by Gypsy Travellers were not working. In France the ongoing tension between localities wanting to remove *nomades* from their jurisdiction, and more general principles of equality were revealed in increasing pressure over stopping places in the 1960s. In a particularly high-profile case the prefect of the wealthy Alpes-Maritimes *département* prohibited stopping in more than 79 of it municipalities. However, this was overturned by the Council of State, which found 'that such a permanent and absolute ban on stopping on all or part of the territory of a department infringed upon individuals' liberties'.

Its decision was to have far-reaching impacts, leading to minister for the interior calls for respect for people stopping (1966) and for local government to build sites for both short- and long-term stopping (1968). The aim was to create new sites in order to preserve public peace by limiting where Gypsies could stop and ensuring that they could 'become accustomed to remaining several months in the same place and also to carrying out regular work'.[52] The following year saw the anthropometric booklet finally being abandoned and replaced by the 'law relating to the exercise of ambulant activities and to the regime applicable to people circulating in France without a fixed abode or residence'. This aimed to enable 'the progressive integration [of nomads] into the national political life' through enshrining a 'right to itinerance', which was no longer seen as 'errance'.[53] The anthropometric booklet was replaced by three different documents: 'circulation cards' which were to be validated at a police station every quarter and were issued to those unable to prove their employment or income; annual 'circulation booklets' for those able to prove their trade but unregistered with the Repertory of Trades or the Registry of Commerce; and the 'special booklet' for registered traders which only needed renewing every five years.

Meanwhile Britain, where the government finally accepted that the status quo was unsustainable, passed the Caravan Sites Act of 1968. This was similar in both intention and outcome to the French legislation. The act required local authorities to provide official sites for 'Gypsies residing in or resorting to' their area, but once provided, councils were granted stronger powers to evict those resorting to unauthorized sites in their district. Not only did the law fail to set a date by which sites needed to be constructed, but it also failed to resolve a fundamental difference in attitude over the function of sites. Local authorities had grudgingly accepted them on the understanding that they were a step towards long-term settlement and assimilation, while site users welcomed them as a means of enabling them to continue their traditional patterns of life in an increasingly circumscribed world. [54]

While both the British and French responses to the existence of Gypsies, and particularly travelling families, appeared to be different to those under Communism in that they apparently supported rather than undermined nomadism, in fact the motivations were remarkably similar. Whether an apparently liberal democracy or a socialist state, the emphasis was on trying to 'normalize' the relationship between Gypsies and wider society by expecting Gypsies to change and conform, often deploying prejudicial attitudes in the process. In part the French law of 1969 confirmed ongoing state insistence to treat Gypsies on the basis of behaviour rather than ethnicity. The *nomades* or 'person of nomadic origin' of the 1950s and '60s became after 1969 someone *sans domicile fixe* (SDF – 'no fixed abode'), and over the 1970s were gradually replaced by *gens du voyage* (travelling people).[55] The title may have changed, but behind official insistences that difference was no deeper than lifestyle there were lingering traces of racialized attitudes. The new circulation documents still kept space for a photo, height and 'particular signs', and regulations set out that Gypsies were not to comprise more than 3 per cent of any particular commune due to supposed fears of electoral manipulation.

Prejudice was expressed in other ways too. The law created the concept of a 'commune of attachment' to which *nomades* were obliged to return to fulfil administrative tasks (which are not few under the French statist model), but rather than the standard six months' residency qualification, Gypsies needed to be attached to a municipality for three years in order to be able to vote. Here we see the reality behind French state assertions of equality: the provision of sites and a loosening of the yoke of the anthropometric notebook went hand in hand with significant reservations about, and specific powers over, Gypsies. As Interior Minister Fouchet argued during the presentation of the legislation to the National Assembly, 'the means available to the police and the gendarmerie allow us to take this liberal measure without risk to public order'. It was the expansion of the technologies of state control, rather than a shift in attitudes towards Gypsies, which ensured the new measures were passed. They remained the only French citizens whose liberty to come and go was conditional and conditioned.[56]

It is important here to pause and pay attention to how this period saw the emergence of a more publically audible Gypsy voice. The 1960s saw the beginning of a rising tide of what might be thought of as 'Gypsy Power' movements, as across Europe Roma, Gypsies and Travellers began to organize politically. This was not completely unprecedented: the Roma workers of Sliven, for example, had long been politically active and organized, although more often as part of national and international labour movements than as 'Gypsies';[57] and in the early 1900s Bulgarian Roma came together to protest about their loss in relation to the removal of the Muslim male franchise. While they were unsuccessful, it created the seeds of a Roma movement, which, aided by increased literacy levels, led to the emergence of civic organizations in the inter-war period. These years also saw political movements inspired by Zionism, with the Polish Roma leaders Michal and Janusz Kwiek arguing for the creation of a Gypsy state – Romanestan – in the newly conquered Italian Abyssinia.[58] Any progress made in Continental Europe, however, had of course been profoundly disrupted by the destruction of Roma and Sinti communities during the Second World War.

Initially then, the germs of political activity in the post-war period across Europe came from non-Gypsies. In Britain, the MP Norman Dodds, whose constituency contained the long-established

Belvedere Marshes site, initially led the way in arguing for the provision of officially sanctioned sites, and in fact established one of
the first licensed sites of the post-war period. In France, Father
Fleury, who had visited the Poitiers internment camp in 1942 and
become concerned about the social position of Gypsies, worked
with Pierre Join-Lambert to form the 'Inter-Ministerial Commission for the Study of the Question relating to Peoples of Nomadic
Origin' in 1948. It aimed 'to assure the quality of life of the Gypsies'
through improvements in accommodation, education, health and
work, as well as ending 'the opposition between two civilizations –
the nomadic and the sedentary'. As with Norman Dodds's work,
the Commission was reformist rather than radical, aiming to help
nomades 'adapt to the real world', with its assumption that Gypsy
lifestyles were inherently opposed to modernity seeming to reinforce the idea that assimilation was the only answer to the 'Gypsy
problem'.[59] Yet from its work came a realization of the lack of basic
knowledge about Gypsy society, culture and experiences, which in
turn prompted the founding of the journal *Études Tsiganes* in 1955.
This rapidly developed an analysis that lobbied for a new approach
to Gypsies, in which they were treated as a specific minority with
particular needs who might be included within the idea of a larger,
national community.

Yet, very quickly, Roma and Gypsies began organizing themselves. During this period, led by Ionel Rotaru, a French-Romanian
Rom, the *Communauté Mondiale Gitane* (World Gypsy Community)
was established, which published a magazine, *The World Voice of
the Gypsies*, and reawakened the idea of Romanestan as well as calling for war reparations from Germany. Although it was banned by
the French government in 1965, its influence was felt as far away as
Bulgaria, where it inspired more clandestine political activity:

> In 1963, we learned from the Serbian Gypsies in Yugoslavia
> that there was a world Gypsy organization with its office in
> Paris . . . We were classmates. We chose people we could
> rely upon because we were afraid of spies. We gathered at
> various homes. We met every Sunday at 10 a.m. We met
> until 1968. We discussed such themes as is there a Gypsy
> alphabet or not. Through the barges that came from
> Yugoslavia, we collected information and magazines.[60]

This form of clandestine organization needs to be seen as separate from the formation of Roma organizations in Yugoslavia, where they were primarily state sponsored. There, in 1969, as a result of the actions of Slobodan Berberski, a Roma with a long and impeccable pedigree as a resistance fighter, communist functionary and member of the Central Committee of the Union of Yugoslav Communists, a Roma Association was formed. A decade later there were more than 60 branches and affiliated Roma organizations that sponsored cultural events, Romani-language television and radio broadcasts.[61] Outside of Yugoslavia, however, socialist governments worked against allowing the expression of separate identity politics, unless it worked within the carefully controlled sphere of party-sponsored organizations, either within or between nations.

We see a more direct form of international cross-fertilization in the formation of the Gypsy Council in Britain in 1966. The active and growing resistance by Gypsy Travellers and people from wider society to a number of high-profile evictions was in no small part encouraged and organized by the activist Gratton Puxon who had experienced resisting evictions alongside Travellers in Ireland. Coming out of this groundswell of resistance, in December 1966, the Gypsy Council held its first meeting: in a Kentish pub displaying a 'No Gypsies' sign. The council's manifesto was a combination of practical requests and demands for an end to prejudicial treatment. It asked for sites in every county, 'equal rights to education, work and houses' and 'equal standing through respect between ourselves and our settled neighbours'.

In its early days non-violent direct action was used repeatedly throughout England at this time to prevent evictions: in Kent, Essex, London, Leeds, Oxford, Birmingham and Bridgewater. In addition, by 1968, more than 300 complaints had been made under the new Race Relations Acts against pubs barring Gypsies and Travellers.[62]

British activism was able to draw strength from, and feed into the growing contemporary international Roma movement through Britain's hosting of the first World Romani Congress in 1971, which showed Gypsies and Travellers not as 'a small minority, as many think, but a proud people 12 MILLION strong, scattered in every country'.[63] By this point the idea of Romanestan had shifted to reflect this, and for many Romanestan now meant, as the Canadian Gypsy activist and writer Ronald Lee put it, 'where my two feet stand'. Lee, as with others, was influenced not only by post-colonial thinkers such as Frantz Fanon, but by the Black Power movements which stressed the importance of pride in their separate identity as well as the importance of radical action to generate change: 'To raise the standard of Rom nationalism is like suddenly shouting a secret in a crowded room.'[64] The Romani congress, which received delegates from fourteen countries, was key in making explicit the need for international unity in both the fight *against* social marginalization and in striving *for* a positive future. In a reflection of the breadth of issues it aimed to tackle, commissions were established to consider war crimes, social and educational conditions, as well as the language and culture of the Roma. The leading role of Yugoslavian Roma in this, and the two subsequent international congresses, was something of a vindication of the benefits of communist state-sponsored support for minority populations. While still experiencing the internal divisions common across the international Roma movements, it was undoubtedly the case that Yugoslavian Roma were better placed than others to articulate their agenda and to take the lead within the International Romani Union up until 1990.

Coming from a different context, within Germany, the role of the state also became important in moulding the shape of its Roma and Sinti civil rights movement. Here, activism was both charged with and motivated by the history of the Holocaust, and as with the demands of the student activist movements of 1968, activists demanded both the German state and individuals to face up to the crimes of the Nazi era. Stimulated by the First World Romani Conference, activists such as Romani Rose and Rudko Kawczynski, who did not carry the silencing shame of their parents' generation, began to organize. The commitment of the German state to make reparations to the victims of Nazism meant that although Roma and Sinti were originally excluded from its terms, a political context existed in which the argument over claims and entitlement might be made. Central to their political agenda was an insistence that they be granted recognition for their special ethnic status and recognition that they were a *German* minority. Initially organization was through the Society for Endangered Peoples, which became instrumental in challenging the use of the word *Zigeuner*, demanding that it be replaced by Sinti and Roma. It also argued strongly that they should be treated as an ethnic group with particular needs rather on the basis of a presumed deviant lifestyle.[65]

A key moment came in 1979 when the Society, alongside Roma and Sinti activists, organized a public demonstration at Bergen-Belsen under the motto *In Auschwitz vergast, bis heute verfolgt* ('Gassed in Auschwitz, persecuted to this day'). This was followed in 1980 by a high-profile hunger strike at Dachau memorial camp, where three of the twelve Roma participants were camp survivors. This protest sought to raise the ongoing marginalized position of Sinti and Roma in German society, but specifically aimed to force the Bavarian Interior Minister to disclose the location of the 'disappeared' vagrant police files. Although they were unsuccessful on this score, the protest created global media coverage, expressions of international solidarity and a raised awareness of the treatment of Sinti and Roma under the Nazis. The hosting of the International Romani Union's third congress in Göttingen in the same year, although mainly organized from outside Germany, 'played a significant role in boosting the self-awareness and public relations of the emerging civil rights movement' in Germany itself. Following the congress a new representative organization was formed – the *Zentralrat Deutscher Sinti und Roma* (Central Council for German Sinti and Roma), taking as its model the national German Jewish Council – which received political recognition and financial support from the Federal government. Accompanying this was a long-awaited statement from the government acknowledging German responsibility for the Roma Holocaust.[66] As in Yugoslavia then, and different from other countries where Roma and Gypsies struggled to find either funding or recognition, German activists were able to benefit from a measure of state support.

In common with the concerns and campaigning of other minority ethnic groups across western Europe from the 1970s, the issue of education became one around which activists and, over time, more proactive academics and practitioners, coalesced. Long seen, and used, as an instrument of assimilation, formal schooling had failed to meet either the needs or aspirations of Roma and Gypsy communities, whether or not they were nomadic. In France, for example, in 1959 compulsory education was extended to sixteen, a measure that went hand in hand with threats to cut family social benefits in cases of poor school attendance. This was seen as highly intrusive by many Gypsy families, whose resentment increased with further regulations that specified that nomadic children had to be sent to school even if a family was only in a commune for half a day. Alongside its other measures of the period, the government introduced four important circulars on the education of Gypsies between 1966 and 1970, measures that culminated in the law of 11 July 1975. Together their strongly assimilationist terms envisaged 'completing' the instruction of the family through constructing an education system with extra 'classes of adaptation'.[67]

Paradoxically, assimilation depends in part on mainstream society accepting minorities in their midst, and evidence suggests that attitudes of schools, teachers and fellow students, their parents and the wider community continued to ensure Gypsy children felt unwanted and stigmatized within the state system. Those interviewed in the early 1980s repeated variations on the phrase 'they put us down at the back of the class and make us do nothing'.[68] It was the same story in Britain where, for most Gypsy Traveller children at the end of the 1960s, the experience of schooling was little different to that of their parents – short-lived, patchy and dominated by bullying from other pupils and disdain from teachers. Jimmy Stockins, left school after two years, aged seven, in the mid-1960s:

> What did I want to go to school for? School was for gorgers [non-Gypsy Travellers]. Why should I learn to read and write? No other person I mixed with could . . . Don't ask me the name of the school . . . I hated it. Sit still. Sit up straight. Single file. Fold your arms. It was like being in a fucking cage. All silly rules and saying prayers . . . I couldn't understand why them calling 'Gypsy' or 'Gypo' across the playground was meant to annoy me. After all, that's what I was . . . Gorger kids seemed to think we didn't like being Travellers for some reason.[69]

In Hamburg, where there was a relatively high concentration of Sinti families, a survey conducted in the city in 1983–4 found that no Roma or Sinti children graduated from high school, with 70 per cent of them being educated in special needs schools. Further, it found that after leaving school one-fifth found waged employment, while the rest went largely into trading, mainly buying and selling carpets and textiles.[70] And despite the pushes made across the Eastern Bloc from the 1960s, although there was a tiny emerging Roma elite, overall, levels of attainment and social integration remained low. An investigation in 1978 concluded that 'only 30% of Gypsy children completed primary school, while the number who finished secondary school was negligible', contributing to more than half of Roma aged over 30 being illiterate.[71]

This led the state to re-emphasize segregation, so that by the 1980s around 80 per cent of Gypsy children in Bulgaria attended segregated schools where the curriculum emphasized 'technical' (vocational) education rather than academic subjects. These schools signed contracts with local firms to produce goods, a portion of the profits going to the students but the bulk to the teachers and the schools. They remained a controversial aspect of Bulgaria's education system, with some arguing that students acquired useful skills while encouraging pupils to stay longer in school. Indeed this policy was seen as the main factor raising the proportion of Roma children going on to secondary schools to between 25 and 30 per cent. Roma rights activists in particular, however, argued how it discriminated against them:

> With this program, Gypsies are destined to be illiterate. They don't learn what children in other schools learn. Even the small numbers who go on to secondary school fail in the first year because they aren't competitive with other students. These special schools exist throughout the country, but only in Gypsy neighbourhoods. Not a single Bulgarian goes to these schools, even if they live in Gypsy neighbourhoods.[72]

As with debates over separate versus integrated schools in other parts of Europe, integrated education also brought problems with it: Gypsy children were perceived as disruptive and lowering the standards of the school, and given the language difficulties experienced by most of them (speaking Turkish and or Romani as their first language rather than Bulgarian), their difficulties within mainstream classrooms were often very real.

In the West, activists and parents, emboldened by the successes of new representational groups such as the Gypsy Council, and seeing the importance of literacy and numeracy in the modern world, began demanding their children's right to education. Leeds, for example, saw a high-profile public campaign that embarrassed the council into finding school places for ten Traveller children within 24 hours.[73] In other areas localized voluntary schemes aimed to bring education onto sites, such as the West Midlands Travellers School, which operated a bus that visited five unauthorized sites during evenings and weekends. By the 1980s, local education authorities, in line with the shift away from assimilation towards multiculturalism, had begun to develop specific Traveller education units, which while varying in quality and practice, provided some acknowledgement of the need to see Gypsy Travellers as a specific group with particular needs.

France too saw similar developments, as it moved away from the traditional French equation of uniformity equalling equality, and towards giving 'more to those who have less'. While not without its limitations, in practical terms this increased funding to schools welcoming students with social or educational difficulties. [74] At the same time, in common with changes across western Europe, there emerged new schooling methods, including building schools on Gypsy sites, as well as introducing mobile 'lorry-schools', often through a mix of state and activist provision. This was not without its problems: some Gypsies did not value mobile or site schools, seeing them as providing lower-quality, piecemeal or paternalistic education, believing that they reinforced the lack of contact with other children.[75] In places where Gypsy children from sites attended mainstream schools in significant numbers, their arrival often led to the removal of sedentary students, creating ghetto-schools.[76]

By the 1980s, then, states of very different political complexions had been making moves no longer simply to remove or assimilate their Gypsy populations, but tentatively to try to implement specialist measures aimed at narrowing the difference between them and wider society. As we have seen, this was not always, and in fact rarely, motivated by concern for the lives of Gypsies themselves, while across the political spectrum very similar measures were used. Often the difference between socialist and non-socialist states was the level of state intervention, rather than the intention behind the measures. And yet, despite the increasing power of states – particularly if we contrast it with that held by early modern, or even the emerging bureaucratic states of the nineteenth century –

what is perhaps most significant is not that states increasingly intervened in the life of Gypsies, but how partial their power actually was. If we look at two very different nations – Britain and Bulgaria – we can see how both states failed either to fully implement their policies towards Gypsies, or to improve their life chances.

In Britain the provision of local authority sites enacted in the legislation of 1968, lacking a timescale by which local authorities might be forced to act, only made slow headway: nearly a decade after its passing there was still over 6,000 caravans with no stopping place. While the next decade did see a slow increase in the number of official sites, it was accompanied by the increasing hardening of popular and official attitudes towards Gypsy Travellers, who were increasingly seen as to blame for their situation. Often offering the only chance of stability open to families, official sites were one place where they could sustain a distinctive culture while being able to access education, health and welfare facilities. And yet they were not unproblematic. Sites were generally designated for residential use only, so that work, such as car-breaking and scrap storage, had to be conducted elsewhere or jeopardize tenancy rights. Kinship networks were weakened as pitches were allocated by wardens on the basis of need or through being known as 'good tenants', so not only were extended families broken up, but families with a history of conflict might be tenanted together. There was no security of tenure as Gypsies and Travellers were exempted from legislation protecting other caravan-dwellers or council tenants from summary eviction, while the physically marginal location of sites reinforced separation from the settled population and promoted a ghetto-like atmosphere.[77] Most crucially, the legislation was enacted at the local level where the weight of public opposition – 'bordering on the frenetic' – against new and existing sites, could erupt into violence and vandalism and was often rooted in stereo-typical assumptions about Gypsies' habits and beliefs. The absence of clear central government direction and the lack of political will at the local level – no councillor ever won a seat through supporting a new caravan site – meant that there was a shortfall of at least 3,500 pitches across the country by the mid-1980s.[78]

For the thousands of Gypsy Travellers who did not want, or were unable, to live on council sites, unauthorized sites trapped families in a cycle of conflict and eviction:

Things are getting worse. Even getting a bit of land is difficult. We go round in a convoy and sometimes we get ten to
fifteen of us on the bit of land and the police come and stop
the rest of us getting on . . . Sometimes they dig a trench all
round with JCB diggers and say we can't get off unless we take
our caravans with us. Well we're trapped then. Can't take out
cars to get food even and we can't get out to get to work . . .
there was one morning at six o'clock when they had warrants
to search for firearms and we were all out of the trailers
standing in a row while they searched . . . Sometimes people
are ill: one time they hitched up a trailer and the midwife
looked out and said that a baby was going to be born . . . The
local people we don't see directly but a few have waved sticks
at us when we try to get onto a piece of land but . . . [the]
worst is what the papers say about us. People panic automatically when we first arrive and too much is written in the
papers to frighten people against us.[79]

If one of the problems of the British legislation was that of reluctant
implementation shaped by local prejudice and the absence of
national direction, what of socialist Bulgaria, which in theory at
least was backed by strong state action?

As ever we need to set policy developments in the wider social
and political climate, particularly the regime's increasingly
sustained attack on Turkish culture and identity culminating in
'the Revival Process' of 1984–9. Bulgaria's long-term move towards
ethnic homogeneity was summed up by the then premier, Todor
Zhivkov, who in 1979 stated that he wished to make Bulgaria the
'Japan of the Balkans'.[80] As in Northern Ireland where Irish
Travellers were doubly suspect – firstly on the grounds of their
Traveller identity, and secondly for being Catholic – the majority
of Bulgarian Gypsies suffered from being both Roma *and* Muslim.
This period saw the forcible renaming of citizens; Turkish cultural
organizations and newspapers banned; Turkish *mahali* (quarters)
broken up and families rehoused; and deliberate ethnic mixing of
military and labour brigades. While we can read this as a specific
attack on minorities, it also operated within the broader political
context of Zhivkov's leadership and what has been called his 'slav-
ish obedience to the Moscow line'. It was most obviously reflected

in the new constitution of 1971 and party programme which stressed how there would be no 'privileges . . . based on ethnic belonging, origin [or] creed' within Bulgaria, but instead a 'unified socialist society' based on 'the amalgamation of urban and rural life, and of physical and mental labour'.[81]

Remarkably, given the resources devoted to these efforts and the regime's near monopoly over civil society, assimilation was commonly both partial and patchy. While by 1974 about 220,000 Bulgarian Muslims had been renamed, Gypsies found ways around the new restrictions through, for example, adopting Bulgarian names for official purposes whilst continuing to use Roma names at home.[82] Ethnographic research, although tightly controlled by the state and usually directed towards demonstrating socialism's successes, in fact revealed how Gypsies sought to maintain their sense of identity in the face of policy.[83] So, by the 1980s the Ljuljin apartment complex in Sofia, for example, which housed a number of dispersed Gypsy families

> amidst concrete terraces, playgrounds, and the hostile stares of Bulgarian neighbours, they still celebrate open-air weddings and baptisms. One weekend they may congregate at one relative's apartment, the next weekend at another's. Although the entire extended family rarely lives together in an apartment, they still gather frequently.[84]

Research also revealed the extent to which travel continued to be a central part of many Gypsies' livelihoods despite holding a fixed address: 'bear and monkey acts, music, ironworking, woodworking, and selling old clothes, trinkets, and black market items' all involved servicing a dispersed customer base, and led to absences of up to a month.[85] This demonstrates that although many Gypsies may have moved more towards a reliance on waged labour, there was space within socialism for private enterprise and trading, particularly on the edges of the economy. The process of 'organizing' goods via a complex network of *vruzki* (connections) had in fact become a key feature of socialist regimes by the 1970s, and was by no means exclusive to Roma. Yet, with a long tradition of self-employment and economic flexibility, they were perhaps better placed than many to exploit the gaps in the socialist system.[86] So, in the mid-1980s:

> Blue jeans from Italy, lingerie from Greece, scarves from
> Turkey or Japan, tee shirts from the United States, and
> electronics from Japan are in great demand. Gypsies with
> relatives in Yugoslavia or Turkey can sometimes establish
> illegal trade routes. If caught they end up in jail, but may
> try to bribe their way out with connections . . . *Vruzki*
> also help obtain scarce Bulgarian goods such as building
> materials and help wade through the bureaucracy.[87]

In engaging in black- or grey-market activities Roma were no
different from the wider population, in that all were attempting to
construct what was often described as a 'normal' life within an
economy of scarcity. And yet, it also supported a distinct cultural
identity in the face of state regulation and the pressures of
assimilation under socialism.

Very quickly, however, things changed. Not simply for Roma,
but right across Europe. The dismantling of the Berlin Wall and
the unexpectedly swift collapse of socialist regimes after 1989
rewrote the political, social and economic map of Europe. Although broadly welcomed for bringing new political freedoms and
increased personal autonomy, including rights to travel abroad, the
precipitous collapse of ex-socialist economies and national boundaries heralded a new and difficult era for the populations of the ex-
Soviet bloc countries. While it would be overstating the case to say
that the changes were calamitous for Roma populations across the
region, events over the subsequent decades suggest that overall
they were among the losers in the new societies. In this period of
often frighteningly rapid change, not only did Gypsies need to
negotiate the new realities facing everyone in the region, but to live
with a right-wing backlash and the rising tide of nationalism which
soon became a feature of daily life.

Having spent four decades needing to accommodate the
regulations imposed by socialism and adapting to an economy of
shortages, as well as becoming used to state-subsidized housing,
education and benefits, the shift to a market economy was socially
traumatic. While affecting all of society, these changes inevitably
hit the more vulnerable the hardest. There was a disproportionate
impact on ethnic minorities, who had sometimes benefited from
targeted programmes, which in the new climate were often entirely

withdrawn, reinforcing marginalization and exclusion. The loss of the wider social benefits which had been tied to waged work was compounded by long-term unemployment. Rural Roma, such as those in Bulgaria who had benefited from the collectivization policies of the 1950s, were now dispossessed under land restitution programmes. Dispossession not only removed access to land but entitlement to pensions and other social benefits, leading to rapid impoverishment and mass out-migration.[88]

Those in urban areas also suffered, with widespread anecdotal evidence suggesting they faced renewed discrimination in the workplace, that they were denied promotions due to their identity or that they were the first to lose their jobs in factories forced to make cutbacks.[89] By 1995, against a national average of 20 per cent, among Bulgarian Roma of working age over three-quarters were unemployed.[90] It was a similar story across the region – unemployment levels habitually hovered around 80 per cent for most of the 1990s and into the 2000s. Although the role some Roma had played in the informal economy under socialism had meant that they were well placed to benefit from the freeing of economic controls, overall a lack of education, social marginalization, high levels of engrained prejudice and massively reduced state support meant that the already low standards of living of the majority of Roma in the region fell to levels social investigators routinely found shocking:

> During winter and early spring, more than half of those living in town relied mainly on the possibility of using discarded fruit and vegetables . . . rotten, disintegrating and nitrate-blackened vegetables smell bad, look bad, and are bad for the health. In spring, they survive on the fresh spring growth of weeds; the women and children pick nettles, docks and sorrel, and this becomes their staple food for 2–3 months. Things are easier in the summer and autumn; they 'privatize' some of the agricultural produce of the neighbouring population, sometimes so successfully that they can sell some of it on the market . . . While carrying out research . . . we were appalled by the appearance of the people in the village. The women and children, as well as a large number of the men were disfigured by facial eczema. It turned out that a quantity of discarded pork and mince

had been found on a rubbish dump near Sliven three days before our arrival . . . there was hardly a house where some-one had not had food poisoning. In Stara Zagora we were told of a family with seven children who had all died after eating a dead sheep, also found on a rubbish dump.[91]

Responding to the difficult economic conditions, for many Roma what often emerged was a patchwork of livelihoods, part of the 'economy of makeshifts' which was to become a major feature of so many people's lives. So some families migrated to the towns, where the men had a better chance of finding temporary work, others to the mountains, where 'entire families gather[ed] mushrooms, herbs, wild fruit and snails'. A sense of this mix of strategies was given by Roma from the Kŭrdzhali region of south-central Bulgaria:

> We've been doing odd jobs for the Bulgarians since we got laid off from the factories five years ago. We beat their carpets, split their logs, render their stonework, and beg from the Turks. The Turks give a lot. The Bulgarians are more stingy.
>
> Fathers have often had to leave the home together with the boys to find casual work in some bigger town. We met many such 'lone' men, accompanied by two or three boys up to 16 years old . . . If the father succeeds in being hired for some job, his sons help him and acquire various skills in this way. If the father stays on the square hoping to be taken on for some employment, the boys wander around sizing up the neighbourhood, at the same time collecting scrap iron and waste paper, empty bottles, discarded clothes and food . . . The girls always stay with the mother. They look after their younger brothers and sisters and the old and the sick, while maintaining order and cleanliness in the home. They are given permanent duties as from 5–6 years old: laundry, cleaning, cooking, baby-sitting etc. [92]

Many turned to the informal sector for the first time, while others, who had already been active in the black market under socialism, extended their activities. Although they were widely depicted in Bulgarian society as the archetypical black-marketeer, and a law of

1991 targeting the illegal economy was seen as being directed solely at Gypsies, in fact black-market activities were common right across the social spectrum. Similarly, the drastic impoverishment and marginalization of a growing proportion of the population combined with an under-funded and ineffectual police force, led to a sharp increase in crime across the region. This was popularly understood to be concentrated among the Roma: the government adviser on ethnic policies in the early 1990s declared that over a quarter of crimes could be 'traced to the Roma'.[93] In-depth research did reveal the extent to that Roma families depended on theft, begging, prostitution and other forms of illegitimate activity for basic survival.[94] However, biased reports in the media rarely contextualized their activities within their extreme poverty, limited employment prospects and extreme social marginalization.

Added into this mix of difficulties was the resentment felt by those in mainstream society, who perceived that under socialism Roma had received disproportionate resources from the state: socialist propaganda had often emphasized the new programmes targeting Roma, without reflecting their partial nature or limited impact. When this became combined with the upsurgence in nationalist politics, particularly in the Balkans, but also the Czech and Slovakian republics and Hungary, it very quickly became translated into anti-Roma prejudice, harassment and violence. In 1992 a group of twelve Bulgarians in Plovdiv staged a hunger strike in protest against being housed amongst Gypsies, but often the hatred was expressed through more violent means. Reports of Gypsy quarters of towns being burnt or attacked by right-wing groups, shootings and stabbings of individuals and of police raids, harassment and brutality became a depressingly familiar feature of life after 1989, as this catalogue of incidents from the Czech Republic suggests:

> Two Romanies were killed in 1993 in the space of one week in September. Also in 1993 Tibor Danihel was drowned, fleeing from a skinhead gang. In 1994 skinheads attacked Gypsies in Breclav and on a train . . . Tibor Berki was killed in May 1995 . . . Roman Zigi was killed in the same year . . . In 1995 altogether more than eighty attacks by skinheads and right-wing groups on Romanies were reported . . .[95]

While there was a particular concentration of anti-Roma violence in the first years of transition, when economic changes, mass unemployment and uncertainty across the region was rife, it by no means disappeared with the gradual bedding down of new political and economic systems. Hungary, for example, which sentenced relatively little anti-Roma activity in the 1990s, experienced a sweep of violence in 2008–9 in which fire bombs and handguns were used in attacks across the country, leading to the deaths of six Roma, and the injury of many more. One of the most notorious events occurred on 23 February 2009 when a 27-year-old man and his five-year-old son were shot dead as they ran out of their burning home in the village of Tatárszentgyörgy. The man's wife and their two other children suffered from severe burns.[96]

The fall-out of anti-Roma feeling was not limited to ex-socialist countries as the combination of the lifting of travel restrictions, a search for better economic conditions and freedom from racial persecution led to large numbers of Roma moving abroad. Despite the noise made by the British tabloid press over the large number 'flooding' the United Kingdom, in actual fact, figures suggest that Germany and Italy attracted some of the largest numbers. While difficult to gain exact figures, 2004 estimates for the Sinti and Roma population of Germany stood at approximately 70,000, with an additional 100,000 Roma carrying foreign citizenship. They were concentrated in the main cities, particularly Berlin and the conurbations around Hamburg, the Rhine–Ruhr region, the Rhine-Main and Rhine–Neckar areas.[97] As in the post-1945 years, their movement was part of a far bigger migration from Eastern Bloc countries to the West, which included the resettlement of ethnic Germans from former communist states.

Their arrival in western Europe revealed the often very partial nature of wider society's acceptance of the presence of Roma and Sinti. Although politically the German state had moved towards full recognition of their persecution under Nazism, this did not translate into more open attitudes towards them.[98] Very quickly virulent anti-Gypsy prejudice became tied up with intensifying debates over both immigration and integration. Owing to its high living standards and relatively liberal refugee laws, Germany saw an increase in immigration and asylum claims from Asia and Africa, at the same time as it was experiencing the socio-economic traumas of reunification. Between January and September 1991 about 91,000 Romanian citizens entered Germany, with Roma activist Nicholae Gheorghe estimating that 81 per cent of them were Roma, and the following year 33,600 Romanian Roma arrived in Germany. By late 1991 the beginning of the conflict in former Yugoslavia had ensured that a steady stream of Roma immigrants entered Germany as asylum seekers.

Often depicted as acting in flagrant defiance of German bourgeois values of stability, order and cleanliness, no other immigrant group attracted the same level of negative attention as the Roma. They were routinely accused of aggressively begging in the street, mugging those who refused to part with their money voluntarily, with Rostock locals, for example, complaining how they 'left rubbish in the streets, stole from shops and threatened shopkeepers'. More generally they were seen as 'poisoning the atmosphere through their misbehaviour'. In common with the actions of far-right groups across Europe, this general atmosphere was used to justify assaults on individuals, attacks on property, arson and harassment: Rostock saw the torching of a building housing Roma asylum seekers in August 1992, an act that received vocal local support.[99] Such 'potent manifestations of racism', which included an increase in support for extreme right-wing parties and 'an enormous upsurge' in the number of racial attacks – from 270 to 1,483 attacks and three deaths in six months in 1991 alone – were not exclusive to Germany.[100]

In Britain, the influx of particularly Bosnian Roma in the early 1990s, while creating a predictable furore in the tabloid media, remained overshadowed by the worsening situation of the British Gypsy Traveller population. Numbers on the road had been swelled by the emergence of growing numbers of 'New Travellers', whose roots lay in the 1960s free-festival movement, but whose numbers increased in the 1980s due to high unemployment and homelessness. By the early 1990s 'New Traveller' culture crossed over with the growing free party scene, adding to public panic about anarchic hordes of 'nomads'. Pressurized by hysterical media reports the government saw a crackdown on travelling as a popular means of reinforcing its position as 'the party of law and order'. Its subsequent 1994 Criminal Justice Act targeted a range of 'unacceptable' activities and lifestyles, and hit the Gypsy Traveller community in fundamental ways: travelling or stopping in groups of more than six vehicles became a criminal offence and crucially the act removed the obligation of local authorities to provide public sites. In its place was the requirement for Gypsies and Travellers to take responsibility for buying and developing their own land, with government asserting that the planning system was 'perfectly capable' of facilitating adequate site provision.[101]

Developments in human rights legislation, the rise of local health and education initiatives sympathetic to Gypsy Traveller culture, and a new wave of research-based political lobbying led by the Traveller Law Research Unit, demonstrated that it was possible for settled society to open up new approaches to Gypsy Travellers. And yet overall these positive developments were outweighed by the post-1994 planning and enforcement regime that proved a disaster for Gypsies and Travellers. Local authorities, many of whom had already proved reluctant to give permission for council-run sites under the act of 1968, were now expected to decide individual planning applications in the face of intense community hostility. On average 90 per cent of Gypsy Traveller applications were rejected and a rapidly growing number faced eviction from their own land for breach of planning regulations, so by 2006 there were around 1,200 such sites subject to council enforcement action.[102] High-profile evictions of Gypsy Travellers from their own land which had not been granted planning permission, such as that of 80 families from Dale Farm in Essex in the autumn of 2011, were the inevitable outcome of leaving site provision in the hands of local authorities driven more by a concern to pacify other residents than to provide stable accommodation options for some of Britain's most marginalized citizens.

The worsening situation across Europe was not passively accepted by Roma, and indeed the hostility faced by them either within their own nations or as migrants spawned a new wave of Roma activists. Within Germany, for example, coming as they did from a refugee perspective, activists often found their natural constituency within a pan-European Romani nationalism that transcended traditional boundaries of clan structure and country of origin. Fighting to legitimize the presence of Roma in western Europe post-1989, they often worked as much with international organizations – Roma, human rights and governmental – as within the structures of the German state. From here there emerged a radical challenge to liberal state policy questioning the automatic coupling of nationhood, citizenship and ethnicity.[103]

Outside the world of activism and within the new parliamentary systems of ex-socialist states, Roma across the region mobilized to form political groupings: the last Czechoslovak elections, held in 1990, saw the Roma Civic Initiative gain two seats in the federal parliament; while in Bulgaria the Democratic Union of Gypsies by May 1990 claimed a membership of 50,000. It was headed by the prominent Roma activist Manush Romanov who won a seat in Parliament the same year, as did a number of Muslim Roma as representatives of the Turkish Party for Rights and Freedom. However, as was the story across Europe, attempts to create a single political voice for Roma rapidly disintegrated; by early 1992 there were three separate Roma political organizations and five more focused on cultural matters. Divisions between Muslim and Christian Roma, and cultural and linguistic differences, continued to ensure that the country's Gypsies had no one representative voice.[104]

Where there was more success, however, was in grass-roots organizations and other NGOs, working as often with national government as in Gypsy quarters, aimed at improving the position of Roma on the ground. This was supported by a new pan-European language of human rights alongside a theoretical respect for minority differences. While often rhetoric rather than reality, human and minority rights legislation within the European Union provided a framework in which activists and NGOs could make claims on national states. It was, for example, through an appeal to the European Court of Human Rights that British Gypsy Travellers on council-run sites were finally granted the same rights as other council tenants. Supported by research and the Council of Europe's Recommendation on Gypsies in Europe of 1993, official recognition was granted to the existence and special position of the large settled Gypsy populations across the Continent, as well as nomadic groups. Recommendations ranging from the teaching of cultural activities, promotion of the Romani language, to particular housing and educational programmes and measures to encourage the participation of Roma and Gypsies in these processes were backed up by EU, or sometimes American, money.[105] While the translation of EU-wide initiatives and money to the local level was not unproblematic, for communities able and willing to act within funding frameworks, they opened up the possibility for material and social improvements.[106] Similarly across ex-socialist states these developments spawned a range of initiatives from trying to challenge the underrepresentation of Roma in the police, to providing funds for small enterprises run by or employing Roma, to initiatives reducing school drop-out rates and fostering a new generation of Roma leaders. Education projects that combined placing Roma children in mainstream schooling with providing free school meals and textbooks and extra language tuition gradually began to bear fruit, a process which was aided by the emergence of a new generation of Roma teachers.[107] Often piecemeal, underfunded and localized, nevertheless these programmes demonstrated that majority society, as much as the Roma themselves, needed to take responsibility for the long-standing marginalization and discrimination faced by Roma.

These years also saw the explosion of a new cultural phenomenon amongst Roma, Gypsy and Traveller communities: an assertive Pentecostalism. First emerging in France in the immediate postwar period, and tied to the annual pilgrimage to 'Saint Sara' at Saintes-Maries-de-la-Mer in the south of France, the movement was centred around the Mission Évangelique Tzigane (MÉT) under its founder, Pastor Clément le Cossec in 1958. By 1985 it claimed 30,000 baptized and 60,000 faithful from all different groups of Gypsies, Gitans, Roma and Manouches.[108] After 1989 the movement spread rapidly among the Roma of former socialist countries, leading to the emergence of a new 'Gypsy evangelical' culture. Unlike nineteenth-century mission movements that positioned Gypsy identity in opposition to Christianity, and where the consequence of conversion was leaving Gypsy culture behind, this movement combined the two. Le Cossec repeatedly emphasized the significance of 'being Gypsy' within the Church. In practical terms this meant promoting Romani translations of the Bible and pushing education and literacy, as well as being involved in anti-racist action alongside Gypsies, and providing the organizational tools to arrange festivals and mass summer conventions.[109] From Irish Travellers in Galway to the Roma of Macedonia and Greece, the movement prompted the creation of new social spaces and ways of interacting, so that religious seminars and larger conferences of the congregation took the place of fairs and other annual gatherings in people's social calendars, suggesting that new ways of 'being Roma' were beginning to evolve.[110]

THE FIRST YEARS of the 21st century saw growing numbers of Roma, Gypsies and Travellers literate, with access to a language of human rights and cultural dignity that stemmed from the Gypsy Power movements of the 1960s as much as it did from a more general shift in society towards multiculturalism. And yet, despite these changes, and alongside official acceptance that assimilatory strategies were neither appropriate nor particularly effective, materially and socially their position seemed little better than in the immediate aftermath of the Second World War. By 2005 an opinion poll revealed that Gypsy Travellers were the minority group British people found most threatening and were most likely to feel negatively towards.[111] This was indicative of how antipathy towards Gypsies, always present in settled society, had increased across the Continent over the course of the late twentieth century. Despite belated developments in legislation giving some limited protection to Roma, Gypsies and Travellers, their position remained vulnerable. A widening gap between their style of living and the mainstream, a reduction in everyday, economic and unproblematic interactions and their growing physical isolation on ghettoized official sites or shanty areas, all reinforced a sense of alienation. In popular imagination Gypsies became delinquent predators on settled communities, bringing criminality, rubbish and antisocial behaviour, with their presence to be resisted at any price. Across Europe the presence of Roma asylum seekers and migrants became emblematic of the uncertainties, economic chaos and explosion of migration brought on by the collapse of the Soviet bloc. More than five centuries after their first arrival on the Continent, in the minds of the mass of the population Gypsies were apparently no more European citizens than when they first presented their letters of penance to the authorities guarding Hildesheim city gates in 1417.

AFTERWORD

IT STARTED WITH A DEATH: on 16 July 2012 a *gens du voyage* was killed by police near Saint-Romain-sur-Cher in central France, prompting rioting from his community and a military force of several hundred being deployed against them. A few days later, in Grenoble, a robbery and shooting at a casino by 'foreign-born French nationals' resulted in two deaths, including that of a policeman. These two events formed the backdrop of Sarkozy's speech talking of the 'failure of a fifty-year period of unregulated immigration': he called for foreigners who killed police officers to be stripped of French citizenship, and for the dismantling of the more than 500 illegal Roma camps across the country. In the time leading up to the evictions and deportations tensions continued to mount on both sides, including high-profile resistance to the eviction of a large camp outside Bordeaux and the leaking of government plans revealing how foreign Roma camps were the focus for the crack-down. In October a further leak confirmed the existence of a database used by the police and maintained by the 'Interministerial task force against travelling crime'.[1] It had been created in 1997 and collected information on three categories of people – 'travelling people (Gypsies)', 'teams from rough urban areas' and 'travelling criminals from eastern Europe (Roma . . .)' – on the grounds that their nomadism allowed them to evade traditional policing and legal borders.

Throughout, the rhetoric of the right-wing government and the popular press conflated Roma and *gens du voyage*, illegal immigration, criminality and nomadism and questioned the basis of all camps in France. Not only were Roma, who were EU citizens and eligible to travel to every Schengen country, positioned as 'illegal immigrants', but the net was cast so wide as to condemn anyone with links to 'Gypsy' communities. By October the clearance of camps had resulted in 1,230 Roma being deported despite protests from Roma activists and the EU, which criticized France for contravening principles of freedom of movement and for singling out the Roma for racist and discriminatory measures.[2]

After going through over 1,000 years of Gypsy and Roma history, this 'summer of shame' holds few surprises, as it contained many of the threads we have followed: fears of nomadism and its ability to evade controls; the idea of 'the Gypsy' as the perpetual foreigner; the willingness of governments to conflate different 'deviant' populations and target repressive measures at them. The inter-ministerial task force was strongly reminiscent of Munich's Gypsy police force, and we have seen how deportations have been one of the state's weapons since the early modern period. But the events were also revealing of some more recent trends: an assertive Roma political voice, and a new Europe-wide regulatory framework accepting both that movement beyond national borders was in principle part of 'normal' behaviour and that ethnic minorities should not be the target of discrimination.

But illuminating as it was, this cannot tell the whole story. So long positioned as outsiders, in fact genetic mapping as much as the genealogies constructed by the Munich police reveal the extent to which, whether settled or mobile, Romani people's heritages are as intimately bound to the European population as they are to an original Indian ancestry. And while dominant over the past 200 years, in fact the idea of the nation state encompassing its 'natural' population is very recent. For most of history Gypsies lived within relatively fluid imperial systems that were less ambitious in terms of how they might manage their populations, and more open to the idea of outsiders. Evidence from the Venetian as well as Ottoman empires shows how they rapidly became integrated into their feudal and military systems. And indeed, that the Ottoman Empire was quite capable of managing nomadism and taxing nomads is revealing of the paucity of imagination of modern bureaucratic states with their insistence on settled residence as a key indicator of citizenship.

This leads us into reflecting just how important were pre-conceived ideas and stereotypes of Gypsies in governing their relationship with states. Although this history has demonstrated the importance of national contexts – not just the toxic combination of factors producing the Roma Holocaust, but equally the British focus on 'respectability' or the seventeenth-century Spanish preoccupation with blood purity – stereotypes across time and place in fact remained remarkably persistent. Ideas of criminality and foreignness fed into their stigmatization and punishment alongside other deviant groups, most often vagrants, but also other minority peoples such as Jews. In turn, as Europe moved into the modern period and states became surer of their powers, the treatment of Gypsies illustrated both the ambitions of liberal states to 'reform' and assimilate marginal groups and a continued and sometimes overwhelming preoccupation with racial determinism.

And within all this, central to Roma experience has been their ability to find gaps and spaces in which they might continue to exist and even sometimes to thrive. We have seen this in their economic activities, where they often exploited niches which settled communities were unable to fulfil; and in their adaption, for example, to the challenges of transportation to the New World. Throughout the early modern period, it was their ability to move to the margins as much as the limitations on state power that enabled them to survive what could have been a devastating wave of legislative repression. And indeed, even at the height of state control over their lives, during Nazism and Communism, testimonies of Roma and Sinti reveal how they were able to evade and sometimes confront repression. These tactics have not been without their costs to communities: everyday resistance in order to evade authoritarian controls or assimilationist policies could also reinforce stereotypes of untrustworthiness and deviance and feed into further justifications for repression or discrimination. The final decades of the twentieth century saw the emergence on the international and national levels of an assertive Roma activism that aimed to give voice and representation to its people. However, long-standing divisions between groups (nomadic/settled, Muslim/Christian, 'citizen'/ 'foreigner'), the material difficulties of organizing a highly dispersed and marginalized community, and the wall of prejudice they have needed to surmount, has meant that their effectiveness has been limited. Despite a gradual embracing of literacy and something of a cultural renaissance, manifested in part by the groundswell of Romani evangelism, Gypsies, Roma and Travellers still find their place in the 21st century contested and uncertain.

Appropriately we will end with the words of Ilona Lacková, a Slovakian Roma whose life was bound up with sweep of the twentieth century. An Auschwitz survivor, she returned to face life under Communism, benefiting briefly from the post-war Roma renaissance before being consigned to the margins. Her career as a writer and spokesperson for the Roma flourished after socialism's collapse in 1989, and she lived to see her memoirs translated into Czech, Slovak, French, Italian and Hungarian: 'It's the end of the war, we've survived. After darkness comes the dawn. But after every dawn also comes the darkness. Who knows what's in store for us.'[3]

REFERENCES

Preface

1 B. Donovan, 'Changing Perceptions of Social Deviance: Gypsies in Early Modern Portugal and Brazil', *Journal of Social History*, XXVI/1 (1992), p. 33.
2 E. M. Hall, 'Gentile Cruelty to Gypsies', *Journal of the Gypsy Lore Society* (hereafter *JGLS*), 3rd series, XI/2 (1932), pp. 49–56.
3 Sinti are a traditionally nomadic group whose presence in Germany dates back at least to the sixteenth century. By the late nineteenth century they had extended their presence to Belgium, the Netherlands, northern Italy, France and Russia.

Introduction: In Search of the 'True Gypsy'?

1 C. Clark, 'Who are the Gypsies and Travellers of Britain?', in *Here to Stay: The Gypsies and Travellers of Britain*, ed. C. Clark and M. Greenfield (Hatfield, 2006), p. 11. The best overview of the debate is contained in D. Mayall, *Gypsy Identities, 1500 to 2000: From Egipcyians and Moon-men to the Ethnic Romany* (London and New York, 2004).
2 Quoted in R. A. Scott Macfie, 'John Sampson, 1862–1981', *JGLS*, 3rd series; VI/1 (1932), pp. 3–23, p. 6. G. Borrow, *Romany Rye* (London, 1948), p. x.
3 See for example G. Hall, *The Gypsy's Parson, his Experiences and Adventures* (London, 1915), pp. 3–4; H. T. Crofton, 'Affairs of Egypt, 1882–1906', *JGLS*, new series, I/4 (1908), pp. 366–7.
4 M. A. Crowther, 'The Tramp', in *Myths of the English*, ed. R. Porter (Cambridge, 1992), pp. 91–113.
5 A. Symons, 'In Praise of Gypsies', *JGLS*, new series, I/4 (1908), pp. 295–9.
6 E. Waugh, 'Children of the Wilderness', in J. Sampson, *The Wind on the Heath: A Gypsy Anthology* (London, 1930), p. 12. See also D. Yates, *My Gypsy Days, Recollections of a Romani Rawnie* (London, 1953), p. 17; and Symons, 'In Praise of Gypsies', p. 296.
7 A. Thesleff, 'Report on the Gypsy Problem', trans H. Ehrenborg, *JGLS* new series, V/2 (1911), pp. 83–85 and continued in *JGLS* VI/4 (1911), p. 266.
8 D. Mayall, *Gypsy-Travellers in Nineteenth Century Society* (Cambridge, 1988), p. 78.
9 Quoted in A. Fraser, *The Gypsies* (Oxford, 1995), pp. 22–3.

10 See J. Sampson, *The Dialect of the Gypsies of Wales* (Oxford, 1926).

11 See for example E. Marushiakova and V. Popov, *Gypsies in the Ottoman Empire* (Hatfield, 2001); D. Kenrick, *Gypsies from the Ganges to the Thames* (Hatfield, 2004), p. 10.

12 E. Marushiakova and V. Popov, *Gypsies (Roma) in Bulgaria* (Frankfurt am Main, 1997) and their *Gypsies in the Ottoman Empire*.

13 Kenrick, *Gypsies from the Ganges to the Thames*, p. 10.

14 I. Medizabal et al., 'Reconstructing the Population History of European Romani from Genome-wide Data', *Current Biology*, XXII/4 (2012), pp. 2342–9.

15 Two contrasting findings are found in M. Nagy et al., 'Searching for the Origin of Romanies: Slovakian Romani, Jats of Haryana and Jat Sikhs Y-STR Data in Comparison with Different Romani Populations', *Forensic Science International*, CLXIX/1 (2007), pp. 19–26; and I. Mendizabal et al., 'Reconstructing the Indian Origin and Dispersal of the European Roma: A Maternal Genetic Perspective', *PLoS One*, VI/1 (2011); D. Gresham et al., 'Origins and Divergence of the Roma (Gypsies)', *American Journal of Human Genetics*, LXIX/6 (2001), pp. 1314–31.

16 I. Hancock, 'Mind the Doors! The Contribution of Linguistics', in *All Change! Romani Studies through Romani Eyes*, ed. D. le Bas and T. Acton (Hatfield, 2010), p. 6.

17 While they differ in their conclusions, probably the two most thorough linguistic overviews for the non-specialist are Fraser's *The Gypsies*, chapter one, and Hancock's, 'Mind the Doors!', pp. 5–26.

18 The different positions may be summed up in Hancock, 'Mind the Doors!' and Kenrick *Gypsies from the Ganges to the Thames*; see also Fraser, *The Gypsies*, chapter one; and R. Turner, 'The Position of Romani in Indo-Aryan', *JGLS*, 3rd series, I/5 (1926), pp. 145–89 on the specific point of departure from India.

19 G. C. Soulis, 'The Gypsies in the Byzantine Empire and the Balkans in the Late Middle Ages', *Dumbarton Oaks Papers*, 15 (1961), p. 163.

20 Soulis, 'Gypsies in the Byzantine Empire', p. 144. See also I. Hancock, *The Pariah Syndrome: An Account of Gypsy Slavery and Persecution* (Ann Arbor, MI, 1987), p. 9.

21 Fraser, *The Gypsies*, p. 35.

22 See E. Kohen, *History of the Byzantine Jews: A Microcosmos in the Thousand Year Empire* (Lanham, MD, 2007), pp. 76–7. For a general account of the iconoclastic period of Byzantine history see J. Herrin, *Byzantium: The Surprising Life of a Medieval Empire* (London, 2007), chapter ten.

23 Soulis provides the best account of the etymological discussion surrounding this word in his 'Gypsies in the Byzantine Empire', pp. 145–6.

24 Kenrick, *Gypsies from the Ganges to the Thames*, p. 35.

25 *The Life of Saint George the Athonite* was written by his disciple George the Small at the Monastery of Iveron in *c.* 1068. The Latin translation of the relevant portion of text and discussion can be found in Soulis, 'Gypsies in the Byzantine Empire', p. 145.

26 This quotation and the subsequent discussion is taken from Soulis, 'Gypsies in the Byzantine Empire', p. 147.

27 See Marushiakova and Popov, *Gypsies in the Ottoman Empire*, p. 38.
28 Fraser, *The Gypsies*, p. 50.
29 Soulis, 'Gypsies in the Byzantine Empire', pp. 153 and 158.
30 *The Pilgrimage of Arnold von Harff*, pp. 82–4, quoted in Soulis, 'Gypsies in the Byzantine Empire', p. 155.
31 Ibid.
32 E. O. Winstedt, 'The Gypsies of Modon and the "Wyne of Romeney"', *JGLS*, new series, 3 (1909–10), p. 61.
33 K. Barkey, *Empire of Difference: The Ottomans in Comparative Perspective* (Cambridge, 2008) pp. 12–13.
34 For a general discussion on the emergence of serfdom in the early modern period see K. Kaser, 'Serfdom in Eastern Europe', in *Family Life in Early Modern Times, 1500–1789*, ed. D. Kertzer and M. Barbagli (New Haven, CT, 2001), pp. 24–62.
35 N. Panaitecscu, 'Gypsies in Wallachia and Moldavia: A Chapter of Economic History', *JGLS*, 3rd series, XX/2 (1941), p. 67.
36 Kenrick, *Gypsies from the Ganges to the Thames*, p. 49.
37 Panaitecscu, 'Gypsies in Wallachia and Moldavia', pp. 58–72.
38 Rumelia literally means 'land of the Romans' and covered the area of the Balkans that had been Byzantine and stayed largely Christian. It essentially covered present-day Greece, European Turkey (Thrace) and Bulgaria. These documents are held at Başbakanlık Osmanlı Arşivi (BBOA), the Oriental Department of the St Cyril and Methodius National Library, Turkey, TD120 and TD370. I am indebted to Prof. Tomova at the Bulgarian Academy of Sciences who made available an early copy of the English version of S. Ivanova's article, 'A Historical Sketch of the Roma in the Bulgarian Lands at the Beginning of the Sixteenth Century' (2012), a version of which can be found at www.ceeol.com, on which much of the following discussion is based.
39 These figures are based on the analysis of the Macedonian historian Alexander Stojanovsky, who used an average of five persons per household to come to the whole population estimate. See Marushiakova and Popov, *Gypsies in the Ottoman Empire*, p. 29.
40 The extent of their migration is reflected in the register of 1523, which shows that a quarter of the Balkan Gypsy population were Muslim by this date. D. Petrovich, 'The Social Position of Gypsies in Some Yugoslav Countries in the Fifteenth and Sixteenth Centuries', *Journal of Yugoslav History* (1976), pp. 48–9. Cited in Ivanova, 'A Historical Sketch'.
41 See BBOA TD 370, c. 109.
42 This analysis is taken from Marushiakova and Popov, *Gypsies in the Ottoman Empire*, pp. 43–4.
43 See A. Stojanovski, *The Roma of the Balkan Peninsula* (Skopje, 1989), p. 141, cited in Ivanova, 'A Historical Sketch'.
44 *Muselem* were a volunteer force that originated in the early period of the Empire that was organized round the principle of the obligations of each ethnic group towards the sultan. Unlike the *sipahis* or the *janissaries* who participated in the elite regular army that was formed later, *muselem* did not receive state money and supported themselves by working. Their

military obligations were compensated through tax reliefs. The members of the corps were grouped into *oçacs* of 25 persons of whom five at any one time were on active service.

45 Petrovich, 'The Social Position of Gypsies', cited in Ivanova, 'A Historical Sketch'.

46 For a broader discussion of the development of the Ottoman bureaucratic system see I. Kunt, *The Sultan's Servants: The Transformation of Ottoman Provincial Government 1550–1650* (New York, 1983).

47 E. Ginio, 'Neither Muslims nor Zimmis. The Gypsies (Roma) in the Ottoman State', *Romani Studies* XIV/2 (2004), p. 118.

48 Marushiakova and Popov, *Gypsies in the Ottoman Empire*, p. 32.

49 See both Kunt, *The Sultan's Servants*, p. 14, and F. Çelik, 'Exploring Marginality in the Ottoman Empire: Gypsies or People of Malice (Ehl-i Fesad) as Viewed by the Ottomans', EUI Working Paper RSCAS, 39 (2004), p. 6 on this point.

50 BBOA TD370, 373. This translation comes from Marushiakova and Popov, *Gypsies in the Ottoman Empire*, pp. 32–3.

51 K. Barkey, *Empire of Difference*, p. 1.

52 Ibid. pp. 1 and 7. This insight also builds on the work of D. Lieven, *Empire. The Russian Empire and its Rivals* (New Haven, CT, 2000). More broadly on state practice see J. Scott, *Seeing Like a State, How Certain Schemes to Improve the Human Condition Have Failed* (New Haven, CT, 1998).

ONE Out of the Medieval World

1 For a general introduction to the period see E. Cameron, *Early Modern Europe* (Oxford, 1999), and his *The European Reformation* (Oxford, 1991); on the Dutch revolt against the Spanish, G. Darby, ed., *The Origins and Development of the Dutch Revolt* (London, 2001); J. Collins, *The State in Early Modern France* (Cambridge, 2010) and M. P. Holt, *The French Wars of Religion* (Cambridge, 2005) provide a good introduction to France in the period, with J. Casey, *Early Modern Spain: A Social History* (London and New York, 1999) and J. N. Hillgarth, *The Mirror of Spain, 1500–1700: The Formation of a Myth* (Ann Arbor, MI, 2000), give useful perspectives on Spain.

2 A. Fraser, *The Gypsies* (Oxford, 1995), chapter five.

3 F. de Vaux de Foletier, *Les tsiganes dans l'ancienne France* (Paris, 1961), p. 48.

4 Anon., *A Parisian journal 1405–1449*, trans. J. Shirley (Oxford, n.d.), pp. 218–19.

5 See for example P. Horden, *Freedom of Movement in the Middle Ages* (Oxford, 2006).

6 P. Spufford, 'Trade in Fourteenth Century Europe', in *New Cambridge Medieval History*, vol VI, ed. M. Jones (Cambridge, 2000), p. 188.

7 Trans. of H. Cornerus, *Chronica novella usque ad annum 1435*, in J. G. Eccard, *Corpus historicum medii aevi* (Leipzig, 1723), 2:1225, in Fraser, *The Gypsies*, p. 67.

8 D. Abulafia, 'The Coming of the Gypsies: Cities, Princes, Nomads', in
   P.C.M. Hoppenbrouwers, A. Janse and R. Stein, eds, *Power and Persuasion.*
   Essays on the Art of State Building in Honour of W.P. Blockmans
   (Turnhout, 2011) pp. 325–42.

9 Argot here is used to describe the informal language or 'cant' used
   generally by vagrants and others. For more detail on the broader
   argument see R Jütte, *Poverty and Deviance in Early Modern Europe*
   (Cambridge, 1994), chapter ten.

10 D. Pym, 'The Pariah Within: Early Modern Spain's Gypsies', *Journal*
   of Romance Studies IV/2 (2004), p. 33.

11 On travel and pilgrimage in this period see for example R. Allen, ed.,
   Eastward Bound: Travel and Travellers, 1050–1550 (Manchester, 2004);
   Horden, *Freedom of Movement*; J. Verdon, *Travel in the Middle Ages,*
   trans. G. Holoch (Notre Dame, 2003).

12 M. Boes, 'Unwanted Travellers? The Tightening of City Borders in Early
   Modern Germany', in T. Betteridge, ed., *Borders and Travellers in Early*
   Modern Europe (Aldershot, 2007), pp. 87–112.

13 The exact words were 'und hetten brieff, wer in nut ir almusen gab, dem
   mochten sy stellen', from E. O. Winstedt, 'Some records of the Gypsies
   in Germany, 1407–1792', *JGLS*, 3rd series, XI/3 (1932), p. 101. The coinage
   of the different German states in this period is highly complex and
   localized, with silver groschens and gold guldens emerging as the most
   common large denomination coins by the early fifteenth century. Gold
   shortages in the mid-fifteenth century resulted in the production of the
   silver guldengroschen, which, by the following century, spread across
   Europe as the thaler. It is likely that Winstedt, in translating these
   documents, made a stab at converting the currencies into pounds, but
   we don't know, however, if he then articulated this in 1930s values. Given
   the large sums he cites, it seems reasonable to suppose that he did.

14 Sigismund (1368–1437) was King of Hungary from 1387; in 1411 the
   electors gave him the German crown, effectively making him Holy
   Roman Emperor, although he was not actually crowned by the pope
   until 1433. During his attempt to end the schism of the Church via
   the Council of Constance (1414–18), the town became a key centre for
   his court.

15 Cited in Fraser, *The Gypsies*, pp. 64–5.

16 *A Parisian Journal*, pp. 217–18; and quoted in F. de Vaux de Foletier, 'Le
   pèlerinage romain des Tsiganes en 1422 et les lettres du Pape Martin V',
   Etudes Tsiganes, 4 (1965), pp. 13–24.

17 Andreas, 'The Gypsy Visit to Rome in 1422', *JGLS*, 3rd series, XI/3–4(1932),
   pp. 111–15.

18 Fraser, *The Gypsies*, p. 64.

19 Boes, 'Unwanted Travellers?', pp. 87–112.

20 E. O. Winstedt, 'Some Records of the Gypsies in Germany, 1407–1792',
   JGLS, 3rd series, XII/3 (1933), p. 123.

21 Vaux de Foletier, *Les tsiganes dans l'ancienne France*, pp. 46 and 49.

22 Boes, 'Unwanted Travellers?', p. 90.

23 M. Montaigne, 'Of Cannibals', trans. J. M. Cohen, in *Essays* (London,
   1958), p. 109. For a reflection on how differences between Europeans and

the people they encountered often became compressed into depictions of cannibals, see T. Betteridge, 'Introduction: Borders, Travel and Writing', in Betteridge, *Borders and Travellers*, pp. 1–14.

24 A. Pagden, *European Encounters with the New World: From Renaissance to Romanticism* (New Haven, CT, 1993), p. 13.

25 Abulafia, 'The Coming of the Gypsies', p. 326. This is not to argue that there was no persecution before this period. See R. I. Moore, *Formation of a Persecuting Society: Power and Deviance in Western Europe, 950–1250* (Oxford, 1987).

26 Boes, 'Unwanted Travellers?', pp. 88–9.

27 For example from Erfurt, 1458; Mainz, 1470; Bamberg, 1478; Magdeburg, 1493; Nuremburg and Ulm, 1499; and Regensburg 1519.

28 Boes, 'Unwanted Travellers?', pp. 93–6.

29 Ibid., pp. 101–3.

30 It is important to note, however, that this period of repression in western Europe coincided with an opening up of society for Jews in Poland in particular, leading to its becoming the centre of Jewish culture and religious development.

31 See R. Muchembled, 'The Witches of the Cambresis: The Acculturation of the Rural World in the Sixteenth and Seventeenth centuries', in *Religion and the People, 800–1700*, ed. J. Obelkevich (Chapel Hill, NC, 1979), pp. 221–76.

32 R. Briggs, *Witches and Neighbours: The Social and Cultural Context of European Witchcraft* (New York, 1996).

33 Jütte, *Poverty and Deviance*, p. 120.

34 M. K. McIntosh, *Controlling Misbehavior in England, 1370–1600* (Cambridge, 1998).

35 Hereford Archives, BG/11/28. Misc. Papers, vol. 6, item 18, 17 August 1530. I am indebted to Tom Johnson not only for drawing this fragment to my attention, but for the analysis.

36 See for example L. Abreu, *Monitoring Health Status and Vulnerable Groups in Europe: Past and Present* (Santiago de Compostela, 2006) on Portugal's harsh treatment of its indigent poor as early as the fourteenth century.

37 C. Dyer, 'Poverty and its Relief in Late Medieval England', *Past and Present*, 216 (2012), pp. 41–78.

38 A. L. Beier, *Masterless Men: The Vagrancy Problem in England, 1560–1640* (London, 1987), p. ix.

39 Dyer, 'Poverty and its Relief', p. 41. This article provides a good overview of the latest thinking on this subject.

40 O. P. Grell and A. Cunningham, eds, *Health Care and Poor Relief in Protestant Europe, 1500–1700* (London, 1997), p. 3. See also Verdon, *Travel in the Middle Ages*, p. 106.

41 Beier, *Masterless Men*, pp. 4–5.

42 Here I have updated the list suggested in Beier, *Masterless Men*, p. 5.

43 L. Abreu, 'Beggars, Vagrants and Romanies: Repression and Persecution in Portuguese Society (14th–18th Centuries)', www.ep.liu.se/ej/hygiea (accessed 14 October 2012).

44 Boes, 'Unwanted Travellers?', p. 99.

45 In addition, legislation governing vagrancy and poor relief was passed in
    Leisning, in 1523–4; Zurich, Mons and Ypres, 1525; Venice, 1527–8; Lyon,
    Rouen, Geneva, between 1531 and 1535; Paris, Madrid, Toledo and London,
    1540; the Netherlands, 1531; England 1531, 1536, 1547; Brandenburg and
    Castile 1540, France 1536 and 1566. See Jütte, *Poverty and Deviance*, p. 105.

46 Pym, 'The Pariah Within', pp. 21–35.

47 A. Bancroft, *Roma and Gypsy-Travellers in Europe: Modernity, Race,
    Space, and Exclusion* (Aldershot, 2005), p. 17.

48 Cited in J. Watts de Peyster, *Gypsies. Information Translated and
    Gathered from Various Sources* (New York, 1885), p. 12.

49 E. O. Winstedt, 'Some Records of the Gypsies in Germany, 1407–1792.
    Conclusion', *JGLS*, 3rd series, XIII/2 (1934), p. 99.

50 R. Pym, *The Gypsies of Early Modern Spain, 1425–1783* (Basingstoke, 2007).

51 For an introduction to this see J. Casey, *Early Modern Spain: A Social
    History* (London and New York, 1999) and Hillgarth, *The Mirror
    of Spain*.

52 A. J. Cruz and M. E. Perry, 'Introduction', in *Culture and Control in
    Counter-Reformation Spain*, ed. A. J. Cruz and M. E. Perry (Minneapolis,
    MN, 1992).

53 B. Donovan, 'Changing Perceptions of Social Deviance: Gypsies in Early
    Modern Portugal and Brazil', *Journal of Social History*, XXVI/1 (1992),
    pp. 33–53.

54 R. Pym 'Law and Disorder: Anti-Gypsy Legislation and its Failures in
    Seventeenth Century Spain', in *Rhetoric and Reality in Early Modern
    Spain*, ed. R. Pym (London, 2006), pp. 41–56.

55 Pym, 'The Pariah Within', pp. 21–35. See also B. Leblon, *Los gitanos de
    España* (Barcelona, 2001), p. 27; and Gil Ayuso Faustino, ed., *Textos y
    disposiciones legales de Castilla impresos en los siglos XVI y XVII*
    (Madrid, 1935), pp. 12–13.

56 C. Pérez de Herrera, *Amparo de pobres* [1598] (Madrid, 1975), p. 177,
    quoted in Pym, 'The Pariah Within'.

57 Pym, 'The Pariah Within', pp. 21–35, and Fraser, *The Gypsies*, p. 161.

58 J. P. Liégois, *Les tsiganes* (Paris, 1971), p. 14.

59 Vaux de Foletier, *Les tsiganes dans l'ancienne France*, pp. 52–3 and 57.

60 Fraser, *The Gypsies*, p. 142.

61 Vaux de Foletier, *Les tsiganes dans l'ancienne France*, pp. 86 and 89.

62 This is a translation of a decree of Sultan Selim II, 1574, to be found in
    E. Marushiakova and V. Popov, *Gypsies in the Ottoman Empire* (Hatfield,
    2001), p. 34.

63 Cited in Ibid., pp. 36–7.

64 Hans Dernschwam, *Tagebuch einer Reise nach Konstantinopel und
    Kleinasien 1553–55*, cited in Marushiakova and Popov, *Gypsies in the
    Ottoman Empire*, p. 49.

65 D. Crowe, *A History of the Gypsies of Eastern Europe and Russia*
    (Basingstoke, 2006), p. 107.

66 Fraser, *The Gypsies*, p. 59.

67 M. Gaster, 'Rumanian Gypsies in 1560', jgls, 3rd series, xii/1 (1933), p. 61.

TWO Breaking Bodies, Banishing Bodies

1 E. O. Winstedt, 'Some Records of the Gypsies in Germany. Conclusion', *JGLS*, 3rd series, XII/3 (1933), p. 101.
2 R. Pym 'Law and Disorder: Anti-Gypsy Legislation and its Failures in Seventeenth Century Spain', in *Rhetoric and Reality in Early Modern Spain*, ed. R. Pym (London, 2006), p. 41.
3 Winstedt, 'Some Records of the Gypsies in Germany. Conclusion', pp. 98–116.
4 Pym, 'Law and Disorder', p. 42.
5 A. Fraser, *The Gypsies* (Oxford, 1995), pp. 161–3.
6 D. Pym, 'The Pariah Within: Early Modern Spain's Gypsies', *Journal of Romance Studies*, IV/2 (2004), pp. 21–35.
7 Winstedt, 'Some Records of the Gypsies in Germany. Conclusion', pp. 100–101.
8 Daranes, 'False Passports', *JGLS*, 3rd series, XII/4 (1933), pp. 214–16. This account is based on the evidence of Fritsch in his *Praeclarissimus Dominus Ahasuerus Fritsch, J.U.C.* (1660).
9 J. Collins, *The State in Early Modern France* (Cambridge, 2010), p. 6; M. P. Holt's, *The French Wars of Religion* (Cambridge, 2005) also provides a good overview of France in this period.
10 See J. P. Liégois, 'Bohémiens et pouvoirs publics en France du XVème au XIXème siècle', *Études Tsiganes* IV/21 (1978), pp. 15–19; and B. Geremek, *Les fils de Cain. L'image des pauvres et des vagabonds dans la littérature européenne du XVe au XVIIe siècle* (Paris, 1991), pp. 78 and 358.
11 F. de Vaux de Foletier, *Les tsiganes dans l'ancienne France* (Paris, 1961), pp. 209–10.
12 H. Asséo, 'Des hommes à part: les Bohémiens en forêt XVIIIe siècle: Forêt, villageois et marginaux, XVIe–XXe siècle', in *Forêt, Villageois et marginaux*, ed. A. Corvol (Paris, 1990), pp. 30–35.
13 Vaux de Foletier, *Les tsiganes dans l'ancienne France*, p. 179.
14 See P. Bamford, *Fighting Ships and Prisons: The Mediterranean Galleys of France in the Age of Louis XIV* (Minneapolis, MN, 1973).
15 See R. Pike, *Penal Servitude in Early Modern Spain* (Madison, WI, 1983), chapter one.
16 L. Lucassen, 'Eternal Vagrants? State Formation, Migration and Travelling Groups in Western Europe, 1350–1914', in L. Lucassen, W. Willems and A. Cottaar, *Gypsies and Other Itinerant Groups: A Socio-historical Approach* (London and New York, 1998), p. 62.
17 F. Redlich, *The German Military Enterpriser and his Work Force: A Study in European Economic and Social History* (Wiesbaden, 1965), pp. 173–4.
18 Lucassen, 'Eternal Vagrants?', p. 63.
19 Winstedt, 'Some Records of the Gypsies in Germany', p. 192.
20 Ibid., 'Conclusion', pp. 103–5.
21 This was J. B. Weissenbruch, *Ausfuhrliche Relation von der famosen Ziegeuner-Diebs-Mord-und Rauber-Bande, welche De. 14. Und 15. Novembr. Ao 1726. zu Giessen durch Schwerdt, Strang und Rad, respective justificirt worden* (Frankfurt and Leipzig, 1727).
22 E. M. Hall, 'Gentile Cruelty to Gypsies', *JGLS*, 3rd series, XI/2 (1932), p. 50.

23 Winstedt, 'Some records of the Gypsies in Germany', pp. 104–5. His
    account is a translation from Karl von Weber's archival account of
    Saxony 1488–1792 entitled *Aus vier Jahrhunderten* (Leipzig, 1861).
24 Winstedt, 'Some Records of the Gypsies in Germany', 'Conclusion',
    pp. 105–7.
25 Hall, 'Gentile Cruelty to Gypsies', pp. 51–2.
26 Winstedt, 'Some Records of the Gypsies in Germany', 'Conclusion', p. 98.
27 Lucassen, 'Eternal Vagrants?', p. 63.
28 Winstedt, 'Some Records of the Gypsies in Germany', p. 193.
29 M. Foucault, *Discipline and Punish: The Birth of the Prison*, trans.
    A. Sheridan (New York, 1977).
30 Hall, 'Gentile Cruelty to Gypsies', pp. 49–56. Her account is based on
    the writings of Dr Weissenbruch who was an assessor at the tribunal.
    See Weissenbruch *Ausfuhrliche Relation von der famosen Ziegeuner-
    Diebs-Mord-und Rauber-Bande.*
31 A reproduction of this picture can be found fronting Hall's 'Gentile
    Cruelty to Gypsies'.
32 See Winstedt, 'Some Records of the Gypsies in Germany', pp. 135–40.
    His account is based on his translation of F. Sauter, *Württembergische
    Vierteljahrshefte für Landesgeschichte*, vol. IV (Stuttgart, 1881), which
    comes from surviving correspondence between the town of Netschetin
    and Casimir Graf von Kupperwaldt.
33 We have similar evidence of repeated legislation from other territories in
    this period too. For example, the Duchy of Silesia passed decrees in 1618,
    1619, 1683, 1685, 1688, 1689, 1695, 1703, 1706, 1708, 1715, 1721 and 1726, all
    of which were variations on Gypsies being banished or threatened with
    death, and that the local police/militia were to be used in order to enact
    the powers. Similarly in Saxony from 1579 to 1722. See Zedler's *Grosses
    Universal Lexicon aller Wissenschaten und Kunste welche, etc.* (Leipzig
    and Halle, 1749).
34 Winstedt, 'Some Records of the Gypsies in Germany', p. 132.
35 This reflection on the severity of the law in England in the eighteenth
    century (the 'Bloody Code') is attributed to George Savile, 1st Marquis
    of Halifax.
36 Cited in J. Watts de Peyster, *Gypsies. Information Translated and
    Gathered from Various Sources* (New York, 1885), pp. 12–13.
37 Winstedt, 'Some Records of the Gypsies in Germany',
    pp. 130–31.
38 Quoted in H. Asséo, *Les Tsiganes: Une destinée européenne* (Paris,
    1994), p. 123.
39 Cited in H.M.G. Grellmann, *Dissertation on the Gypsies, being an
    Historical Enquiry, Concerning the Manner of Life, Economy, Customs
    and Conditions of these People of Europe, and their Origin*, trans.
    M. Rapier (London, 1787), pp. 349–50.
40 Vaux de Foletier, *Les tsiganes dans l'ancienne France*, pp. 182, 185–9;
    R. Pym, *The Gypsies of Early Modern Spain, 1425–1783* (Basingstoke,
    2007).
41 Cited in Grellmann, *Dissertation on the Gypsies*, pp. 349–50.
42 Fraser, *The Gypsies*, p. 181.

43 See Pym, *Gypsies of Early Modern Spain*.

44 The Settlement Act's full title was *An Act for the Better Relief of the Poor of this Kingdom* (14 Car. II c.12). It was based on principles that went back to the 1388 Statute of Cambridge and allowed for the removal from a parish, back to their place of settlement, of newcomers whom local justices deemed 'likely to be chargeable' to the parish poor rates. Exemption was given if the new arrival was able to rent a property for at least £10 a year, but this was well beyond the means of an average labourer. Expensive legal battles often took place between a parish attempting to remove a pauper whom it claimed it had no duty to support, and the parish that it claimed did have responsibility.

45 This is based on a sample of records from Warwickshire, Sheffield, Dorset and Essex. See P. Slack, *Poverty and Policy in Tudor and Stuart England* (London and New York, 1988), p. 92.

46 The following is based on an analysis of the constables' accounts of Repton (Derbyshire); Utoxeter; Market Harborough; Melton Mowbray, Wymeswold and Stathern; and Ecclesfield set out in T. W. Thompson, 'Gleanings from Constables Accounts and Other Sources', *JGLS*, 3rd series, VII/1 (1928), pp. 30–47.

47 Ibid.

48 Ibid.

49 Oxford Quarter Sessions, August 1736, in Anon., 'Gypsies as Highwaymen and Footpads', *JGLS*, 3rd series, VI/2 (1927), pp. 70–72.

THREE The Dark Enlightenment

1 T. Coates, 'Social Exclusion: Practice and Fear of Exile (degredo) in Portuguese History: A Case Study of Castro Marim', *Campus Social: Revista Lusófona de Ciências Sociais*, 2 (2005), pp. 122–4.

2 Alvará of 15 April 1718 cited in B. Donovan, 'Changing Perceptions of Social Deviance: Gypsies in Early Modern Portugal and Brazil', *Journal of Social History*, XXVI/1 (1992), p. 38. The following account is based on this article.

3 M. Moraes, *Os Ciganos no Brasil: Contribuição ethnographica* (Rio de Janeiro, 1886), pp. 23–4.

4 A. de St-Hilare, *Viagem a provincial de Sao Paolo*, trans. R. Regis Junqueira (Sao Paolo, 1976), pp. 102–3, quoted in Dovovan, 'Changing Perceptions', p. 42.

5 M. Graham, *Journal of a Voyage to Brazil, and Residence There, During Part of the Years 1821, 1822, 1823* (London, 1824), pp. 253–4, quoted in Donovan, 'Changing Perceptions', p. 44.

6 Donovan, 'Changing Perceptions', pp. 33–53.

7 A. T. Sinclair, *American Gypsies: Edited from Manuscripts in the New York Public Library, with Additions, by George F. Black* (New York, 1917), p. 17.

8 See 'American Gypsies', *The Family Magazine, or Monthly Abstract of General Knowledge*, 2 (1835), pp. 86–7; and M. Sway, *Familiar Strangers: Gypsy Lives in America* (Champaign, IL, 1988), pp. 37–9.

9 Cited in B. Belton, *Questioning Gypsy Identity: Ethnic Narratives in Britain and America* (Walnut Creek, CA, and Oxford, 2005), pp. 73–5.

10 Ibid.

11 Ibid.

12 Statutes, 39 Eliz., c. 4., cited in ibid.

13 Donovan, 'Changing Perceptions', p. 39.

14 F. L. Olmsted, *Journey to the Seaboard Slave States* (New York, 1856), cited in Sinclair, *American Gypsies*, p. 18.

15 Anon., 'The Gypsies of Aleppo', *JGLS*, 3rd series, IX/2 (1930), p. 95. Quotes from A. Russell, *The Natural History of Aleppo* (London, 1756), p. 104, and R. Pococke, *A Description of the East* (London, 1745), pp. 207–8.

16 Translation published in 'Two Rumanian Documents concerning Gypsies', trans. M. Gaster, *JGLS*, 3rd series, IX/4 (1930), pp. 179–82.

17 'Two Rumanian Documents', pp. 179–82.

18 Phanariots were an Ottoman Christian elite that claimed a Byzantine heritage and who, despite structural impediments, imperial ideology and religious doctrine, ascended to power in the region from the mid-seventeenth century. For a discussion of their role in Ottoman strategies to maintain control of the Balkans in the eighteenth century see C. Philliou, 'Communities on the Verge: Unravelling the Phanariot Ascendancy in Ottoman Governance', *Comparative Studies in Society and History*, 51 (2009) pp. 151–81.

19 Mavrocordato ruled Moldavia on four occasions and Wallachia five times. D. Crowe, *A History of the Gypsies of Eastern Europe and Russia* (Basingstoke, 2006), pp. 110–11.

20 'Two Rumanian Documents', pp. 179–82.

21 Panaitecscu, 'The Gypsies in Wallachia and Moldavia: A Chapter of Economic History', *JGLS*, 3rd series, XX/2 (1941), pp. 69–70.

22 I. M. Zeitlin, *Jews. The Making of a Diaspora People* (Cambridge, 2012), p. 85.

23 For newer, critical approaches to the idea of 'the Enlightenment' see D. Goodman, *The Republic of Letters: A Cultural History of the French Enlightenment* (Ithaca, NY, 1994); C. Hesse, *The Other Enlightenment: How French Women Became Modern* (Princeton, NJ, 2001); J. Israel, *Enlightenment Contested: Philosophy, Modernity, and the Emancipation of Man, 1670–1752* (Oxford, 2006).

24 A controversial but useful introduction to primary sources on this topic is E. Chukwudi Eze, *Race and the Enlightenment: A Reader* (Cambridge, 1997).

25 E. Filhol, 'La Bohemienne dans les dictionnaires francais (XVIIIe–XIXe siècles): discours, histoire et pratiques socio-culturelles', in *La Bohemienne; figure poetique de l'errance aux XVIIIe et XIXe siècles*, ed. P. Auraix-Jonchiere and G. Loubinoux (Clermont-Ferrand, 2005), pp. 21–44.

26 W. Willems, *In Search of the True Gypsy: From Enlightenment to Final Solution* (London and Portland, OR, 1997).

27 H.M.G. Grellmann, *Dissertation on the Gypsies, being an Historical Enquiry, Concerning the Manner of Life, Economy, Customs and Conditions of these People of Europe, and their Origin*, trans. M. Rapier (London, 1787), p. i.

28 Ibid., pp. ix–xi and xv–xvi.

29 Ibid., pp. 83–4.

30 Ibid., pp. 83–4.

31 Ibid., pp. 84–5.

32 Willems, *In Search of the True Gypsy*, p. 30.

33 See D. Beales, *Enlightenment and Reform in Eighteenth Century Europe* (London and New York, 2005), and M. Hochedlinger, *Austria's Wars of Emergence: War, State and Society in the Habsburg Monarchy, 1683–1797* (Harlow and London, 2003) for a general history of the period.

34 Willems, *In Search of the True Gypsy*, pp. 31–2.

35 Ibid., pp. 34–5.

36 Grellmann, *Dissertation on the Gypsies*, pp. 70–71.

37 Ibid., p. 80.

38 Although this was a partial process, with the central authority of the state often resisted or ignored. See for example R. Mackay, *The Limits of Royal Authority: Resistance and Obedience in Seventeenth-Century Castile* (Cambridge, 1999).

39 Fraser, *The Gypsies*, pp. 163–4.

40 A. Gómez Alfaro, *The Great 'Gypsy' Round-up in Spain* (Strasbourg, n.d). See also his *The Great Gypsy Round-up: Spain; The General Imprisonment of Gypsies in 1749* (Madrid, 1993).

41 Zygmunt Bauman, *Modernity and the Holocaust* (Cambridge, 1989).

42 My analysis of the round-up is based on Gómez Alfaro, *Great 'Gypsy' Round-up*. For his full consideration of this topic see his *The Great Gypsy Round-up: Spain; The General Imprisonment of Gypsies in 1749*.

43 Gómez Alfaro, *Great 'Gypsy' Round-up*, p. 5.

44 An appeal from Bernardo Martínez de Malla, Cristóbal Bermúdez, Miguel Correa, Salvador Bautista and Pedro González quoted in Gómez Alfaro, *Great 'Gypsy' Round-up*, p. 101.

45 Gómez Alfaro, *Great 'Gypsy' Round-up*, p. 8.

46 Fraser, *The Gypsies*, pp. 166–7.

47 Ibid., p. 145.

48 F. de Vaux de Foletier, *Les tsiganes dans l'ancienne France* (Paris, 1961), p. 211; Fraser, *The Gypsies*, p. 147.

49 O. Hufton, 'Begging, Vagrancy, Vagabondage and the Law: an Aspect of the Problem of Poverty in Eighteenth-century France', *European History Quarterly*, 2 (1972), pp. 97–123.

FOUR Nationalism, Race and Respectability

1 T. Kontje, 'Gypsies and Orientalism in German Literature and Anthropology of the Long Nineteenth Century by Nicholas Saul: Review', *Modern Language Review*, CIII/4 (2008), pp. 1154–5.

2 Quoted in X. du Crest, 'Bohemiens, Gitans, Tsiganes et Romanichels dans la peinture francaise du XIXe siecle' in *Le mythe des Bohemiens dans la littérature et les arts en Europe*, ed. S. Moussa (Paris, 2008), p. 246.

3 T. Tetzner, *Geschichte der Zigeuner; ihre Herkunft, Natur und Art. Für gebildete Leser dargestellt* (Weimar and Ilmenau, 1835).

4 E. Filhol 'La Bohemienne dans les dictionnaires francais (XVIIIe–XIXe siècles): discours, histoire et pratiques socio-culturelles', in *La Bohemienne; figure poetique de l'errance aux XVIIIe et XIXe siècles*, ed. P. Auraix-Jonchiere and G. Loubinoux (Clermont-Ferrand, 2005), pp. 24–38.

5 L. Lucassen, 'A Blind Spot: Migratory and Travelling Groups in Western European Historiography', *International Review of Social History*, 2 (1993), pp. 209–35.

6 B. Whyte, *The Yellow on the Broom* (Edinburgh, 1979); and N. Joyce, *Travellers: An Autobiography* (Dublin, 1985).

7 J. Bloch, *Les Tsiganes*, (Paris, 1969).

8 A. Sutre, '"Les Bohémiens du pays": une inscription territoriale des Bohémiens dans le Sud-Ouest de la France au XIXème et au début du XXème siècle', unpublished MA thesis, Ecole des hautes études en sciences sociales (EHESS), 2010, pp. 159–60.

9 Ibid., p. 159.

10 F. de Vaux de Foletier, *Les bohémiens en France au 19ème siècle* (Paris, 1970), pp. 63–73 and 105.

11 L. Charnon-Deutsch, 'Travels of the Imaginary Spain Gypsy', in J. Labanyi, *Constructing Identity in Twentieth Century Spain: Theoretical Debates and Cultural Practice* (Oxford, 2002), pp. 22–40.

12 W. Willems. *In Search of the True Gypsy: From Enlightenment to Final Solution* (London and Portland, OR, 1997), p. 76.

13 In P. Panayi, *Ethnic Minorities in Nineteenth and Twentieth Century Germany: Jews, Gypsies, Poles, Turks and Others* (London, 2000), p. 53.

14 Ibid.

15 J. Baird, *The New Statistical Account of Roxburghshire* (Edinburgh, 1841).

16 Brunel was a civil servant for the French Council of Hygiene. E. Braga, 'Les Bohémiens de la Région Parisienne: entre fantasmes et réalités (1850–années 1930)', unpublished MA thesis, Université de Paris I, 2011, pp. 40–42.

17 G. Borrow, *Romano Lavo-Lil* (London, 1874), pp. 207–37.

18 A. Harding, *East End Underworld: Chapters in the Life of Arthur Harding*, ed. R. Samuel (London, 1981), pp. 220–21, 223.

19 J. Walton, 'Municipal Government and the Holiday Industry in Blackpool', in *Leisure in Britain, 1780–1939*, ed. J. Walton and J. Walvin (Manchester, 1983), pp. 159–85.

20 S. G. Boswell, *The Book of Boswell: The Autobiography of a Gypsy*, ed. J. Seymour (London, 1970), pp. 19–20.

21 P. Robert, 'La migration des Sinté piémontais en France au XIXème siècle', *Etudes Tsiganes* (2004), pp. 18–51.

22 A. Reyniers, 'Pérégrinations des Jénis en France au XIXe siècle', *Etudes Tsiganes*, II/2 (1991), pp. 19–25.

23 Vaux de Foletier, *Les bohémiens*, p. 101.

24 Reyniers, 'Pérégrinations des Jénis', p. 20.

25 A. Paspati, 'Turkish Gypsies', *JGLS*, 1st series, I/1 (1889), pp. 3–5; and more generally his *Études sur les Tchingianés ou Bohémiens de l'Empire Ottoman* (Constantinople, 1870).

26 E. Marushiakova and V. Popov, *Gypsies in the Ottoman Empire* (Hatfield, 2001), p. 69.

27 S.G.B. St Clair and C. A. Brophy, *A Residence in Bulgaria; or Notes on the Resources and Administration of Turkey: The Condition and Character, Manners, Customs and Language of the Christian and Mussulman Populations, with Preference to the Eastern Question* (London, 1869), pp. 7–11.

28 See for example N. Hampson, 'The Idea of Nation in Revolutionary France', in *Reshaping France: Town, Country and Region during the French Revolution*, ed. A. Forrest and P. Jones (Manchester, 1991), pp. 13–25.

29 M. Biondich, *The Balkans: Revolution, War, and Political Violence Since 1878* (Oxford, 2011). The most famous and cogent discussion of this 'invention' is Eric Hobsbawm and Terence Ranger's *The Invention of Tradition* (Cambridge, 1983).

30 For more on the political ideologies sustaining the Ottomans, see D. Goffmann, *The Ottoman Empire and Early Modern Europe* (Cambridge, 2002) and S. Deringil, *The Well Protected Domains: Ideology and the Legitimation of Power in the Ottoman Empire, 1876–1909* (London and New York, 1998).

31 An introduction to the different writings and perspectives on this complex topic can be found in M. Turda, 'National Historiographies in the Balkans, 1830–1989', in *The Contested Nation. Ethnicities, Class, Religion and Gender in National Histories*, ed. S. Berger and C. Lorenz (Basingstoke, 2011), pp. 463–89. See also T. Georgieva, 'Migrations in the History of Multi-ethnicity and Multiculturalism in the Balkans: Bulgarian Sources', in E. Popova and M. Hajdinjak, *Forced Ethnic Migrations in the Balkans: Consequences and the Rebuilding of Societies*, conference proceedings, Sofia, February 2005, pp. 13–20.

32 See their works, J. A. Vaillant, *Les Romes, histoire vraie des vrais Bohémiens* (Paris, 1857), and F Colson, *De l'etat present et de l'avenir des principautes de Moldavie et de Valachie; suivi des traits de la Turquie avec des puissances Europeannes, et d'une carte des pays Roumains* (Paris, 1839).

33 Vaillant *Les Romes*, quoted in E. Pons, *De la robie la asimilare* (1999), http://adatbank.transindex.ro, accessed 8 November 2012.

34 M. Kogălniceanu, *Esquisse sur l'histoire, les moeurs et la langue des Cigains* (Berlin, 1837), p. 16.

35 D. Crowe, *A History of the Gypsies of Eastern Europe and Russia* (Basingstoke, 2006), p. 115.

36 For a general introduction to the significance of the 1848 revolutions see J. Sperber, *The European Revolutions, 1848–51* (Cambridge, 2005).

37 A. Fraser, *The Gypsies* (Oxford, 1995), pp. 224–6.

38 Marushiakova and Popov, *Gypsies in the Ottoman Empire*, p. 86.

39 S. Tabakov, *An Attempt at a History of the Town of Sliven* (Sofia, 1911), quoted in Marushiakova and Popov, *Gypsies in the Ottoman Empire*, pp. 57–9.

40 Crowe, *History of the Gypsies*, pp. 7–8.

41 Ibid., p. 162.

42 C. Delclitte, 'Nomades et nomadisme : le cas de la France 1895–1912', unpublished MA thesis, Université de Paris VIII, 1994, p. 17.

43 Fraser, *The Gypsies*, p. 228.

44 Vaux de Foletier, *Les bohémiens*, pp. 123–4.

45 I. Hancock, *The Pariah Syndrome: An Account of Gypsy Slavery and Persecution* (Ann Arbor, MI, 1987), p. 37.

46 I. Brown, 'The Gypsies in America', *JGLS*, 3rd series VIII/4 (1929), p. 148.

47 Circular issued by the minister for the interior to prefects, 19 November 1864.

48 26,885 people were arrested as part of this coup. For details of their experiences of transportation see M. Spieler, *Empire and Underworld: Captivity in French Guiana* (Cambridge, MA, 2012).

49 Circular issued by the minister for the interior to prefects, 19 November 1864.

50 Vaux de Foletier, *Les bohémiens*, pp. 172 and 178.

51 Fraser, *The Gypsies*, p. 253.

52 W. A. Barbieri, *Ethics of Citizenship: Immigration and Group Rights in Germany* (Durham, 1998) 13.

53 Panayi, *Ethnic Minorities*, p. 10.

54 B. Vick, 'The Origins of the German Volk: Cultural Purity and National Identity in Nineteenth-Century Germany', *German Studies Review*, XXVI/2 (2003), pp. 241–56.

55 W. Solms, 'On the demonising of Jews and Gypsies in Fairy Tales', in, *Sinti and Roma: Gypsies in German-speaking Society and Literature*, ed. S. Tebbutt (New York and Oxford, 1998), pp. 91–104.

56 M. Fulbrook, *A Concise History of Germany* (Cambridge, 1999), pp. 114–15; K. Bade and J. Oltmer, 'Germany', in *The Encyclopedia of Migration and Minorities in Europe from the Seventeenth Century to the Present*, ed. K. Bade et al. (Cambridge, 2011), pp. 65–82. Between 1816 and 1914 around 5.5 million Germans emigrated to the USA.

57 'Bittschrift des Allgemeinen Deutschen Handels- und Gewerbevereins an die Bundesversammlung vom 20. April 1819 gemäss Friedrich List', *Schriften, Reden Briefe, Bd. 1* (Berlin 1929), in M. Görtenmaker, *Deutschland im 19. Jahrhundert* (Opladen, 1994).

58 Hessisches Staatsarchiv, Darmstadt, Germany (hereafter HStAD), G 15 Friedberg Q/Nr. 279, *Großherzoglich Hessische Zeitung*, Darmstadt, 17 April 1819.

59 HStAD/G 15 Friedberg Q/Nr. 279, The Grand Duchy Hessian Cabinet of the Province Upper Hesse to the various district administrations and police administrations in the province, Giessen, 8 December 1821.

60 See for example A. Green, *Fatherlands: State-building and Nationhood in Nineteenth-century Germany* (Cambridge, 2001). Thomas Mann's classic novel *Buddenbrooks* gives a fictionalized account of regional differences and social change from the 1830s to the 1870s.

61 R. Brubaker, *Citizenship and Nationhood in France and Germany* (Cambridge, MA, 1992), pp. 13–15.

62 Panayi, *Ethnic Minorities*, p. 52.

63 Quoted in Fraser, *The Gypsies*, p. 249.

64 L. Lucassen, 'Harmful Tramps: Police Professionalization and Gypsies in Germany, 1700–1945', in L. Lucassen, W. Willems and A-M. Cottaar, *Gypsies and other Itinerant Groups: A Socio-historical approach* (London and New York, 1998), p. 84.

65 A. K. Fahrmeir, 'Nineteenth Century German Citizenships.
    A Reconsideration', *Historical Journal* XL/3 (1997), pp. 721–52; see
    also Lucassen, 'Harmful Tramps'.

66 Foreigners might also become Prussian, but they had to prove, among
    other things that they had led an 'irreproachable life'. Brubaker,
    Citizenship and Nationhood, p. 13.

67 R. Salillas, *El delincuente espanol: el lenguaje* (Madrid, 1896), pp. 208–9,
    quoted in Charnon-Deutsch, 'Travels of the Imaginary Spanish Gypsy',
    pp. 24–5.

68 Lucassen, 'Harmful Tramps', p. 76.

69 Ibid., pp. 81–2.

70 HStAD: No. 42. Resolution of the Royal Ministry of the Interior II. Police
    treatment of Gypsies, April 1885.

71 See R. Kedward, *La vie en bleu* (London, 2005), p. 11; and R. Price,
    A Concise History of France (Cambridge, 2005), pp. 228–9 and 239.

72 D. Mayall, *Gypsy-Travellers in Nineteenth Century Society* (Cambridge,
    1988), p. 20.

73 Fraser, *The Gypsies*, p. 216.

74 Mayall, *Gypsy-Travellers*, Appendix 1, provides a summary of legislation
    affecting Travellers from 1530 to 1908.

75 Braga, 'Les Bohémians de la Région Parisienne'.

76 Vaux de Foletier, *Les bohémiens*, p. 170.

77 J-M. Berlière, 'La république et les nomades (1880–1914)', *Etudes Tsiganes*
    (2004), pp. 18–57.

78 G. Smith, *I've Been a'Gipsying* (London, 1882), Preface.

79 Report of the Select Committee on the Temporary Dwellings Bill
    (London 1887), pp. 45–6; detailed discussions of the earlier phase of
    Moveable Dwellings Bills can be found in Mayall, *Gypsy-Travellers*,
    chapter six, and G. K. Behlmer, 'The Gypsy Problem in Victorian
    England', *Victorian Studies*, XXVIII/2 (1985), pp. 231–55; and the later
    phase in B. Taylor, *A Minority and the State: Travellers in Britain in the
    Twentieth Century* (Manchester, 2008), chapter two.

80 Smith, *I've been a'Gipsying*, p. 242.

81 The National Archives, Kew (hereafter TNA), HO45/10529/147162/7,
    Pedder's notes on Select Committee, 24 October 1910.

82 Ibid.

83 Delclitte, 'Nomades et nomadisme', p. 73; Berlière, 'La république et les
    nomades', p. 52; and P. Lawrence, 'Images of Poverty and Crime: Police
    Memoirs in England and France at the End of the Nineteenth Century',
    Crime, Histoire et Sociétés, IV/1 (2000), pp. 73–4.

84 Following the annexation of Alsace-Lorraine residents were given fifteen
    months to choose between emigrating to France or remaining and
    legally becoming German. By 1876, about 100,000 (approximately 5 per
    cent) of the population had emigrated to France.

85 Berlière, 'La république et les nomades', p. 57; and Vaux de Foletier, *Les
    bohémiens*, p. 167.

86 Vaux de Foletier, *Les bohémiens*, 183.

FIVE Into the Flames

1 The term *porrajmos* ('tearing apart' or 'devouring' in Romani) has emerged as one way of describing the experience of Roma and Sinti during the Second World War. However, it is rejected by major segments of the Roma community as completely unacceptable because in a number of Romani dialects it is 'a term associated with rape; is obscene; is unmentionable in mixed company; and is regarded as highly inappropriate in the context of memorializing the events of mass murder'. See C. Cahn, 'The Roma: A Minority in Europe. A Review', *Romani Studies* 5, XIX/1 (2009), p. 72. Consequently I use the term Roma Holocaust. There has been increasing scholarly interest in this subject, most recently A. Weiss-Wendt, *The Nazi Genocide of the Roma: Reassessment and Commemoration* (Oxford and New York, 2013). Susan Tebbutt's 'History and Memory. The Genocide of the Romanies', in D. Kenrick, *The Gypsies During the Second World War: 3 The Final Chapter* (Hatfield, 2006), pp. 179–95 offers a good introduction to the fraught debates within this field. The leading work in German is M. Zimmermann's *Rassenutopie und Genozid: Die nationalsozialistische 'Lösung der Zigeunerfrage'* (Hamburg, 1996), with a summary of his main arguments provided in M. Zimmermann, 'The National Socialist Persecution of the Jews and Gypsies: Is a Comparison Possible?', trans. B. Templer, in Kenrick, *The Final Chapter*, pp. 135–48. More controversial is G. Lewy's *The Nazi Persecution of the Gypsies* (Oxford, 2000). The Interface collection's *The Gypsies During the Second World War, Vols 1–3* edited by Donald Kenrick provides an excellent examination of the situation in different countries, as well as life in the local authority camps and the extermination camps.

2 See D. Crowe, *A History of the Gypsies of Eastern Europe and Russia* (Basingstoke, 2006), pp. 84–5.

3 Report on Habitual Offenders etc. (Scotland), xxxii. Section 118 of the 1908 Act required these children to attend school, or the parents be fined 20 shillings, with the additional possibility of the child being sent to an Industrial School.

4 'Education of Gypsy Children', *Surrey Advertiser* (21 December 1912); National Archives of Scotland, Edinburgh (hereafter NAS), HH55/237, Letter from Home Office to under-secretary of state for Scotland, 19 November 1918.

5 Highland Council Archive, Inverness, CI/5/7/9, Staff Committee notes, 10 June 1914.

6 'Report of the Departmental Committee on Tinkers in Scotland, 1918' (Edinburgh, 1918), p. 16.

7 'Tinkers in Scotland', p. 16.

8 P. Panayi, *Ethnic Minorities in Nineteenth and Twentieth Century Germany: Jews, Gypsies, Poles, Turks and Others* (London, 2000), p. 97.

9 A. Fraser, *The Gypsies* (Oxford, 1995), p. 250.

10 J. Perkins, 'Continuity in Modern German History? The Treatment of Gypsies', *Immigrants and Minorities*, XVIII/1 (1999), p. 70; L. Lucassen, 'The Clink of the Hammer was Heard from Daybreak until Dawn: Gypsy

Occupations in Western Europe (Nineteenth and Twentieth Centuries)', in L. Lucassen, W. Willems and A-M. Cottaar, *Gypsies and other Itinerant Groups: A Socio-historical Approach* (London and New York, 1998), pp. 153–73.

11 E. Sitou, 'L'affaire des Gitanos: Chronique d'une flambée raciste à Toulouse à la fin du XIXe siècle', *Etudes Tsiganes*, XXX/1 (2008), p. 16. More generally, the uncertainties of the period and the conditions within the mining towns of the north are captured in Zola's *Germinal*. See also L. P. Moch, 'France', in *The Encyclopedia of Migration and Minorities in Europe from the Seventeenth Century to the Present*, ed. K. Bade et al., p. 55. For an introduction to the Dreyfus trial and its wider impact see E. Cahm, *The Dreyfus Affair in French Society and Politics* (London, 1996).

12 European Roma Rights Centre (hereafter ERRC), *Always Somewhere Else: Anti-Gypsyism in France* (Budapest, 2005), p. 49.

13 J-M. Berlière, 'La république et les nomades (1880–1914)', *Etudes Tsiganes* (2004), p. 59.

14 Archives Nationales de France, Paris (hereafter ANF), C7487/5739, Rapports faits au nom de la Commission relative à la répression du vagabondage et de la mendacité, 13 June 1910, 'Vagabondage et medacité: rapports Réville (cf. 9e législature).

15 ANF, C7415/2500-2505, Urgence déclaré 'Vagabondage et medacité: assistance, répression, nomades', n.d.

16 Quoted in C. Delclitte, 'Nomades et nomadisme: le cas de la France 1895–1912', unpublished MA thesis, Université de Paris VIII, 1994, p. 101. As in Britain, which saw the creation of the Showmen's Guild, fairground workers managed to escape the most stringent surveillance of the law through self-organization. In the run-up to the 1912 law they ran a campaign under the banner of 'Equality for All'.

17 E. Aubin, 'A propos d'un texte de Marcel Waline: "Un problème de sécurité publique: les Bohémiens"', *Etudes Tsiganes*, VII/1 (1996), p. 37.

18 Information was required in the following categories: height, size of chest; width, length and size of head; bizigomatic (face) diameter; length of right ear; length of the middle and little fingers of the left hand; left elbow and left foot; and eye colour. Fingerprints and photographs (front and profile) were also required. Children under thirteen were not included in this, as their details could fluctuate too much – they were 'only' fingerprinted.

19 ERRC, *Always Somewhere Else*, p. 50.

20 Berlière, 'La république et les nomades', pp. 63–4.

21 Estimates put the numbers of Gypsies across all of Germany at the beginning of the twentieth century at around 2,000, increasing rapidly to 8,000 in 1906 owing to migration from the Balkans.

22 A. Dillmann, *Zigeuner-Buch* (Munich, 1905); H. Heuss, 'German Policies of Gypsy Persecution, 1870–1945', in K. Fings et al., *From 'Race Science' to the Camps. The Gypsies During the Second World War* (Hatfield, 1997), p. 23.

23 L. Lucassen, 'Harmful Tramps: Police Professionalization and Gypsies in Germany, 1700–1945', in L. Lucassen, W. Willems and A-M. Cottaar, *Gypsies and other Itinerant Groups: A Socio-historical Approach* (London and New York, 1998), p. 86.

24 HStaD, R12 U Nr. 210, The Regional Prosecutor of the Grand Duchy Higher Regional Court, to Civil Servants of the Regional Prosecution Department, letter 'The Gypsy pest', Darmstadt, 18 November 1911. Emphasis added.

25 Lucassen, 'Harmful Tramps', p. 85.

26 Fraser, *The Gypsies*, p. 250.

27 See Andreas, *Gypsy Coppersmiths in Liverpool and Birkenhead* (Liverpool, 1913) and E. O. Winstedt, 'The Gypsy Coppersmiths Invasion of 1911–13', *JGLS*, new series, VI/4 (1913), pp. 244–303.

28 Lucassen, 'Harmful Tramps', p. 87.

29 Z. Barany, *The Eastern European Gypsies: Regime Change, Marginality and Ethno-politics* (Cambridge, 2002), p. 95.

30 D. Yates, *My Gypsy Days, Recollections of a Romani Rawnie* (London, 1953), pp. 110–11; Whyte, *The Yellow on the Broom* (Edinburgh, 1979), p. 2; F. Cowles, *Gypsy Caravan* (London, 1948), p. 111.

31 Crowe, *History of the Gypsies*, p. 43.

32 NAS: HH55/237, Letter from Rev. George A. Jeffrey to the Secretary of Scotland, 4 December 1916.

33 For example see 'Gypsy's Fire', *Sussex Express* (3 November 1916).

34 NAS: HH55/237, Eva Campbell Colquhoon, 'Welfare of Tinkers: An explanatory booklet', Munro Press (Perth, n.d., probably 1918).

35 O. Brown and D. McNab, 'The Shack Dwellers of the New Forest', *Journal of the Royal Sanitary Institute*, VI (1952), p. 717.

36 Brown and McNab, 'The Shack Dwellers'.

37 NAS: HH55/240, notes of meeting between Scottish Board of Health, Joint Scottish Churches, Scottish NSPCC, Miss Eva Campbell Colquhoun and others in regard to welfare of Tinkers, 4 June 1925.

38 H. Mauran, 'Un camp d'Alsaciens-Lorrains romanichels dans la Drôme (Crest, 1915–1919)', *Etudes Tsiganes*, XIII/1 (1999), pp. 90–119.

39 E. Filhol, '"Le prix de la liberté" itinéraire d'une famille tsigane internée: dans les camps français durant la Première Guerre Mondiale', *Etudes Tsiganes* (2004), pp. 18–19 and 67–8.

40 Mauran, 'Un camp d'Alsaciens-Lorrains romanichels', pp. 92–4.

41 Quoted in Filhol, 'Le prix de la liberté', p. 76.

42 Crowe, *History of the Gypsies*, p. 45.

43 Anon, 'Užhorod, January 1933', *Lidové Noviny*, 27 January 1933, trans. S. E. Mann, quoted verbatim as 'In a Gypsy School', *JGLS*, 3rd series, XIII/2 (1934), pp. 117–19.

44 The following account is taken from E. Marushiakova and V. Popov, 'Roma History: Soviet Union Before World War Two', http://romafacts. uni-graz.at, accessed 15 May 2013.

45 For this broader context see T. Martin, *The Affirmative Action Empire: Nations and Nationalism in the Soviet Union, 1923–1939* (Ithaca, NY, 2011).

46 J-M. Berlière et al., *Fichés? Photographie et identification 1850–1960* (Paris, 2011), p. 97; 'Vos Papiers! Identités de papier dans les Basses-Alpes de 1789 à 1944' (2012); Dignes les Bains: Catalogue de l'exposition Archives départementales des Alpes-de-Haute-Provence 26 January– 26 May 2012.

47 A. Sutre, '"Les Bohémiens du pays": une inscription territoriale des

Bohémiens dans le Sud-Ouest de la France au xixème et au début du xxème siècle', unpublished MA thesis, EHESS, 2010, pp. 96 and 101.

48 Crowe, *History of the Gypsies*, p. 45.

49 The ICPC was founded in 1923 at the Second International Police Congress in Vienna as the International Criminal Police (ICP). Founding members were Poland, Austria, Belgium, China, Egypt, France, Germany, Greece, Hungary, Italy, the Netherlands, Romania, Sweden, Switzerland and Yugoslavia. The United States joined in 1923 and the United Kingdom joined in 1928. Following the *Anschluss* in 1938, the organization was controlled by Nazi Germany, and its headquarters were moved to Berlin in 1942.

50 TNA, MEPO 3/2047, tenth session of ICPC, Vienna, 17–21 September 1934, statement 'Fight Against the Gypsies'.

51 TNA, MEPO 3/2047, ICPC outline from International Central Office, n.d., possibly January 1936.

52 Panayi, *Ethnic Minorities*, p. 129. On this period generally see D. Peukert, *The Weimar Republic: The Crisis of Classical Modernity* (New York, 1991) and H. Heiber, *The Weimar Republic* (Oxford, 1993).

53 HStAD/G15 Schotten, Nr. Q85 'The Gypsy Plague', *Oberhessischer Anzeiger und Friedberger Zeitung*, 27 April 1926.

54 See for example HStAD/G15 Schotten, Nr. Q85, Hessian Ministry of the Interior, to all district administrations, Darmstadt, 25 June 1920; and Dieburg Nr. Q4 Dieburg district administration, Hesse, memo to all local police stations, 27 April 1926.

55 I. Hancock, 'Gypsy History in Germany and Neighbouring Lands. A Chronology Leading to the Holocaust and Beyond', in *The Gypsies of Eastern Europe*, ed. D. Crowe and J. Kolsti (New York and London, 1992), p. 14.

56 HStAD/G15 Schotten, Nr. Q85, letter from Hessian Ministry of Labour and Economy to district administrators, 13 February 1925.

57 Panayi, *Ethnic Minorities*, p. 144.

58 Lucassen, 'Harmful Tramps', p. 88.

59 Ibid.

60 HStAD/G15 Schotten, Nr. Q 85 Ministry of the Interior to district administrators, 16 November 1927. Gypsy children over the age of six were fingerprinted but not photographed.

61 HStAD/G15 Schotten, Nr. Q85. Forwarded letter from the State Police of Baden to Hessian district administrators, police departments, etc., 20 August 1928.

62 Panayi, *Ethnic Minorities*, p. 143.

63 F. Sparing, 'The Gypsy Camps', in Fings et al., *From 'Race Science' to the Camps*, p. 40.

64 Lucassen, 'Harmful Tramps', p. 90.

65 A helpful introduction to the highly fraught issue of the uniqueness of the Holocaust and the position of Jews and other groups within this can be found in A. S. Rosenbaum, ed., *Is the Holocaust Unique? Perspectives on Comparative Genocide*, 3rd edn (Boulder, CO, 2009). See also D. Stone, ed., *The Historiography of Genocide* (Basingstoke, 2010).

66 On this argument see P. Longerich, *Holocaust: The Nazi Persecution and*

Murder of the Jews (Oxford, 2010), and T. Snyder, 'A New Approach to the Holocaust', *The New York Review of Books* (23 June 2011).

67 Sparing, 'The Gypsy Camps', pp. 58–9.

68 Gypsies were classified according to how 'racially pure' they were deemed to be with a scale ranging from Z (Zigeuner – 'pure Gypsy'), through ZM+, ZM, ZM- (Zigeunermischling, with the plus and minus indicating if gypsy blood was dominant or not), to NZ (Nicht-Zigeuner).

69 W. Wippermann, 'Compensation Withheld: The Denial of Reparations to the Sinti and Roma', in Kenrick, *The Final Chapter*, p. 174.

70 B. Muller-Hill, *Murderous Science: Elimination by Scientific Selection of Jews, Gypsies, and Others in Germany, 1933–1945* (Oxford, 1988), p. 57.

71 M. Burleigh and W. Wipperman, *The Racial State: Germany, 1939–45* (Cambridge, 1991), p. 54.

72 HStAD/G 15 Schotten, Nr. Q85, Nr. 22 Ausgabe B, Ministerial Paper of the Reich- and Prussian Ministry of the Interior, 25 May 1938.

73 Sparing, 'The Gypsy Camps', pp. 58–9.

74 Z. Bauman, *Modernity and the Holocaust* (Cambridge, 1989), is a good introduction to this argument. On the basis that around 100 people were killed as a result of Kristallnacht he calculated that it would have taken 200 years for six million Jews to be killed through pogroms.

75 HStAD/G15 Dieburg Nr. Q4, President of Hesse State Police to district administrators, 10 July 1933; and G28 Butzbach G451 Hessian Police Department, Darmstadt to local police stations, 12 May 1936.

76 Panayi, *Ethnic Minorities*, pp. 175–6.

77 HStAD/G15 Dieburg Nr. Q4 Gross-Umstadt Police to district administration, 7 October 1934.

78 HStAD/G15 Schotten, Nr. Q85 Reichsstatthalter in Hesse to district administrators and police departments re deportation costs of Gypsy families, 23 September 1937.

79 W. Winter, *Winter Time: Memoirs of a German Sinto who Survived Auschwitz*, trans. S. Robertson (Hatfield, 2004), p. 24.

80 Sparing, 'The Gypsy Camps', pp. 59–60.

81 These Gypsies and Sinti came from Cologne, Dusseldorf, Hannover, Bremen, Frankfurt and Stuttgart. See Sparing, 'The Gypsy Camps', pp. 60–62.

82 See Fraser, *The Gypsies*, p. 261; Sparing, 'The Gypsy Camps', pp. 64–5; E. Thurner, *Nationalsozialismus und Zigeuner in Österreich* (Vienna, 1983), pp. 174–9. Of the 130,000 female prisoners in Ravensbrück, 15,000–32,000 survived. Owing to the burning of camp records in the final days of the war, the exact numbers are not known.

83 D. Kenrick and G. Puxon, *The Destiny of Europe's Gypsies* (London, 1972), pp. 183–4; G. Puxon, 'Forgotten Victims: Plight of the Gypsies', *Patterns of Prejudice* (1977), pp. 11 and 26.

84 Figures for Chełmno are hard to come by, but it is possible that only three people survived this camp.

85 See for example M. Tyagly, 'Nazi Occupation Policies and the Mass Murder of the Roma in Ukraine', and M. Holler, 'The Nazi Persecution of Roma in North-western Russia: The Operational Area of the Army Group North, 1941–1944', in Weiss-Wendt, *The Nazi Genocide of the*

Roma. Some survivors from this massacre joined partisan units, including Jefrosinja (Ruzha) Tumarshevic, whose husband and daughter were executed. See V. Kalinin, 'Roma Resistance in the Soviet Union', in Kenrick, *The Final Chapter*, pp. 112–13.

86 Quoted in J. Sigot, 'Camp Allemand ou Camp Français?', *Etudes Tsiganes*, VI/2 (1995), p. 37.

87 S. Fogg, 'They Are Undesirables': Local and National Responses to Gypsies during World War II', *French Historical Studies*, XXXI/2 (2004), pp. 327–58.

88 D. Peschanski, *Les Tsiganes en France 1939–1946* (Paris, 1994), p. 27.

89 M. C. Hubert, 'Les Tsiganes pendant la Seconde Guerre Mondiale', in Cercle d'étude de la déportation et de la Shoah, *La persécution des Tsiganes: histoire et mémoire* (Paris, 2005), pp. 3–12.

90 Anon., 'Role de la sedentarisation dans l'adaptation des Tsiganes', *Etudes Tsiganes*, 1 (1961), pp. 26–7.

91 Fogg, 'They Are Undesirables', p. 353.

92 Cited in M. Pernot, ed., *Un camp pour les Bohémiens: Mémoires du camp d'internement pour les nomades de Saliers* (Arles, 2001), p. 5. This is the fullest account of conditions at the Saliers camp.

93 J. Sigot, 'Le Camp de Montreuil-Bellay (Maine-et-Loire)' in Cercle d'étude de la déportation et de la Shoah, *La persécution des Tsiganes: histoire et mémoire* (Paris, 2004), p. 29.

94 M. Debelle, 'Les persécutions des Tsiganes en Languedoc-Roussillon: pendant la seconde guerre mondiale', *Etudes Tsiganes* XXIII–XXIV/3–4 (2005), p. 213.

95 Kenrick and Puxon, *The Destiny of Europe's Gypsies*, p. 107.

96 The fullest first-hand account of this comes in J. Yoors, *Crossing. A Journal of Survival and Resistance in World War Two* (London, 1971).

97 Fogg, 'They Are Undesirables', pp. 355–7.

98 R. J. Crampton, *Concise History of Bulgaria* (Cambridge, 2005), pp. 165–6.

99 Although most Jews were effectively hounded out of the country in 1948. The most accessible account of Jews during the war in Bulgaria is M. Bar-Zohar, *Beyond Hitler's Grasp: The Heroic Rescue of Bulgaria's Jews* (Holbrook, MA, 1998). See also A. Wachtel, *The Balkans in World History* (Oxford, 2008), p. 110.

100 Crowe, *History of the Gypsies*, p. 19.

101 K. Kanev, 'Law and Politics on Ethnic and Religious Minorities in Bulgaria', in *Communities and Identities in Bulgaria*, ed. A. Krasteva (Ravenna, 1999), p. 69; D. Kenrick, *The Romani World* (Hatfield, 2004), pp. 43–4; Marushiakova and Popov, 'Ciganska politika i ciganski izsledvania v Bulgaria' (1919–89), in Marushiakova and Popov, *Studii Romani*, vol. 7 (Sofia, 2007), pp. 122–3.

102 Evidence over the experiences of Roma in Italy during the war remains fragmented and more research needs to be done. The current best overview is Giovanna Boursier's work that can be found at http://romafacts.uni-graz.at, accessed 19 May 2013.

103 D. Reinhartz, 'The Genocide of the Yugoslav Gypsies', in Kenrick, *The Final Chapter*, pp. 87–95.

104 The best overview of this period can be found ino A. Korb, *In the Shadow of the World War: Mass Violence by the Ustaša Against Serbs, Jews and*

Roma in Croatia, 1941–45 (Hamburg, 2013).

105 Wachtel, *The Balkans*, p. 109; Reinhartz, 'The Genocide of the Yugoslav Gypsies', pp. 92–4, and D. Kenrick, 'Resistance', p. 106, both in Kenrick, *The Final Chapter*.

106 G. Făcăoaru, Câteva date în jurul familiei si statului biopolitic, București (1941), trans. in V. Ionescu, 'Deportations from Romania', http://romafacts.uni-graz.at (accessed 19 May 2013). See also V. Solonari, 'Ethnic Cleansing or "Crime Prevention"? Deportation of Romanian Roma', in Weiss-Wendt, *The Nazi Genocide of the Roma*, chapter four.

107 Survivor testimony of Ferenc Horváth in K. Katz, 'The Roma of Hungary in the Second World War', in Kenrick, *The Final Chapter*, p. 69.

108 Quoted in Tebbutt, 'History and Memory', pp. 179–95.

109 For other survivor testimonies see the United States Holocaust Memorial Museum, Fortunoff Video Archive, Washington, D.C.; the SHOAH Video Testimony Collection, Yale University. J. von dem Knesebeck, *The Roma Struggle for Compensation in Post-war Germany* (Hatfield, 2011), chapter two, gives a valuable overview of the extent and meaning of Roma survivor testimonies. Katz, 'The Roma of Hungary', pp.47–85, is based on first-hand accounts.

110 The following is taken from his autobiography, *Winter Time*.

111 The following account is taken from the reconstruction of his story, which was in part written down while in hiding in 1944 and in part was told to Alexander Ramati, who published it as *And the Violins Stopped Playing. A Story of the Gypsy Holocaust* (London, 1985).

112 Ramati, *And the Violins Stopped Playing*, p. 112.

113 On this point see von dem Knesebeck, *The Roma Struggle*, pp. 57–9.

114 More details of Nazi experiments on Gypsies can be found in L. Eiber, 'The persecution of the Sinti and Roma in Munich, 1933–45', in Tebbutt, *Sinti and Roma*, pp. 17–33.

115 Yale University: Fortunoff Video archive for Holocaust Testimonies, Testimony of Anna W, www.library.yale.edu/testimonies/excerpts/annaw.html. Recorded between 1979 and 1981 (accessed 15 November 2012).

116 See C. Bernadac, *L'Holocauste oublié* (Paris, 1979); see also Fraser, *The Gypsies*, pp. 256–69.

SIX A New Dawn?

1 M. Marrus, *The Unwanted: European Refugees from the First World War Through the Cold War* (Philadelphia, PA, 2002), pp. 296–308.

2 See for example I. Connor, *Refugees and Expellees in Post-war Germany* (Manchester, 2007); P. Panayi, *Ethnic Minorities in Nineteenth and Twentieth Century Germany: Jews, Gypsies, Poles, Turks and Others* (London, 2000), chapter six.

3 M. Brenner, *After the Holocaust: Rebuilding Jewish Lives in Post-war Germany* (Princeton, NJ, 1997), pp. 60–63. More generally, a comprehensive introduction to Germany in this period can be found in M. Fulbrook, *German National Identity after the Holocaust* (Cambridge, 1998).

4 P. Sander, 'Criminal Justice Following the Genocide of the Sinti and Roma', in D. Kenrick, *The Gypsies During the Second World War: 3 The Final Chapter* (Hatfield, 2006), pp. 154–8.

5 W. Wippermann, 'Compensation Withheld: The Denial of Reparations to the Sinti and Roma', in Kenrick, *The Final Chapter*, pp. 171–7; S. Milton, 'Persecuting the Survivors', in S. Tebbutt, ed., *Sinti and Roma: Gypsies in German-speaking Society and Literature* (New York and Oxford, 1998), p. 38.

6 W. Winter, *Winter Time. Memoirs of a German Sinto who Survived Auschwitz*, trans. S. Robertson (Hatfield, 2004), p. 119.

7 Milton, 'Persecuting the Survivors', p. 39. Full German passports lasted ten years and were issued free of charge.

8 J. von dem Knesebeck, *The Roma Struggle for Compensation in Post-war Germany* (Hatfield, 2011), pp. 59–61.

9 Otto Pankok quoted in G. Margalit, *Germany and its Gypsies: A Post-Auschwitz Ordeal* (Madison, WI, 2002), pp. 58–9.

10 HStAD/H 1 Nr. 6392, Head of Alsfeld district administration to all district mayors, 27 March 1947, re Decree from the Ministry of the Interior, 3 March 1947.

11 Panayi, *Ethnic Minorities*, p. 233; Milton, 'Persecuting the Survivors', pp. 36–7.

12 J. Sigot, 'Camp Allemand ou Camp Français?', *Etudes Tsiganes*, VI/2 (1995), pp. 55–6.

13 S. P. Imbert, *Les tsiganes: analyse d'une politique d'insertion à Toulouse* (Toulouse, 1999), p. 47.

14 J-P. Liégois, 'Tsiganes, Nomades et Pouvoirs Publics en France au 20e siècle: du rejet a l'assimilation', *Pluriel débat*, 19 (1979), pp. 74–5.

15 S. Nicholas, 'From John Bull to John Citizen: Images of National Identity and Citizenship in the Wartime BBC', in *The Right to Belong: Citizenship and National Identity in Britain, 1930–60*, ed. R. Weight and A. Beach (London, 1998), p. 45.

16 B. Taylor, *A Minority and the State: Travellers in Britain in the Twentieth Century* (Manchester, 2008), p. 158.

17 TNA, AST 7/1480, Arbroath Area Office, 'Tinkers'.

18 Taylor, *A Minority and the State*, pp. 174–6.

19 Z. Barany, *The Eastern European Gypsies: Regime Change, Marginality and Ethno-politics* (Cambridge, 2002), pp. 114–15.

20 Quoted in D. Crowe, *A History of the Gypsies of Eastern Europe and Russia* (Basingstoke, 2006), p. 55.

21 Ibid., p. 20.

22 S. Pashov, *Romano esi* (1949) 1:1, n.p.

23 Crowe, *History of the Gypsies*, p. 20.

24 A. Fraser, *The Gypsies* (Oxford, 1995), p. 270.

25 Crowe, *History of the Gypsies*, pp. 54–5.

26 I. Tomova, *The Gypsies in the Transition Period* (Sofia, 1995), p. 17.

27 E. Marushiakova and V. Popov, 'State policies under communism', fact sheets on Roma, Council of Europe, http://romafacts.uni-graz.at, accessed 29 April 2013.

28 A fictionalized account of her life can be found in C. McCann's *Zoli* (New York, 2007).

29 R. Gronemeyer and G. Rakelmann, *Die Zigeuner. Reisende in Europa* (Köln, 1988), p. 121.

30 Fraser, *The Gypsies*, p. 280.

31 R. J. Crampton, *Concise History of Bulgaria* (Cambridge, 2005), p. 191; Crowe, *History of the Gypsies*, p. 21.

32 E. MacColl and P. Seeger, *Till Doomsday in the Afternoon: The Folklore of a Family of Scots Travellers, the Stewarts of Blairgowrie* (Manchester, 1986), p. 16.

33 Fraser, *The Gypsies*, pp. 272–4; A. Reyniers, 'Quelques jalons pour comprendre l'économie tsigane', *Etudes Tsiganes*, XII/2 (1998), p. 7.

34 TNA HLG71/1650, background notes for Parliamentary Question, 19 June 1956. Note the automatic assumption that when Gypsy Travellers adopted seemingly urban, and definitely not picturesque, scrap-metal-dealing, they could not be 'pure-bred gypsies'.

35 TNA HLG 71/2267, internal MHLG memo, 10 October 1956.

36 HStAD/H1 Nr. 1953, district president of Darmstadt to Hessian minister of the interior, 10 April 1956.

37 HStAD/H1 Nr. 1953, Hessian minister of the interior to district presidents of Darmstadt, Kassel and Wiesbaden, 7 May 1953.

38 Milton, 'Persecuting the Survivors', pp. 36–7.

39 J. Connors, 'Seven Weeks of Childhood: An Autobiography', in J. Sandford, *Gypsies* (London, 1973), pp. 166–7.

40 Central Public Archive: Sofia, Bulgaria (hereafter CPA), f. 1, op. 6, minutes #A182, Secretariat of the Central Committee of the Bulgarian Communist Party, 4 June 1959, letter appended to minutes, 16 June 1959.

41 Ibid.

42 D. Crowe, 'The Gypsies in Hungary', in *The Gypsies of Eastern Europe*, ed. D. Crowe and J. Kolsti (New York and London, 1992), pp. 120–21.

43 Crowe, 'Gypsies in Hungary', pp. 122–3.

44 CPA, f. 1, op. 6, a.e. 3753, Law Against Vagrancy and Begging, 1 November 1958. It did however specifically exclude the seasonal nomadism of farmers from its terms.

45 CPA, f. 1, op. 6, a.e. 3753, 'Project Decree for the Arrangement of the Issue of the Gypsy Population in Bulgaria', 1 November 1958, pp. 10–11.

46 Ibid., pp. 11–12.

47 Ibid., p. 13.

48 Helsinki Watch, *Destroying Ethnic Identity* (New York and Washington, DC, 1991), p. 13; C. Silverman, 'Bulgarian Gypsies: adaptation in a socialist context', *Nomadic Peoples* (1986), p. 53.

49 Crowe, *History of the Gypsies*, p. 22.

50 CPA, Decision of the Secretariat of the Central Committee of the Bulgarian Communist Party, approved in minutes #850 of the Secretariat, 27 September 1978; Helsinki Watch, *Destroying Ethnic Identity*, pp. 29–34.

51 E. Marushiakova and V. Popov, 'State Policies under Communism', http://romafacts.uni-graz.at, accessed 14 May 2013.

52 Quoted in ERRC, *Always Somewhere Else: Anti-Gypsyism in France* (Budapest, 2005), p. 57.

53 Quoted in E. Aubin, '1912–1969: La liberté d'aller et venir des nomades:

l'idéologie sécuritaire', *Etudes Tsiganes*, VII/1 (1996), p. 16; and E. Aubin, 'L'évolution du droit français applicable aux Tsiganes: Les quatres logiques du législateur républicain', *Etudes Tsiganes* (2000), pp. 15 and 33.

54 Taylor, *A Minority and the State*, 188.

55 Imbert, *Les tsiganes*, p. 13.

56 Recorded details included skin/eye/hair colour, body type and other defining physical features. ERRC, *Always Somewhere Else*, pp. 64 and 70; Imbert, *Les tsiganes*, pp. 86–7; Aubin, 'L'évolution du droit français', pp. 32–3 and '1912–1969', p. 36; M. Bidet, 'Will French Gypsies Always Stay Nomadic and Out of the Law-making Process?' in N. Sigona and R. Zetter, *Romani Mobilities in Europe: Multidisciplinary Perspectives*, Refugees Study Centre, University of Oxford, 14–15 January 2010, p. 22.

57 They had, for example, in 1927 taken the lead in Bulgaria in petitioning against the United States' execution of the two anarchists Nicola Sacco and Bartolomeo Vanzetti.

58 D. Kenrick, *The Romani World* (Hatfield, 2004), p. 106.

59 Quoted in Imbert, *Les tsiganes*, pp. 66–9.

60 Helsinki Watch, *Destroying Ethnic Identity*, p. 14.

61 Marushiakova and Popov, 'State Policies under Communism'.

62 T. Acton, *Gypsy Politics and Social Change. The Development of Ethnic Ideology and Pressure Politics among British Gypsies from Victorian Reformism to Romani Nationalism* (Oxford, 1974), p. 167.

63 Ibid., p. 163.

64 G. Puxon, 'Gypsies: The Road to Liberation', *Race Today* (June 1971). He is here, of course, adapting the words of Stokely Carmichael.

65 Y. Matras, 'The Development of the Romani Civil Rights Movement in Germany, 1945–96', in Tebbutt, *Sinti and Roma*, p. 52.

66 Matras, 'Romani Civil Rights', p. 55.

67 Directorate of Judicial affairs quoted in V. Repaire, 'La construction du lien social à l'école ou les enjeux de la scolarisation des enfants tsiganes', unpublished PhD thesis, Université de Paris V, 2004, p. 116.

68 A. Cotonnec and A. Chartier, 'Ils nous mettent au fond des classes: parole preliminaire sur l'ecole', *Etudes Tsiganes*, 4 (1984), p. 9.

69 J. Stockins with M. King and M. Knight, *On The Cobbles: Jimmy Stockin: The Life Of A Bare-Knuckle Gypsy Warrior* (Edinburgh, 2000), pp. 46–7.

70 D. Lüken-Klaßen and S. Meixner, *Roma in Public Education* (Bamberg, 2004), p. 5.

71 CPA, Decision of the Secretariat of the Central Committee of the Bulgarian Communist Party, approved in minutes #850 of the Secretariat, 27 September 1978; Helsinki Watch, *Destroying Ethnic Identity*, pp. 29–34.

72 Manush Romanov, quoted in Helsinki Watch, *Destroying Ethnic Identity*, p. 31.

73 P. Saunders, J. Clarke and S. Kendall, eds, *Gypsies and Travellers in their Own Words: Words and Pictures of Travelling Life* (Leeds, 2000), pp. 10–11.

74 See Repaire, 'La construction du lien social', pp. 167–8 for a discussion of the limitations of this approach.

75 J.-P. Liégois, 'L'accès aux droits sociaux des populations tsiganes en

France: rapport d'étude de la Direction générale de l'action sociale'
(Rennes, 2007), pp. 102–3.

76 A. S. Spinelli, 'La scolarisation des enfants tsiganes', in *Tsiganes à l'école: Pédagogie interculturelle pour l'accès aux apprentissages*, ed. F. Malique (Paris, 2003), pp. 40–42; N. Lafaurie, 'L' école des Cailloux Gris D'Herblay: une école tsigane à part entière, récupération ou abandon?', *Etudes Tsiganes*, 4 (1984), pp. 31–4.

77 Taylor, *A Minority and the State*, p. 199.

78 D. Hawes and B. Perez, *The Gypsy and the State: The Ethnic Cleansing of British Society* (Bristol, 1996), pp. 30–32.

79 Association of Chief Police Officers Archive, Open University, Milton Keynes: ACPO, DOE, 'The accommodation needs of long-distance and regional Travellers: a consultation paper', February 1982, Appendix 3.

80 Crowe, *History of the Gypsies*, p. 25.

81 Crampton, *Concise History of Bulgaria*, pp. 193–4.

82 P. Gocheva, 'The Mysteries of the Last Census', *Duoma* (27 April 1993); Crowe, *History of the Gypsies*, p. 25.

83 For an insight into controls governing research under socialism see Helsinki Watch, *Destroying Ethnic Identity*, p. 13.

84 Silverman, 'Bulgarian Gypsies', p. 53.

85 Ibid.

86 This was a feature across socialist countries. See for example J. Wedel, *The Unplanned Society: Poland During and After Communism* (New York, 1992).

87 Silverman, 'Bulgarian Gypsies', p. 54.

88 I. Tomova, *Ethnic Dimensions of Poverty in Bulgaria* (Washington, DC, 1998).

89 Helsinki Watch, *Destroying Ethnic Identity*, p. 38.

90 Tomova, *Gypsies in the Transition*, p. 50.

91 Ibid., pp. 9, 17 and 21–2.

92 Ibid.

93 Crowe, *History of the Gypsies*, p. 27.

94 Tomova, *Gypsies in the Transition*, p. 55.

95 Kenrick, *The Romani World*, p. 57.

96 An introduction to anti-Roma violence can be found in M. Stewart, ed., *The Gypsy Menace: Populism and the New Anti-Gypsy Politics* (London, 2012). Also see separate country entries in Kenrick, *The Romani World*.

97 Lüken-Klaßen and Meixner, 'Roma in Public Education', p. 6.

98 Quoted in van dem Knesebeck, *The Roma Struggle*, p. 227.

99 Barany, *The East European Gypsies*, pp. 243–7.

100 P. Panayi, 'Racial Violence in the New Germany, 1990–93', *Contemporary European History*, III/3 (1994), pp. 265–87.

101 Hawes and Perez, *The Gypsy and the State*, p. 122.

102 According to evidence introduced at later court cases, South Bucks v Porter, Wrexham CBC v Berry and Chichester DC v Keet and Searle, see 'Rights of Gypsies and Travellers: Planning Permission for Caravan Sites', www.yourrights.org.uk (accessed 17 December 2008); R. Home, 'The planning system and the accommodation needs of Gypsies', in *Here to Stay: The Gypsies and Travellers of Britain*, ed. C. Clark and

M. Greenfield (Hatfield, 2006), pp. 90–107, p. 97.

103 Matras, 'Romani Civil Rights', pp. 60–63.

104 Crowe, *History of the Gypsies*, pp. 28–9.

105 Kenrick, *The Romani World*, pp. 54.

106 See for example I. Chorianopoulos et al., 'Residential Segregation and the EU Social Exclusion Discourse: Greek Roma and the Participatory Governance Lock in', *Antipode* (2014, forthcoming).

107 Kenrick, *The Romani World*, pp. 45–6.

108 M. Bordigoni, 'Sara aux Saintes-Maries-de-la-Mer: métaphore de la présence gitane dans le "monde des gadjé"', *Etudes Tsiganes*, XX/4 (2004), pp. 25 and 31; P. Williams, 'Le miracle et la nécessité: à propos du développement du pentecôtisme chez les Tsiganes', *Archives de sciences sociales des religions*, LXXIII/1 (1991), pp. 81 and 98.

109 C. le Cossec, '"Phénomène pentecôtiste" ou réveil réligieux?', *Etudes Tsiganes*, 1 (1985), pp. 19–21.

110 M. Slavkova, 'Evangelical Gypsies in Bulgaria: Way of Life and Performance of Identity', *Romani Studies*, XVII/2 (2007), pp. 205–46.

111 Stonewall, *Profiles of Prejudice* (MORI UK opinion poll service, 2005), p. 1.

Afterword

1 'Underclass Gypsies: An Historical Approach on Categorisation and Exclusion in France in the Nineteenth and Twentieth Centuries', in *The Gypsy Menace: Populism and the New Anti-Gypsy Politics*, ed. M. Stewart (London, 2012), pp. 95–114.

2 Ibid.

3 I. Lacková, *A False Dawn: My Life as a Gypsy Woman in Slovakia* (Hatfield, 1999).

FURTHER READING

Abreu, L., 'Beggars, Vagrants and Romanies: Repression and Persecution in Portuguese Society (14th–18th Centuries)', www.ep.liu.se/ej/hygiea (accessed 14 October 2012)

Abulafia, D., 'The Coming of the Gypsies: Cities, Princes, Nomads', in *Power and Persuasion. Essays on the Art of State Building in Honour of W. P. Blockmans*, ed. P.C.M. Hoppenbrouwers, A. Janse and R. Stein (Turnhout, 2011), pp. 325–42

Acton, T., *Gypsy Politics and Social Change. The Development of Ethnic Ideology and Pressure Politics among British Gypsies from Victorian Reformism to Romani Nationalism* (Oxford, 1974)

Asséo, H., 'Des hommes à part les Bohémiens en forêt XVIIIe siècle: Forêt, villageois et marginaux, XVIe–XXe siècle', in *Forêt, Villageois et marginaux*, ed. A. Corvol (Paris, 1990), pp. 30–35

Bancroft, A., *Roma and Gypsy-Travellers in Europe: Modernity, Race, Space, and Exclusion* (Aldershot, 2005)

Barany, Z., *The Eastern European Gypsies: Regime Change, Marginality and Ethno-politics* (Cambridge, 2002)

Beier, A. L., *Masterless Men: The Vagrancy Problem in England, 1560–1640* (London, 1987)

Belton, B., *Questioning Gypsy Identity: Ethnic Narratives in Britain and America* (Walnut Creek, California and Oxford, 2005)

Berlière, J-M., 'La république et les nomades (1880–1914)', *Etudes Tsiganes* (2004), pp. 18–57

Bernadac, C., *L'Holocauste oublié* (Paris, 1979)

Boes, M., 'Unwanted Travellers? The Tightening of City Borders in Early Modern Germany', in *Borders and Travellers in Early Modern Europe*, ed. T. Betteridge (Aldershot, 2007)

Boswell, S. G., *The Book of Boswell: The Autobiography of a Gypsy*, ed. J. Seymour (London, 1970)

Burleigh, M. and W. Wipperman, *The Racial State: Germany, 1939–45* (Cambridge, 1991)

Clark, C. and M. Greenfield, eds, *Here to Stay. The Gypsies and Travellers of Britain* (Hatfield, 2006)

Crowe, D., *A History of the Gypsies of Eastern Europe and Russia* (Houndmills, 2006)

Crowe, D. and J. Kolsti, eds, *The Gypsies of Eastern Europe* (New York and London, 1992)

Donovan, B., 'Changing Perceptions of Social Deviance: Gypsies in Early Modern Portugal and Brazil', *Journal of Social History*, XXVI/1 (1992), pp. 33–53

European Roma Rights Centre (ERRC), *Always Somewhere Else: Anti-Gypsyism in France* (Budapest, 2005)

Fings, K., et al., *From 'Race Science' to the Camps. The Gypsies During the Second World War* (Hatfield, 1997)

Fogg, S., 'They Are Undesirables': Local and National Responses to Gypsies during World War II', *French Historical Studies*, XXXI/2 (2004), pp. 327–58

Fraser, A., *The Gypsies*, 2nd edn (Oxford, 1995)

Ginio, E., 'Neither Muslims nor Zimmis: The Gypsies (Roma) in the Ottoman State', *Romani Studies*, XIV/2 (2004), pp. 117–44

Gómez Alfaro, A., *The Great Gypsy Round-up. Spain: The General Imprisonment of Gypsies in 1749* (Madrid, 1993)

Hawes, D. and B. Perez, *The Gypsy and the State: The Ethnic Cleansing of British Society* (Bristol, 1996)

Helsinki Watch, *Destroying Ethnic Identity: The Gypsies of Bulgaria* (New York and Washington, DC, 1991)

Joyce, N., *Travellers: An Autobiography* (Dublin, 1985)

Jütte, R., *Poverty and Deviance in Early Modern Europe* (Cambridge, 1994)

Kenrick, D., *The Romani World* (Hatfield, 2004)

——, *The Gypsies During the Second World War: 3 The Final Chapter* (Hatfield, 2006)

Lacková, I., *A False Dawn: My Life as a Gypsy Woman in Slovakia* (Hatfield, 1999)

Lewy, G., *The Nazi Persecution of the Gypsies* (Oxford, 2000)

Liégois, J-P., *Les tsiganes* (Paris, 1971)

Lucassen, L., W. Willems and A. Cottaar, *Gypsies and Other Itinerant Groups A Socio-historical Approach* (London and New York, 1998)

MacColl, E., and P. Seeger, *Till Doomsday in the Afternoon: The Folklore of a Family of Scots Travellers, the Stewarts of Blairgowrie* (Manchester, 1986)

Marushiakova, E., and V. Popov, *Gypsies in the Ottoman Empire* (Hatfield, 2001)

——, 'Roma History: Soviet Union Before World War Two', http://romafacts. uni-graz.at [AQ: access date?]

Mayall, D., *Gypsy-Travellers in Nineteenth Century Society* (Cambridge, 1988)

Moussa, S., ed., *Le mythe des Bohemiens dans la littérature et les arts en Europe* (Paris, 2008)

Muller-Hill, B. *Murderous Science: Elimination by Scientific Selection of Jews, Gypsies, and Others in Germany, 1933–1945* (Oxford, 1988)

Panayi, P., *Ethnic Minorities in Nineteenth and Twentieth Century Germany: Jews, Gypsies, Poles, Turks and Others* (London, 2000)

Pym, R., *The Gypsies of Early Modern Spain, 1425–1783* (Basingstoke, 2007)

Ramati, A., *And the Violins Stopped Playing: A Story of the Gypsy Holocaust* (London, 1985)

Reyniers, A., 'Pérégrinations des Jénis en France au XIXe siècle', *Etudes Tsiganes*, II/2 (1991), pp. 19–25

Sandford, J., *Gypsies* (London, 1973)

Silverman, C., 'Bulgarian Gypsies: adaptation in a socialist context', *Nomadic Peoples* (1986), pp. 22–53

Soulis, G. C., 'The Gypsies in the Byzantine Empire and the Balkans in the Late Middle Ages', *Dumbarton Oaks Papers*, 15 (1961), pp. 142–65

St Clair, S.G.B., and C. A. Brophy, *A Residence in Bulgaria; or Notes on the Resources and Administration of Turkey: The Condition and Character, Manners, Customs and Language of the Christian and Mussulman Populations, with Preference to the Eastern Question* (London, 1869)

Stewart, M., ed., *The Gypsy Menace: Populism and the New Anti-Gypsy Politics* (London, 2012)

Stockin, J., with M. King and M. Knight, *On The Cobbles: Jimmy Stockin: The Life Of A Bare-Knuckle Gypsy Warrior* (Edinburgh, 2000)

Sway, M., *Familiar Strangers: Gypsy Lives in America* (Champaign, IL, 1988)

Taylor, B., *A Minority and the State: Travellers in Britain in the Twentieth Century* (Manchester, 2008)

Tebbutt, S., ed., *Sinti and Roma: Gypsies in German-speaking Society and Literature* (New York & Oxford, 1998)

Vaux de Foletier, F., *Les bohémiens en France au 19ème siècle* (Paris, 1970)

von dem Knesebeck, J., *The Roma Struggle for Compensation in Post-war Germany* (Hatfield, 2011)

Weiss-Wendt, A., *The Nazi Genocide of the Roma: Reassessment and Commemoration* (Oxford and New York, 2013)

Whyte, B., *The Yellow on the Broom* (Edinburgh, 1979)

Willems, W., *In Search of the True Gypsy: From Enlightenment to Final Solution* (London and Portland, OR, 1997)

Winter, W., *Winter Time: Memoirs of a German Sinto who Survived Auschwitz*, trans. S. Robertson, (Hatfield, 2004)

Yoors, J., *Crossing. A Journal of Survival and Resistance in World War Two* (London, 1971)

ACKNOWLEDGEMENTS

Over the extended period of writing this book I have benefited from the rich intellectual atmosphere of Birkbeck and the generous support of many colleagues: Fred Anscombe, John Arnold, Ludivine Broch, David Feldman, Vanessa King, Aphrodite Papayianni, Pam Pilbeam, Jessica Reinisch and Julian Swann. Tom Johnson presented me with the fantastic Tudor document out of the blue. A school research grant paid for my able team of research assistants, whose languages made accessible a wealth of new archival: Dorina Reichhold for the German material; St John O Donnabhain's research, translation and work drafting and talking through the French material went far beyond the call of duty and funds; Martyn Weeds led the Bulgaria research and his initial writing allowed me to make sense of unfamiliar territory. In Bulgaria thanks also to Veronica Dimitrova, Nevena Germanova, the intellectual generosity of Plamen Makariev (Sofia University), Ilona Tomova (Bulgarian Academy of Sciences), Emil Buzov and Vassil Chaprazov. Other academics who have written in this small but thankfully growing field of research generously shared their material with me: David Abulafia; Maria Boes; Richard Pym.

Particular thanks to comrades Mike Berlin and Ben Rogaly for ongoing friendship, academic conversations and support within and outside the academy. The writing of this book was both delayed and enriched through my repeated trips to Dale Farm: Elby, Teresa, Michelle and John, Michelle, Patrick and family and Richard Sheridan have remained close to my heart throughout the writing of this book. Many thanks to Will and the Liberton household for hospitality in Edinburgh, Ludo in Leeds, and to all my fellow co-op members, especially Hayley and my walk fellowes at No. 4. Special mention must go to the unfailing presence of The Ginger Shadow, and the blithe interruptions of Jack and Rosa. And finally, for walking alongside me through the darkness (and the map), thanks to the sweet dreamer in my life.

The map on page 10 is courtesy of the University of Texas Libraries, The University of Texas, Austin.

INDEX